Disabled Children and the Law

Second Edition

of related interest

Law, Rights and Disability
Edited by Jeremy Cooper
ISBN 1 85302 836 3

Community Care Practice and the Law
Third Edition
Michael Mandelstam
ISBN 1 84310 233 1

Surviving the Special Educational Needs System
How to be a 'Velvet Bulldozer'
Sandy Row
ISBN 1 84310 262 5

Supporting South Asian Families with a Child
with Severe Disabilities
Chris Hatton, Yasmeen Akram, Robina Shah, Janet Robertson and Eric Emerson
ISBN 1 84310 161 0

The Views and Experiences of Disabled Children
and Their Siblings
A Positive Outlook
Clare Connors and Kirsten Stalker
ISBN 1 84310 127 0

Quality of Life and Disability
An Approach for Community Practitioners
Ivan Brown and Roy I. Brown
Foreword by Ann and Rud Turnbull
ISBN 1 84310 005 3

Disabled Children and the Law
Research and Good Practice
Second Edition

*Janet Read, Luke Clements
and David Ruebain*

Jessica Kingsley Publishers
London and Philadelphia

Table 5.1 is reproduced from p.52 of *Delivering Housing Adaptations for Disabled People: A Good Practice Guide* (2004) by Office of the Deputy Prime Minister, Department for Education and Skills and Department of Health. © Crown copyright. Reproduced with the permission of the Controller of HMSO and the Queen's Printer for Scotland.

First published in 2006
by Jessica Kingsley Publishers
116 Pentonville Road
London N1 9JB, UK
and
400 Market Street, Suite 400
Philadelphia, PA 19106, USA

www.jkp.com

Library of Congress Cataloging in Publication Data

Read, Janet, 1947-
    Disabled children and the law : research and good practice / Janet Read, Luke Clements, and David Ruebain.— 2nd ed.
        p. cm.
    Includes bibliographical references and index.
    ISBN-13: 978-1-84310-280-9 (pbk.)
    ISBN-10: 1-84310-280-3 (pbk. : alk. paper) 1. Children with disabilities—Legal status, laws, etc.—Great Britain. I. Clements, L. J. (Luke J.) II. Ruebain, David. III. Title.
    KD3313.R43 2006
    344.4203'24083—dc22

                        2006004552

British Library Cataloguing in Publication Data
A CIP catalogue record for this book is available from the British Library

ISBN-13: 9781843102809
ISBN-10: 1 84310 280 3

Printed and bound in Great Britain by
Athenaeum Press, Gateshead, Tyne and Wear

Acknowledgements

In writing this edition we have had invaluable assistance from Julie Doughty of Cardiff University Law School, particularly in relation to the revisions to Chapter 8. We are also grateful to Sara Ryan, University of Warwick, for her assistance in updating the literature review.

We welcome critical feedback, suggestions and information. These should be sent to Janet Read at J.M.Read@warwick.ac.uk.

CHAPTER I

Introduction

What is this book about?

There are three basic principles underpinning this book:

- Disabled children and their families have a right to a quality of life comparable to that enjoyed by others who do not live with disability.

- If we are to ensure that the rights of disabled children and their families are protected and promoted, then it is essential to have an integrated approach to research, good practice and the law.

- The law should be seen as a tool that can be used to help achieve practice that research indicates is valued and meets important needs.

Accordingly, throughout the book, the three elements of research, good practice and the law are considered along a continuum, in the following order:

- What research has to tell us about the needs of disabled children and those close to them.

- What research has to tell us about valued services to meet those needs and how this is reflected in current policy and practice.

- How the law can be used as a tool to make valued and appropriate services available to meet need.

In other words, in relation to different topics, we start with the issues that research tells us are significant for the children and those close to them; we move on to strategies that may make a difference; and then we consider how the law might help. Wherever possible, we use the best research evidence available. It is important to recognise, however, that some significant areas of disabled children's lives remain under-researched. In addition, we also draw on literature that may not have an empirical research base but that has offered important theoretical insights or new perspectives that have helped us to appreciate the lives of disabled children and those close to them.

Who is this book for?

Disabled children and young people and those close to them often lack essential information about matters that substantially affect their lives. We hope that this book helps to tackle this problem. It is written with disabled young people and their families in mind, and we hope that some may have direct access to it and find that it contains material that is useful to them. After the publication of the first edition of *Disabled Children and the Law: Research and Good Practice*, we were delighted with the numbers of families who told us that they had read the book and found it useful. We realise, however, that others may find that the various handbooks and websites that we recommend are much more to their liking than a research-based text. In addition, we hope that the book will be of value to organisations, lawyers, advisors and advocates assisting disabled children and their families or representing their interests. In this way, the children and their families may benefit indirectly from the information that we have provided.

This book is also aimed at practitioners and managers providing and planning services for disabled children and their families, and at students training for the relevant professions. In recent years, there has been a growing expectation that the best available research evidence should inform practice and service development. It can prove very difficult, however, for even the most conscientious of practitioners to keep abreast of current research. Similarly, there is evidence that some practitioners and managers find aspects of the law related to disabled children complex and demanding (Read and Clements 1999). This book is intended to give service providers access both to a substantial range of research and to related legislation.

How this book is organised

There is no easy way to lay out a book of this nature. A law book would deal with each statute in succession and a practice book might deal with the duties of each public authority separately (i.e. social services, education, the National Health Service (NHS), and so on). Since we challenge the inappropriate compartmentalisation of issues that arise in the lives of disabled children, we have not favoured either arrangement. We have opted instead (after trying many alternatives) for a layout based primarily on important stages in a child's lifecourse.

Such an approach has caused slight difficulty with this new edition, as we seek to highlight and incorporate the legal changes arising from the Children Act 2004. In our opinion, however, the Act's impact is not likely to be so fundamental as to require a change to the book's overall structure. We address the key changes of the 2004 Act in Chapter 4.

The book is organised in two parts: Part I is the main body of the text on research, good practice and the law. Part II contains more detailed legal source materials and precedent letters.

In Part I, following this introduction, there is a chapter on human rights, ethics and values. Chapters 3 and 4 provide an overview of research, policy, practice and the law in relation to all disabled children and their families. These chapters form an essential background and are intended to be read in conjunction with others on specific topics. Chapters 5 to 7 follow the children's lifecourse and deal with issues that routinely become important for them and their families at particular times. Finally, Chapter 8 focuses on children who live away from their families. Each of these chapters is divided into two parts: the first part consists of a review of research and policy in relation to need and services and the second part comprises a legal commentary on those findings. The sources cited in the sections concerned with research and good practice are to be found in the list of references at the end of the book. Following the convention in law publications, the references for the legal commentaries are to be found as endnotes at the end of a particular commentary.

Taking this approach to the three elements, research, good practice and the law, has undoubtedly created considerable problems of organisation. In relation to any topic, we have had to draw on a range of research and legislation, appreciating, however, that most people will not read this book from cover to cover. We have, therefore, tried to find a way of giving readers the best possible access to material that they may need without either being too repetitive or risking a serious omission. Some issues, for example the need for an effective means of communication for each disabled child, could have been explored in almost every section. Choices had to be made, however, and some matters are dealt with in a particular chapter, not because they belong there exclusively but because, on balance, that seems the most appropriate place for them to be. We have tried to help the reader by providing extensive cross-referencing and a detailed index.

Note

Although this book is concerned throughout with the safety and well-being of disabled children, it does not deal specifically with procedures in relation to child protection. Similarly, it does not offer information and advice on income maintenance benefits. Reference is made, however, to texts and guides on these topics.

PART I

Research, the Law
and Good Practice

CHAPTER 2

Human Rights, Ethics and Values

Introduction

In this chapter, we outline briefly some of the values that underpin our approach. These principles and related theoretical work appear in one form or another throughout this book, but the aim of this chapter is to make them explicit.

Quality of life and human rights

Our approach is founded on a very simple assumption. We believe that it should not be regarded as an exotic idea for disabled children and those close to them to aspire to a quality of life comparable to that enjoyed by others who do not live with disability. In our view, it should be seen as unacceptable in the twenty-first century for the lives and experiences of disabled children and their families to be bereft of those features that many others take for granted, features that make an essential contribution to an ordinary and reasonable quality of life. This is not, of course, the same as saying that all children, disabled or not, need or want exactly the same personal, social and material experiences in exactly the same form. What we are suggesting is that we should aim for basic equality of opportunity and recognise that children and their families will take very different routes and need markedly different supports if there is to be any chance of achieving it.

We should, therefore, never start from the assumption that an experience that is taken for granted by many non-disabled children and their families should be ruled out on the grounds of a child being disabled. By contrast, if we start by assuming that disabled children and their families should have access to experiences that others routinely expect, then the issue becomes one of finding the route to achieve it and the services that will enable it to happen. To assume that

disabled children and their families have the same basic social and human rights
as other people is fundamental.

This idea is not new. Increasingly, researchers and disability activists have
highlighted situations and experiences that are often fundamental to the lives of
disabled children and their families but that would be regarded as intolerable for
those who are non-disabled (e.g. Hirst and Baldwin 1994; Morris 1995). They
have pointed to differential standards that apply to the two groups and to the size
of the gap between them. Since the 1990s, we have seen increasing challenges to
the notion that it is acceptable for such a gap to exist between the expectations
and experiences of disabled and non-disabled children and young people. Russell
(2003, p.216) draws our attention to 'a compelling body of evidence from
research and inspection reports that many disabled children and their families
continue to face multiple discrimination, low expectations and many physical
and social barriers to full participation in society'.

Our experience as both researchers and practitioners has taught us that
although children and their families may have to compromise as they focus their
attention on managing the day-to-day rigours of life, many retain a sense of
injustice or disquiet about the gap that exists between their own quality of life
and that of others who do not live with disability. We cannot be the only people
who have been asked by disabled children how we think that others of their age
would like it if they had to put up with things that are integral to the experience
of growing up with disability. Parents of disabled children whom we know also
frequently draw an implied or explicit comparison between their own children's
lives and the lives of others. When faced with a battle to get something that they
feel would improve their disabled child's quality of life, they often challenge what
they regard as taken-for-granted restrictions and low standards. In doing so, they
sometimes use the language of fairness and unfairness and pose questions such as
'Why shouldn't she have what other children have?'

Some of the questions asked by disabled children and young people and their
parents should not be assumed to be simply rhetorical. When we attempt
seriously to answer questions that begin 'How would they like it if...?' or 'Why
shouldn't she have the same...?', the unacceptable quality of the opportunities
afforded to many disabled children and their families is brought home to us. If,
for example, we were to come to the conclusion that it would be unbearable and
damaging for a non-disabled child to be without a means of communication or a
consistent way of expressing preference or dissent, then we immediately have to
ask why it is routinely regarded as acceptable for many disabled children to be in
that position. Furthermore, if the answer is a resounding 'No' to a question about
whether some aspect of the quality of life experienced by disabled children would

be good enough for non-disabled children, we need then to interrogate why it should be contemplated. The onus must be on having to explain and to justify it.

One group of practitioners known to the authors used a rough and ready but effective yardstick in relation to these issues. The team undertook a review of services offered to disabled children with complex support needs with the aim of extending the children's opportunities and enhancing their quality of life. The staff dubbed the project 'Good Enough for Me: Good Enough for You' as a reminder of one guiding principle: if the children's quality of life did not meet the standards and expectations that staff might have for their own and that of their families, then they should immediately question what could be done.

We are aware that some disabled children and young people and their families may feel sceptical about an assertion that there is nothing exotic about the idea that they should have aspirations comparable to those of others. They may wonder, understandably in our view, whether those who suggest it have any idea of what they are up against most of the time. Similarly, hard-pressed practitioners and managers in services with few resources may, equally understandably, argue that such notions are fine in an ideal world but, sadly, the world is far from ideal. It is precisely because things are so taxing for many disabled children and their families, and because good services are so thin on the ground, that it is crucial to be emphatic about the principle. Although it may not yet be possible always to achieve the goal of a comparable quality of life and opportunity, the consequences of lowering our sights may be that we work to inferior standards and achieve less. In addition, it needs to be acknowledged that in circumstances where people are offered little, there is a danger that an often quite limited service that makes only a marginal difference to their lives may be presented as more significant than it actually is. We do not wish to suggest that small or incremental gains are always unimportant, and we certainly do not want to diminish the efforts of families and conscientious practitioners to create as much room for manoeuvre as they can with whatever limited resources they have at their disposal. We recognise, too, that like all individuals and families, disabled children and those close to them make compromises. Nevertheless, it would be dangerous to lose sight of the useful yardstick of how the child's and family's quality of life compares with that of others in the general population. One way of making a difference is to focus on reducing the gap between the two. In doing so, it is worth remembering that studies have indicated that children and their parents frequently aspire to rather basic things that they feel would enhance the quality of their personal and social lives. Some of these are familiar and important to us all, such as age-appropriate community-based leisure activities and interests, the chance to meet and make friends, some choice and independence, and so on (Mitchell and Sloper 2001).

Parents frequently point out, however, that they feel it is unwise to spend all their time concentrating on what they regard as the injustices in their lives and their children's lives. Many regard it as essential to emphasise positive strategies and to carve out those defensible spaces in their lives that foster and enhance the well-being of all family members (Beresford 1994; Read 2000). This does not mean, of course, that they are unaware of or unaffected by the gap between their lives and those of others who do not live with disability. Throughout this book, we shall be detailing the hardships that children and families face and the positive and creative aspects of their lives, and services and strategies that can make a difference.

Understanding disability

The approach outlined so far is predicated on an assumption that it is possible to make a difference so that the lives of disabled children and their families are improved. This in turn rests on a further set of assumptions about the nature of the difficulties that disabled children and adults and their families face. Later in the book there is more detailed reference to work that has been undertaken since the 1980s on defining and theorising disability. Much of this work has been developed by disabled academics and activists and lays emphasis on the social oppression of children and adults who live with impairment (e.g. Morris 1991; Oliver 1996). Those writers and activists who developed what became known as the 'social model of disability' tended to use the term 'impairment' to refer to physical, sensory or intellectual limitations and the term 'disability' to encompass the socially created restrictions experienced by the children and adults concerned. At this point, we want to take time only briefly to summarise our understanding of disability and the things that affect the lives of disabled children and adults in both positive and negative ways. A more extended discussion can be found in Chapter 3.

There can be no doubt that some of the most restrictive and difficult features in the lives of disabled children and their families are not a necessary or inevitable consequence of having impairments. Some of the most devastating and eroding factors are socially or politically constructed and can be changed by social and political means. Consequently, in this book we place a great deal of emphasis on the part that can be played by child, family and community support services to enhance opportunity and reduce restriction. These tend to focus on reducing material and social barriers in order to create a supportive and enabling environment in which a child may flourish. We also recognise, however, that like other children, those who are disabled can benefit from sensitive and high-quality interventions that aim to enhance their individual cognitive and physical development. Although some might argue that there has often been too great a focus on changing the child and too little focus on reducing the negative impact of social barriers, we assume that individual and social change are not necessarily mutually exclusive. It is important to state, however, that if we do not appreciate the immense impact of social factors on disabled children and the disabling nature of the structural problems that they face, then we fundamentally misunderstand their situation and do them and their families an enormous disservice.

Whose perspectives?

One of the most significant influences in aiding understanding of disability has been the oral and written contribution of disabled children and adults and those close to them. Throughout this book, we rely heavily on research and other accounts shaped by these perspectives.

It has to be recognised that although families may be significant social groupings for most people, in all households individuals have different needs and perspectives. Some of these may be difficult to reconcile all of the time. Consequently, it is important to hear the accounts or to gain access to the perspectives of all children and adults intimately involved in the issues that we discuss. Although one version of events may take precedence at a particular time, it is crucial that individuals who have a significant stake in a situation are not silenced. It is only too easy for one version or one account to become privileged over another. Because the opinions of disabled children have so often been neglected, considerable emphasis needs to be placed on measures to offset this. Such an assumption, however, carries with it no implication that their fathers, mothers, brothers and sisters need no voice or that their opinions are unimportant. Like other parents, those with disabled children assume a major degree of responsibility for their children's health, development and well-being. Many develop extensive knowledge and expertise in relation to both their own children and the provision that would meet their needs. They also find very effective coping strategies and ways of living their lives in given circumstances. It is clearly essential that their voices are heard.

In addition to variations within households, there is also a wide gamut of perspectives and needs across the total population of disabled children and adults and their families. There may be some commonality of experience and views, but there is also great diversity. Individuals and groups develop their own distinctive perspectives on disability, the needs derived from it and the interventions that would bring about improvement. These diverse perspectives and the language used to characterise them change and develop in the light of experience. It would be surprising if this were not the case. However, although some people expect and accept a range of views, diverse perspectives can sometimes cause conflict. A passionately held belief that is self-evident to one individual or group can seem like dogma to someone else. What is regarded as the voice of authority and leadership by some will be experienced as authoritarianism by others. In this book, we try to draw on as wide a range of perspectives as possible.

The significance of social groupings and social divisions

Individuals derive their perspectives, attitudes and values from a variety of significant social and personal experiences, and the diversity of this experience will in part be a reflection of the range of social groupings or divisions to which individual children and their families belong. Issues related to socioeconomic status, gender, ethnic origin, culture, age and sexuality have a profound and complex influence in all people's lives. Research on health inequalities demonstrates that social circumstances and inequality across the entire lifecourse have a major impact on health and well-being (Ahmad 2000; Shaw *et al.* 1999). Unsurprisingly, therefore, these factors also powerfully shape the experiences of disability. Throughout this book, we draw attention to the different experiences of children and their families from a range of social groupings, and to some of the ways in which their life chances and access to services are significantly affected. Without adopting an over-deterministic position, it is our view that for many families, issues related to, for example, social exclusion and material hardship are so significant that they structure their opportunities, lifestyles and coping strategies in major ways. The impact of these social factors on the needs of disabled children and their families is a key issue for all practitioners involved in service provision.

Relationships between service users and providers

There has been a growing official recognition in recent years of the necessity to provide more responsive and sensitive services for the diverse population of disabled children and those close to them (e.g. Ball 1998; DH 2000a). Within the social care field in particular, this focus has included an increased emphasis on developing services and professional practice aimed specifically at countering discrimination and social exclusion (Thompson 1993). Since the early 1990s, the notion of the user of public and voluntary sector services as a consumer or customer with comparable rights to those of any other consumers has become common currency and, increasingly, there are requirements, particularly in the public sector, for service users and patients to participate in setting the agendas of service provision. This may be seen as something of a challenge to the traditional authority and power of professionals and managers.

Although we would not wish to undermine any attempts to ensure that disabled children and their families are treated with respect and offered services that are responsive to their needs, it is essential to be clear about the difference between prevailing rhetoric, no matter how well intentioned, and what is often delivered. There is no doubt that some families become particularly cynical about approaches that appear to promise much but can only deliver a lot less in the way of tangible benefits. From the service user's point of view, the repetition of mantras about partnerships between service professionals and children and their parents cannot conceal the frequently uncomfortable complexities of these relationships (Murray 2000) and the unequal power relations that almost invariably exist between those who use services and those who provide them. For disabled children and their families, for example, no amount of 'user-centred' or 'needs-led' terminology will disguise an assessment that is covertly resource- or provision-driven.

This presents dilemmas for many conscientious practitioners who know only too well the limitations on resources within their services. These realities are also appreciated by many families. When we characterise them primarily as service users, it is easy to forget that they are also readers of their local newspapers, council-tax payers and so on. The whole orientation of this book is to help raise the level of expectations that disabled children and their families may have, but we recognise that few people assume that service providers' resources are unlimited.

It needs to be recognised, however, that in addition to facing often severe resource limitations, service users and practitioners frequently find themselves trying to achieve something important and worthwhile in an environment that is continually changing and where there are few constant points of reference. At the time of writing, children's services, including those for disabled children, are undergoing a major reorganisation underpinned by the Children Act 2004. However good the intentions driving this Act, it is not unlikely that, for a time at least, the resolve of both practitioners and service users will be tested by almost inevitable organisational turbulence. This turbulence is not limited to that caused by this new legislation, however. For some time, a significant problem for service users and providers in this field has concerned the large volume of new initiatives and guidance emanating from central government. Coote (2005, p.18) referred to this as 'hyperactive policy-making' when describing the upheavals in children's services. It frequently appears to be the case that no programme or initiative is given time to bed down before being replaced with something new. The detrimental impact of constant bureaucratic upheaval has long been recognised by commentators and practitioners and long ignored by policy-makers (Clements and Smith 1999; Webb and Wistow 1986). It has been argued that all too often the alleged benefits promised by a new initiative or reorganisation prove to be of dubious practical value when weighed against the harm done in terms of the fracturing of existing practices and the confusion and demoralisation of staff and service users. In addition, substantial financial resources and staff time are given over to the task of instituting the new system and training staff to work within it. In this situation, it is all too easy for professional staff to find themselves increasingly inhabiting a world of jargon and procedures while spending less and less time in face-to-face contact with disabled children and those close to them. Lord Laming in his inquiry report into the death of Victoria Climbié argued: 'The performance of managers and their effectiveness should be judged against the efficiency, reliability and standards of services delivered to vulnerable children and families, rather than in the maintenance of bureaucratic procedures' (Laming 2003, Para. 17.85). He also noted that he had heard 'too much evidence of organisational confusion and "buck passing"...to believe that the safety of a child can be achieved simply through issuing more guidance' (Para. 17.86).

These issues make it all the more important to reconsider the basic attitudes and approaches that families with disabled children value in practitioners. A range of research on which we draw more fully later in this book indicates that parents and children are likely to appreciate practitioners whose values mean that they:

- treat them with courtesy and sensitivity and take their concerns and points of view seriously
- approach their way of life, culture and beliefs in a respectful manner
- approach them in as straightforward and honest a way as possible
- do what they say they will do, when they say they will do it
- respect their privacy by, for example, starting with a practical approach and focusing on more personal matters only when invited to do so or when a relationship is established
- are well informed or prepared to find out about matters essential to the well-being of the child and family
- demonstrate that they have an accurate appreciation of the taxing and busy nature of their lives
- demonstrate that they appreciate the positive aspects of their experience
- do not hold them responsible, even by implication, for factors beyond their control.

Such an approach, and the values that underpin it, form only a baseline, but one that can be adhered to by any informed and competent practitioner. In the chapters that follow, we shall refer frequently to other standards and responses that families ought to be able to expect. While many parents may have a realistic view of restricted public-sector resources and the constraints under which practitioners work, we assume that their primary responsibility is to represent their own child's interests in the best way that they can. It is therefore entirely reasonable for any parent to make the most of any lawful opportunity to ensure that their child's needs are met in the best way possible.

Even when practitioners, parents and children share common aims and values in relation to the quality of life that should be available to disabled children, the process of working towards this is, by its very nature, challenging. Pumpian (1996), exploring the goal of self-determination across the lifespan, suggests that there are three deceptively simple questions that disabled people should have the right to be asked:

- Where do you want to spend your time living, working, learning and socialising?
- What activities are important to you in those settings?
- Which people are important to interact with in these environments and activities?

He points out, however, that the complexity of the questions is revealed only once we try to work out what concepts such as self-determination and choice mean in practice:

> At first, answering these questions seems simple until we deal with real people in complex situations. Then these questions cause us to question and clarify our values. Our values will be challenged and conflict will be unavoidable. When is a dream, or a choice, a bad dream or just not ours? When is a goal unrealistic or just beyond our ability or willingness to be creative, inconvenienced, engaged, or effective? When is an activity too risky and irresponsible, and when is it a risk worth taking and a necessary part of a person's growth and development? (p.xv)

The struggle to make sense of these issues and others like them will be familiar territory to many disabled young people, their families and practitioners.

The law and its application

Throughout this text, the review of research and good practice precedes the legal analysis. Our basic premise is that the way that the law should be approached and used is dictated by good practice. Law is not freestanding and separate, and, indeed, like good practice and research findings, it is not always clear. If, therefore, the law and good practice appear to conflict, then one's interpretation of the law should generally be guided by good practice. In general, the law in relation to disabled children has been drafted with the aim of reinforcing good practice and promoting certain ideals. If, then, the law is believed to be dictating a course that conflicts with the best interests of the child, then almost certainly the law has been misunderstood. Mahatma Gandhi (who was by training a barrister) expressed this concept as 'if we take care of the facts of a case, the law will take care of itself' (Gandhi 1982, p.132).

The law is an active and adaptable tool. Although principles and procedures may be written down in law books, the law itself is alive and is something that happens in daily life. It is what regulates actions and guides decision-making. Some of the same principles that inform social and healthcare practice also inform the law, not least of which is a fundamental respect for human dignity and human rights and a respect for the right of people to be different and to hold different views. Laws concerning fundamental human rights and civil liberties include both international documents, for instance the United Nations (UN) Convention on the Rights of the Child 1989, and domestic documents, such as the Human Rights Act 1998, the Children Act 1989 (Parts I and III) and the anti-race and sex discrimination legislation. In addition, we have UK laws for which (arguably) there are no equivalent international covenants, for instance the Disability Discrimination Act 1995.

The impact of the European Convention on Human Rights (ECHR; incorporated into domestic law via the Human Rights Act 1998) is becoming increasingly evident. The rights of most relevance to disabled children and their families/carers are Articles 3 and 8. Article 3 is concerned with the prohibition of degrading treatment and Article 8 with privacy and family life. The courts' review of these rights frequently resorts to concepts such as 'civilised values' and to 'dignity'. In *Price* v. *United Kingdom* [2002],[1] for example, Judge Greve held that:

> In a civilised country like the United Kingdom, society considers it not only appropriate but a basic humane concern to try to improve and compensate for the disabilities faced by a person in the applicant's situation. In my opinion, these compensatory measures come to form part of the disabled person's physical integrity.

Likewise, Baroness Hale of Richmond has observed:

> …human dignity is all the more important for people whose freedom of action and choice is curtailed, whether by law or by circumstances such as disability. The Convention is a living instrument… We need to be able to use it to promote

respect for the inherent dignity of all human beings but especially those who are most vulnerable to having that dignity ignored. In reality, the niceties and technicalities with which we have to be involved in the courts should be less important than the core values which underpin the whole Convention. (Hale 2004)

Although in this book we make reference to the relevant human rights case law, for an extended analysis of the potential impact of the ECHR on the rights of disabled people reference should be made to Clements and Read (2003).

The courts have generally considered that the Disability Discrimination Act 1995 demands a similar, although subtly different, analysis. The rights that the Act protects are of a narrower kind (i.e. relating to specific subject areas, e.g. employment, education, goods and services, etc.), although once the Act's provisions are engaged the courts' approach is to assess the proportionality of the response made to the disabled person's needs: did the response, for instance, seek to accommodate the legitimate needs of the disabled person (in the parlance of the legislation, to make a 'reasonable adjustment')? The impact of the 1995 Act is considered in more detail on p.157.

The law, as with good social and healthcare practice, frequently requires attention to detail, i.e. the doing of small things well. This is particularly so in those areas where there is a significant risk of harm to individuals. Here, the concern is about not only the risk of active abuse but also the risk of neglect or 'drift'. In such situations, the law demands that professionals adhere to clearly defined procedures, routines and practices that seek to protect and promote individual rights and freedoms. Laws concerning these matters are frequently labelled 'due process' provisions. They do not lay down rights but impose restrictions and administrative obligations upon the state. Into this category one might put the Children Act 1989 (Part VI), the Mental Health Act 1983 and most of the detailed procedural regulations under the Children Acts and Education Acts. The law gives public officials very little discretion in relation to the discharge of these obligations. Where vulnerable people are reliant upon the good behaviour and diligence of people discharging public functions, experience has shown that meticulous compliance with certain administrative procedures is one mechanism that helps to reduce the risk of abuse and neglect.

Note

1 [2002] 34 EHRR 1285, 1296.

CHAPTER 3

Research and Good Practice

Overview

Russell (1991) suggests that when we attempt to understand the experience of disabled children and their families, it is helpful to see disability as a major and potentially damaging life event that is amenable to intervention and compatible with a good quality of family life. One advantage of such a balanced view is that it neither minimises the problems faced by parents and their sons and daughters nor adopts a stance in relation to disablement that is inevitably negative. Instead, it proposes an approach that identifies both the factors that generate difficulty and the nature of support services and other arrangements that can alleviate the strain and open up positive opportunities.

Although it is important never to lose sight of the individuality of disabled children and their families, there is now a large body of research and other literature that has a great deal to tell us about social trends that may affect them, their most common experiences and needs, the problems they encounter, and services and other supports that generally are found to be positive and helpful. Within the literature and policy documents, a number of themes consistently come to the fore that are relevant to children of all age groups and their families. Such themes may, however, have different significance at particular times in their lives. Some of these themes and findings refer to matters that have a very direct effect on their ways of living. Others deal with issues that have an equally signifi-cant but sometimes more indirect impact.

In this chapter, we review those overarching themes before turning in later chapters to experiences more particularly linked with different periods in the lifecourse. We suggest that the following themes should be seen as a backdrop when any of those particular experiences are considered:

- Key debates and social trends:
  - the population of disabled children
  - understanding disability, exclusion and lack of opportunity
  - disabled children's perspectives.
- Common needs and problems of disabled children and their families:
  - caring in the home: mothers, fathers and siblings
  - needs to be met at home
  - material, financial and practical problems
  - families' experiences of services
  - the need for information
  - critical transitional periods
  - personal consequences for parents, disabled children and their siblings.
- Valued service provision:
  - a needs-led approach to assessment and integrated family service provision
  - improving information
  - coordination of services
  - key working and advocacy
  - interventions to enhance children's development
  - assistance with financial and practical problems of daily living
  - homecare, support workers and short-term breaks.

The majority of this chapter will focus on the situations of children who live at home with either or both of their parents; this is the experience of the vast majority (91.2%) (Gordon *et al.* 2000b). Because it is clear, however, that disabled children have a far greater likelihood than non-disabled children of living away from home for substantial periods, a later chapter is devoted entirely to the experience of being away from their families of origin (see Chapter 8).

Key debates and social trends

The population of disabled children

There is a consensus that there is a lack of accurate data at a national level on the prevalence of disability in children and young people and on trends within this population (Gordon *et al.* 2000b; ONS 2004). Data are currently collected at local and national levels for a range of purposes and by a number of different organisations. Because of the way that these data are collected and because of a lack of standardisation of categories and definitions, there is no straightforward way of aggregating data from different sources in order to obtain a reliable overall estimate of the numbers of disabled children in Britain. There is, for example, considerable overlap between data sources, with the result that some children may appear in different guises more than once.

The most comprehensive national disability surveys were undertaken by the Office of Population, Census and Surveys (OPCS) between 1985 and 1989 (Bone and Meltzer 1989; Meltzer, Smyth and Robus 1989; Smyth and Robus 1989) and consequently are now out of date. Gordon *et al.* (2000b) undertook a reanalysis of the OPCS data and, for some purposes, policy-makers and researchers still regard this analysis as the most robust national data currently available. The Family Fund Trust (FFT) database is one of the most frequently used and highly regarded national sources of information on disabled children and their families. The FFT is a government-funded independent organisation that gives grants and information to those severely disabled children and their families who are relatively disadvantaged financially. It holds data on all families who apply. Prevalence estimates and data related to the characteristics of disabled children and their households that draw on the FFT register of applicants tend to be adjusted to take account of both the under-representation of middle- and higher-income families (ONS 2004) and the estimated rate of applications by those who are eligible (Glendinning *et al.* 2001; Lawton and Quine 1990).

More recently, the Department for Work and Pensions (DWP) Family Resources Survey has collected data on disabled children based on definitions of disability used in the Disability Discrimination Act 1995 (DDA). Other government departments have now adopted the estimates from the Family Resources Survey (DfES/DH 2004).

Gordon *et al.* (2000b), drawing on the reanalysis of the OPCS data of 1985–89, indicate that there were an estimated 327,000 disabled children under the age of 16 years living in Britain. The majority of these (91.2%) lived at home with their parents. Other children were being cared for by a relative (0.6%), 2.5 per cent were looked after by foster carers and 4.4 per cent were at boarding school on a termly or weekly basis. A smaller number (1.5%) lived in communal establishments on a permanent basis. It is also often estimated that between 110,000 (Russell 2003) and 150,000 (Roberts and Lawton 2001) of these children may be defined as severely disabled. The Family Resources Survey, using the DDA definition, has estimated a larger overall population of disabled children: 700,000. This estimate includes all children under the age of 16 years and, in addition, those in the 16–18 years age group who are unmarried, living at home and in full-time education.

The population of disabled children has changed significantly over the period since the early 1980s (McConachie 1997; Russell 2003). In addition to the marked reported increase in numbers identified as having autistic-spectrum disorders and attention deficit/hyperactivity disorder (ADHD), greater numbers of low-birthweight babies and babies with severe and complex disorders are surviving and being cared for at home. Some children may have a substantial range of impairments. The issue of multiple impairment has significant implications for the children and their families as well as for services attempting to meet their needs. The lives of a growing number of children with complex impairments are sustained by means of technological procedures and equipment usually managed by their parents at home. These include, for example, tube feeding, assisted ventilation and resuscitation procedures (Glendinning *et al.* 2001; Noyes 1999; Social Services Inspectorate 1998). Again, there is a limited amount of reliable national data, but some estimates suggest that there may be as many as 6000 technology-dependent children in the UK (Glendinning *et al.* 2001). These children may frequently require a high level of sensitive, integrated social care and healthcare on an ongoing basis. It is not unusual for there to be problems over the organisation of medical care, disputes or uncertainty about the respective responsibilities of different service providers in relation to these complex needs, as well as issues related to the adequacy of staff training (Ball 1998; Kirk and Glendinning 2004; Social Services Inspectorate 1998; Townsley and Robinson 2000).

Understanding disability, exclusion and lack of opportunity

Debates on appropriate ways of theorising disability more generally have affected understandings of the experience of childhood disability. As we have suggested in Chapter 2, it has increasingly been acknowledged that some of the most restricting and damaging features in the lives of disabled children and adults and those close to them are not an inevitable or necessary consequence of having physical impairment or learning disability (Baldwin and Carlisle 1994; Barnes and Mercer 1996; Morris 1991; Oliver 1996). A greater focus on the oppressive and exclusionary nature of social and contextual factors has led to the development of what is often termed the 'social model of disability'. Some writers and activists who adopt this approach have sought fundamentally to redefine disability solely in terms of those extrinsic factors that are seen to oppress and restrict people living with impairment (Oliver 1996). Others who are sympathetic to the notion that social, political and ideological forces can be overwhelmingly damaging on the lives of disabled people have expressed reservations about some interpretations of the social model that has appeared to give limited attention to the potentially restricting nature of impairment (Crow 1996; Read 1998, 2000; Williams 1996). Despite some differences in analysis and emphasis, there has, nevertheless, been a growing consensus about the fact that some of the greatest restrictions and limitations experienced by disabled children and adults are undoubtedly created by the way that society is organised to exclude them, by other people's damaging attitudes, by limited and unequal opportunities and by inadequate service provision. There has been an increasing emphasis on the need to challenge these features in the lives of the disabled children and adults concerned and to develop provision that offsets their effects and creates positive opportunities.

These shifts in understanding show through clearly in the literature, research and official policy documents on disabled children and young people and their families (e.g. Baldwin and Carlisle 1994; Ball 1998; Beresford *et al.* 1996; DH 2000a; DH *et al.* 2000; PMSU 2005; Sloper 1999; Social Services Inspectorate 1998). Increasingly, there has been a challenge to what is seen as the over-medicalisation of children and their experiences, and it has been argued that services have often been constrained by too narrow a medical and educational focus (McConachie 1997). The tensions between biomedical and social models of disability do not exist simply at a theoretical level. Both the formal and work-a-day definitions that people use affect how children are viewed and, sometimes, the type and level of service that is provided or withheld. ADHD provides just one example of the tensions between different ways of defining disabled children and the consequences for those involved. As we have already seen, increasing numbers of children are being given a medical diagnosis of ADHD, and some of these are prescribed medication designed to control their behaviour. Although some parents may be unhappy about the idea of defining their children in this way, others may regard it as potentially helpful to have such a diagnosis, particularly if it appears instrumental in helping them to access supportive services. It may also come as a relief to some parents if a diagnosis appears to imply that the child's challenging or unconventional behaviour may be attributed to biomedical origins rather than to their upbringing. Even when parents accept the notion of their child having such a medicalised definition, however, this does not always result in the provision of services. Two of the authors (the lawyers) commonly meet families whose local authorities do not accept that a diagnosis of ADHD places the child within a category of disabled children for whom they have a duty to provide services, an issue that will be discussed in the legal commentaries later in this book. In addition to the possibility that this may be seen as an effective way to ration resources, it also appears that some non-medical practitioners have reservations about the increasing numbers of children being given this diagnosis.

In recent years, there has been considerable debate on the different standards that have been applied in making judgements about what is regarded as acceptable for disabled children compared with non-disabled children. In almost all aspects of their lives, experiences that would be regarded as too narrow, unsettling, exclusionary or damaging for a non-disabled child have often not even seemed to require justification for their disabled peers. The repeated questioning of such assumptions and arguing for disabled children and their rights to be governed by the same standards as those applied to their non-disabled peers can be seen as a major breakthrough in policy, research and other literature in the last decade (Clements and Read 2003; DH 2000a; Hirst and Baldwin 1994; Morris 1995, 1998a, 1998b, 1998c).

Related to this general trend has been a greater focus on policies and practices that create opportunities for the inclusion of children with diverse needs and characteristics in mainstream services and facilities (Booth 1999; Booth et al. 1992; Reisser and Mason 1992; Russell 2003; Social Services Inspectorate 1994). Substantial work on inclusion in education began to emerge in the early 1980s, but initiatives in this and other fields have accelerated in more recent times (Booth 1999; Russell 2003; Sebba and Sachdev 1997; Shaw 1998).

While the whole population of disabled children and their families shares some common experiences, it is of course made up of individuals and groups with very diverse backgrounds and characteristics. Recent years have seen a growing awareness in research and other literature of the way in which gender, ethnic origin, age and socioeconomic status should be seen as major mediating factors that differentially structure the experience of disability (e.g. Ahmad 2000; Butt and Mirza 1996; Connors and Stalker 2003; Gordon et al. 2000b; McCarthy 1999; Russell 2003; Sloper and Turner 1992; Twigg and Atkin 1994). This has frequently been given less attention than it merits, and it has been salutary for service providers and policy-makers to realise the degree to which social and ethnic background and characteristics affect children's and their families' access to services that meet their needs. Research has shown consistently that families on low incomes and families from minority ethnic groups, for example, can be very disadvantaged in this respect (Ahmad and Atkin 1996; Baxter et al. 1990; Butt and Mirza 1996; Chamba et al. 1999; Dyson 1992, 1998; Gordon et al. 2000b; Hatton et al. 2004; Shah 1992, 1997; Sloper and Turner 1992). Many families with disabled children have to work very hard indeed to find out their entitlements, and even when they have done so there is no guarantee that what is available will fit what the children and adults require. Sometimes, however, those under the greatest pressure because of a combination of stressful life events, social exclusion and very limited resources are least likely to be able to find their way through the maze and come out at the other end with something that really meets their needs. Some of these will be children and families with the greatest needs for support. Consequently, increased attention has been given to practice and service organisation designed to challenge and redress such discriminatory experiences (Baxter *et al.* 1990; Begum 1992; Chamba *et al.* 1999; Dalrymple and Burke 1995; Hatton *et al.* 2004; Jones, Atkin and Ahmad 2001; Shah 1992, 1997; Thompson 1993).

Another theme that has emerged consistently over recent times is related to the growing disquiet about the ways in which disabled children have been represented in some professional literature, the media and charity advertising. There have been increasing challenges to the tendency to misrepresent disabled children as tragedies or burdens and a greater consensus about the need to be vigilant in protecting the disabled child's right to dignity and respect in all situations (Beresford 1994; Goodey 1991; Hevey 1992; Ward 1997).

Disabled children's perspectives

A theme that is embedded in this book is the importance of listening to parents and appreciating their perspectives and wishes. As we have suggested, this approach has been emphasised in research and policy for a considerable time. In the past few years, however, awareness has grown about the limited degree to which the opinions and perspectives of disabled children have been sought in both research and practice. Some researchers have argued that disabled children have been consigned to a passive role rather than being seen as active subjects who should be included fully in those processes that have a bearing on their lives (Priestley 1998). There is increasing recognition that it can never be assumed that disabled children 'have nothing to say', even though they may be living with complex impairments and have significant barriers to communication (Russell 1998). In addition, since the early 1990s, there has been a challenge to the notion that it is sufficient for anyone seeking to further the interests of children to rely solely on the views of adults who are close to those children. Consequently, we have seen a growth in work that seeks to obtain disabled children's accounts and opinions directly and gives status to their perspectives. This has included attempts to involve the children as active participants in research, development and service evaluation (Beresford 1997; Beresford *et al.* 2004; Cavet and Sloper 2004; Connors and Stalker 2003; Kennedy 1992; Lewis 1995; Marchant and Page 1992; Mitchell and Sloper 2003; Rabiee, Sloper and Beresford 2005; Minkes, Robinson and Weston 1994; Russell 1998; Ward 1997). Because disabled children's voices have routinely been ignored for a very long time, it may prove necessary, for a while at least, to give counterweight to the established order of things by placing the need to consult with them high on the agenda.

There is clearly no reason, however, why more sustained attempts to seek the perspectives of disabled children need be seen to devalue the opinions or contributions of parents and significant others in their households and families. Listening seriously to disabled children does not carry with it any assumption that their mothers, fathers and siblings need no voice or that the disabled child's perspectives are inevitably privileged over others. While acknowledging that the needs and perspectives of children and parents should not be viewed as indistinguishable, research also recognises that, particularly in the case of young children living at home, their own and their parents' needs and well-being are often linked inextricably (Beresford 1994). Consequently, in most circumstances, parents of disabled children, like any others, should be asked for consent and kept fully informed when their children's opinions are being sought (Ball 1998; Russell 1998).

Disabled children and their families: common needs and problems

If we are to provide services that are sensitive and effective, it is essential to appreciate what research tells us about the common needs of disabled children and young people, the care and assistance they require, who usually provides support and what are the problems routinely encountered by everyone involved. By doing this, we have a greater chance of understanding what is needed, where it should be targeted and how we may provide an integrated system of family support that takes into account the needs, activities and resources of all members of households.

Caring in the home: mothers, fathers and siblings

The majority of disabled children are brought up at home in their families of origin; parents, particularly mothers, have the main responsibility for their care. The patterns of care for disabled children reflect childcare arrangements in families more generally, with women tending to assume primary responsibility (Abbott and Sapsford 1992; Atkin 1992; Beresford 1995; Read 1991, 2000). In two-parent households where there is a male partner, however, fathers frequently play a significant and active role in relation to both the disabled and other children. Fathers are often identified by mothers as their most important source of practical and emotional support (Atkin 1992; Beresford 1995; Read 2000).

Mothers undertake a greater volume of the work overall. This cannot be explained fully simply by the fact that in two-parent households fathers are more likely than mothers to undertake paid employment outside the home. Even when fathers are unemployed or at home for other reasons, the caring workload and responsibility usually remain weighted towards mothers (Atkin 1992).

Fathers and mothers also tend to undertake different types of caring tasks. The ongoing day-to-day care, particularly intimate personal care, most often falls to mothers, who, in addition, frequently undertake physical and practical tasks. Fathers tend to take on some of those practical and physical jobs that do not include personal care and assistance. They may also undertake tasks related to the children's leisure activities from time to time or on a regular basis (Atkin 1992).

As in many other families, mothers tend to take ultimate responsibility for orchestrating things that need to be done in relation to both the disabled child and other children and for attending to issues related to emotional and physical well-being. It appears that mothers often assume the role of jugglers and mediators who balance out the interests of different individuals within the household (Glendinning 1983; Graham 1985; Read 2000).

The key role played by mothers of disabled children as mediators between the child and the formal healthcare and social-care system is well documented (Beresford 1995; Glendinning 1983, 1986; Read 1991, 2000; Sloper and Turner 1992). In two-parent households, fathers may have difficulty in attending appointments on behalf of the children (Beresford 1995) but may become involved in non-routine matters that have been identified as significant (Strong 1979; Read 2000).

It is important to emphasise that there are large numbers of women who, as lone parents, carry the full responsibility for the care and upbringing of their disabled children. The majority of lone-parent households are headed by women (ONS 2004) and, compared with the general population, a greater proportion of households with disabled children have a lone parent (Beresford 1995). These findings are important because of the limitations on household income that often accompany lone parenthood and because of the support that many women in two-parent households acknowledge they receive from a partner (Beresford 1995). Whether the lone parent is a man or a woman, managing everything single-handed may prove enormously taxing.

The caring tasks to be accomplished may change over time, but many mothers find themselves having a very intimate and protracted involvement with their sons and daughters. As time progresses, the experience of the mother of the disabled child can diverge considerably from that of her peers who have non-disabled children. In the present circumstances, whatever mothers and their disabled sons and daughters might otherwise wish, the options to live independently of each other are drastically reduced compared with the experience of non-disabled young people and their families (Hirst and Baldwin 1994; Read 2000). Reliable and appropriate childcare for disabled children is not found easily, and adequate externally provided support services to meet the needs of older sons and daughters are simply not readily available (Kagan *et al.* 1999; Russell 2003). The Council for Disabled Children's survey of the childcare needs of over 2000 parents with a disabled child found that 85 per cent wished to work full- or part-time. The majority reported substantial barriers caused by a lack of affordable and suitable childcare for their disabled children (Russell 2003). Parents in other studies have reported that few nurseries and childminders have accessible buildings or the training and expertise needed to cope with children with complex needs (Kagan *et al.* 1999).

This means that it often falls to mothers to continue to provide care and assistance to their sons and daughters on an ongoing and long-term basis. This state of affairs may persist simply because mothers and their sons and daughters have been offered no other positive and viable alternative. Mothers' opportunities to have a career or to undertake any paid work outside the home are consequently very restricted indeed (Baldwin and Glendinning 1983; Beresford 1995). The situation not only has personal implications for the women and their sons and daughters but also has a negative effect on the total household income.

Fathers' labour-market participation generally appears to be affected in different ways from that of mothers. Nevertheless, it may still have repercussions for the household income and for the career and job prospects of the individual men concerned. Fathers who are employed do not tend to give up their jobs but many report that their work is affected adversely by having to take time off to attend to matters related to their disabled child (Atkin 1992).

Although the pivotal role of parents, particularly mothers, has been recognised for some time, in recent years there has been a recognition of the amount of support, care or assistance that many siblings offer on a regular basis to their disabled brothers and sisters (Atkinson and Crawforth 1995; Dearden and Becker 2004). Sometimes this can take the form of directly helping a disabled brother or sister or by undertaking tasks that assist the parent providing most of the care. In a survey of children and young people known to young carers projects in the UK, 31 per cent were defined as offering care or assistance to a disabled brother or sister (Dearden and Becker 2004).

Some young people may feel happy with what they do in this respect. Some may baulk, particularly at any suggestion that they be given the label of 'young carer', feeling that it places an unwelcome connotation on their personal identity or their relationship with a disabled brother or sister. They may also worry about the implications of calling their situation to the attention of those in authority.

Others may believe, however, that what is asked of them goes beyond what they think of as reasonable, places too great a restriction on their lives or skews their relationship with the disabled child or young person. As a result, some may welcome formal or semi-formal recognition of what they do.

Needs to be met at home

While the upbringing of all children may prove taxing at times, it has to be recognised that the care of a disabled child frequently makes demands that exceed what is usually required of parents of non-disabled children (Baldwin and Carlisle 1994; Baldwin and Glendinning 1982; Beresford 1995; Glendinning 1983; Roberts and Lawton 2001; Sloper and Turner 1992). The volume of work to be undertaken directly with the child on both a routine and a non-routine basis tends to be greater and the caring tasks more complex. A combination of factors related to circumstances and human and practical resources may make balancing the needs of disabled and non-disabled family members a challenging proposition. Trying to be even-handed in meeting the sometimes incompatible needs of different children in the household and making sure that nobody misses out is something that undoubtedly preoccupies many parents and may be a cause of stress (Glendinning 1983; Read 2000).

Beresford's (1995) national survey of 1100 families with a disabled child confirmed the findings of many other studies on the high levels of personal care and assistance being offered by mothers to their severely disabled sons and daughters of all ages. Help is frequently needed with bathing, washing, eating, toileting, mobility and communication. Special dietary needs have to be met, medication has to be administered, and physiotherapy and other programmes need to be undertaken. Some children need to be watched over or require a great deal of attention and stimulation if frustration is to be kept at bay. In addition, social, communication and behavioural problems are identified as significant in the lives of substantial numbers. It has to be remembered, as other studies have shown, that this work is not confined to the daytime. For a range of reasons, many disabled children need attention during the night (Atkinson and Crawforth 1995; Haylock, Johnson and Harpin 1993; Roberts and Lawton 2001; Sloper and Turner 1992), and this can result in disrupted sleep not only for the main caregiver but also for other members of the household.

The literature describes graphically the ongoing and long-term nature of the caring commitments. Although some children's needs for care and assistance are undoubtedly reduced as they mature, for large numbers this is not the case. For example, in Beresford's (1995) research, four in five young people in the 12–14 years age group still needed help with self-care. In addition, one in two needed substantial assistance with washing, dressing, toileting and mobility. Two-thirds needed to be supervised and kept occupied. The point has been made frequently that as a child gains in height and weight, the physical demands on many mothers and other carers become greater.

In addition, Beresford's (1995) survey indicated that behavioural, social and communication problems tended to increase in prevalence and severity as children grew older. The negative impact that they were seen to have on a range of necessary or desirable daily tasks and activities also became more marked. Challenging behaviour in an older and bigger child can be much more difficult to accommodate and manage than in a child who is younger and smaller.

Getting out and about and undertaking activities that others take for granted can require a great deal of planning, organisation and energy for families with disabled children of all ages. Notwithstanding issues related to the children's mobility or behaviour, going shopping or taking a daytrip can be made difficult by a combination of transport problems, an inaccessible built environment, a restricted budget, the need to transport equipment and parental fatigue (Beresford 1995; ONS 2004). It is also by no means unusual for parents and children to have to face negative or insensitive reactions by other members of the public (Glendinning 1983; Read 2000).

We have already indicated how difficult it is for parents to obtain appropriate childcare provision for their disabled children. They may also find that the measures that other parents use to offset the demands of childrearing are less available to them. Babysitting, 'child swaps' and other informal systems of moral and practical support that prove crucial for many parents do not come their way so easily (Read 1991; Russell 1991). Such arrangements are often based on reciprocity and on participants having agreed needs and circumstances in common. The child who is viewed as markedly different and who sometimes has unusual needs to be met may not fit within the informal rules governing such arrangements. In addition, many people may feel uncomfortable with disabled children and uncertain as to whether they can offer them care. As families with disabled children are not unlikely to find themselves living on a limited budget, parents may not have the choice of buying in childcare or other practical sources of help and diversion for both adults and their children. Consequently, the social lives of all members of the households of disabled children may become more restricted, and there is an ever-present danger of their feeling a sense of isolation or exclusion.

Material, financial and practical problems

There is an association between socioeconomic background and prevalence rates of childhood disability. The prevalence rates of mild and severe childhood disabilities are higher in children whose parents are manual workers (ONS 2004). In addition, it has long been established that the presence of a disabled child has a significant financial impact on the household (Baldwin 1985; Dobson and Middleton 1998, 2001; Russell 2003). This is as a result of two main factors: increased expenditure and reduced income. The costs of disabled living are high and therefore household expenditure increases. Simultaneously, as we have already indicated, the child's need for care reduces the opportunities that parents, particularly mothers, have for earning income outside the home. Even when families are aware of their full benefit entitlements, research has demonstrated that in relation to children of a range of ages and with a variety of impairing conditions, there is a substantial shortfall between the maximum benefit entitlement and the minimum essential costs associated with disability (Dobson and Middleton 1998; Russell 2003). For example, in Dobson and Middleton's (1998) work, the shortfall was estimated on average to be around 20 per cent for primary-school-age children who are unable to walk and as much as 50 per cent for children under five years of age regardless of impairment. Dobson and Middleton conclude that even when children in the sample are in receipt of maximum entitlements, benefit levels would need to be increased substantially in order to offset the minimum essential costs of living with disability. Many families simply do not receive their full entitlements, however (Audit Commission 2003; Preston 2005). Research has also drawn attention to high levels of debt among some families with disabled children (Harrison and Woolley 2004).

As a result of these factors, living standards in households with a disabled child are lower than those of comparable families in the general population, and it has to be recognised that some such families are living in conditions of extreme material hardship. Russell (2003) draws attention to the fact that around 55 per cent of families with a disabled child are judged to be living in poverty or on its margins. Some of those have been described quite simply as 'the poorest of the poor' (Gordon et al. 2000b). Again, the fragile financial position in this respect of lone-parent households cannot be stressed too strongly. Research has also drawn attention to the particularly vulnerable population of more than 7500 families in the UK who have more than one disabled child (Lawton 1998; Tozer 1999). In these families, there is an increased rate of unemployment among parents, a greater incidence of lone parenthood and a greater likelihood of being dependent on income support.

Restricted financial resources are also partly responsible for another major material problem in the lives of families with disabled children. Such families are likely to be living in accommodation of a poorer standard than families with similar incomes but non-disabled children. Many families find themselves living in housing conditions that are very restrictive and unsuitable for both child and carers (Beresford 1995; Beresford and Oldman 2002; Oldman and Beresford 1998; Sloper and Turner 1992). Some of the most severe housing problems are to be found among low-income families and families from ethnic minority communities. Some are living in accommodation that is hazardous and of very poor quality. Even when families have a place to live that might be judged reasonable when general criteria are applied, it often does not have the space, layout and adaptations suitable for the needs of a disabled child, the carers and other family members. Disabled children are frequently precluded from participating in ordinary activities associated with childhood simply by the existence of physical barriers within their home environment (Oldman and Beresford 1998). In the face of serious shortfalls in public financial assistance and the absence of suitable public housing, families frequently overstretch themselves financially by moving house or undertaking adaptations at their own expense (Oldman and Beresford 1998). In a national survey of 3000 households of disabled children, nine in ten identified at least one problem area that made the home unsuitable for disabled children and their families while one in four identified six or more problem areas (Beresford and Oldman 2002).

Ownership of both special equipment and standard consumer durables can also prove to be a problem. Research tells us that low-income families are disadvantaged in their access to disability aids and equipment (Gordon *et al.* 2000b). It has also been argued repeatedly that the ownership of ordinary consumer durables and systems such as cars, refrigerators, telephones, freezers, washing machines and central heating is essential for the families because such items can help to offset the additional demands of bringing up and meeting the needs of a disabled child (Baldwin and Carlisle 1994; Beresford *et al.* 1996). There is evidence, however, that the rate of ownership of these important items is lower among families of disabled children than the general population, with lone-parent households being particularly disadvantaged (Baldwin and Carlisle 1994; Beresford *et al.* 1996). For example, transport is a very significant resource for most families with disabled children. There are serious and well-documented difficulties associated with use of public transport, making car ownership extremely important (Beresford *et al.* 1996). This can prove to be a major problem for already overstretched households. Suitable cars that are big enough to accommodate growing children and their essential equipment tend to be more expensive. In addition, once a car has been purchased, wear and tear and running costs are likely to be higher than for other families. A national survey indicated that only half of parents with disabled children had access to a car compared with two-thirds of those in the general population (Beresford 1995). There is some variation in research findings on this issue, however, as one study of 300 disabled children and their households suggests a slightly higher rate of car ownership and, consequently, higher associated costs (Dobson and Middleton 1998). Other research reported that a third of a sample of 37,000 families with severely disabled children who had received financial assistance from the Family Fund had been given grants for transport-related costs (Roberts and Lawton 1999). It is argued that this not only indicates the importance of transport in the lives of many but also points to the inadequacy of current levels of related statutory financial assistance.

Research indicates, then, that some of these households that have irrefutably high levels of need for practical and financial support and both ordinary and specialist equipment frequently cannot access even those things that many people in the general population regard as basic to an ordinary standard of living.

Giving consideration to the material and financial problems encountered by families with disabled children is important in its own right. In addition, however, it is important to be aware that there is substantial research evidence of a clear association between high levels of parental stress and concerns about money, housing, transport and other vital material assets (Beresford *et al.* 1996). It is crucial not to underestimate the eroding nature of this level of stress on those parents who experience it over substantial periods as their children grow towards adulthood. It is also important to be aware of the fact that those who do not have a little extra money to buy in something that makes life easier or more enjoyable for children or adults, or who cannot afford decent transport or housing adaptations, frequently have only their own resilience, energy and muscle power to fall back on yet again.

Families' experiences of services

In addition to the direct caring work at home and the practical and material problems that have been identified, becoming the parent of a disabled child also necessitates involvement with a multiplicity of different agencies and professionals (Glendinning 1986; Sloper 1999; Sloper and Turner 1992; Yerbury 1997). This in itself constitutes tiring, time-consuming and often frustrating work. Since the mid 1990s, we have witnessed significant attempts by central government, the NHS and local government to improve services to disabled children (Russell 2003); however, there remain wide variations in the quality and availability of provision to meet the needs of disabled children and their families.

Accessing and dealing with services undoubtedly remains a major problem for children and their parents (Audit Commission 2003).

For 20 years, a wide range of literature and official reports record considerable levels of unmet needs and substantial parental difficulty and dissatisfaction with many services (Appleton *et al.* 1997; Audit Commission 1994, 2003; Ball 1998; Baxter *et al.* 1990; Beecham *et al.* 2002; Beresford 1995; Butt and Mirza 1996; Chamba *et al.* 1999; Glendinning 1986; Gordon *et al.* 2000b; Hall 1997; Haylock *et al.* 1993; Kirk and Glendinning 2004; McConachie 1997; Sloper and Turner 1992; Social Services Inspectorate 1994, 1998). A number of recurring findings emerge from these studies and policy documents. Provision that parents regard as suited to their own and their children's needs often is simply not available or is provided inconsistently. Innovative, sometimes valued projects do not always turn into long-term financially secure provision. Many families have lengthy waits first for assessment and subsequently for the provision of basic equipment, adaptations and other services. The Audit Commission (2003) reports that waiting times were frequently so lengthy that children had outgrown the provision or had missed an essential opportunity for the enhancement of their development. Services are also delivered by a range of specialists working within organisational systems of baffling complexity. There are problems associated with coordination and joint planning between key agencies and disciplines at all levels and an ever-present danger that disabled children and their parents fall through the gaps or become marginalised. Only a minority have a key worker or individual practitioner who acts as a point of contact to help them through the maze (Greco and Sloper 2004). The significance of these issues for children who have complex impairments as well as their parents cannot be stressed too strongly (Cass *et al.* 1999; Kirk and Glendinning 2004; Noyes 1999).

Many parents of disabled children experience enormous difficulty in finding their way through the terrain and report conflict and frustration with professionals. Good services can undoubtedly be powerful mediators of stress, but the difficulties they encounter can actually make parents feel worse, particularly if their views on needs differ from those of the professionals (Beresford 1995; Dyson 1987; Goodey 1991; Gough, Li and Wroblewska 1993). It has been shown that parents have to be extremely active and persistent if they are to gain access to what they regard as appropriate information and provision (Audit Commission 2003). There is a strong sense of their having to find out about, negotiate and fight for quite basic things. Even when they know what could be available, parents, in particular mothers, need to be very active indeed if they are to access the services they want. Those families under the greatest pressure because of a combination of stressful life events and very limited resources are least likely to be able to take on these formidable tasks (Sloper and Turner 1992).

A number of studies have highlighted children and families from black and ethnic minority communities, lone parents and parents on low incomes as being vulnerable to having unmet needs for support (Baxter *et al.* 1990; Beresford 1994; Chamba *et al.* 1999; Hatton *et al.* 2004; Robinson and Stalker 1993; Shah 1992, 1997). In some services, the under-representation of poorer children and their families and families from black and ethnic minority communities is a cause for concern (Robinson and Stalker 1993; Butt and Mirza 1996).

Parents report that they have to overemphasise their own and their children's problems and deficits in order to get a response from a service (Ball 1998). Family-support services also tend to be provision-led. It has also been reported that many children and their families receive multiple and duplicate assessments (Audit Commission 2003; Ball 1998; McConachie 1997; Social Services Inspectorate 1998; Townsley, Abbot and Watson 2003). The purpose of these assessments is not always clear to families, and telling one's story over and over again can be painful and very wearing (Audit Commission 2003). Most children and families appear to be assessed for existing provision only, and comprehensive assessments of their needs for family support tied in with consistent follow-up action still seem quite rare (Ball 1998; Social Services Inspectorate 1998). In the light of these findings, it is not surprising that parents report that they regard dealing with service providers as one of the most stressful aspects of bringing up a disabled child (Beresford 1995).

The need for information

Across the whole of childhood and the transition to adulthood, disabled children and their families need information in an accessible and usable form. This information can be about the child's condition, the responsibilities of various agencies, entitlements to benefits, practical support and other services. It has been reported consistently that parents and children have difficulty finding information that is essential to their well-being (Audit Commission 2003; Ball 1998; Beresford 1995; Chamba *et al.* 1999; Sloper and Turner 1992; Social Services Inspectorate 1998). Sadly, many families do not seem to have access even to the basics.

Parents' and children's needs for information as well as their ability to absorb it vary across time and circumstances. Families are more likely to make use of material that is geared to events and circumstances that are a priority to them at a particular point. For example, when they are entering a new phase in their lives, their need for specific information may be particularly acute. Aside from any concerns that budget holders may have about generating increased demand on limited resources, it has proved difficult for agencies to develop information systems that are sophisticated and user-friendly enough to cope with both the complexity of the information to be delivered and the diversity of circumstances of those needing to receive it. The plethora of voluntary agencies offering specialist information to parents of disabled children may be seen as both an indication and a recognition of unmet need in this respect. In addition to the general shortfall, it is clear that the availability of culturally appropriate information, as well as interpreting and translation facilities for those whose mother tongue is not English, presents problems (Baxter *et al.* 1990; Chamba *et al.* 1999; Shah 1997).

Critical transitional periods

Another general theme that can be pieced together from research and other literature is that of critical transitional periods in the lives of disabled children and their families. These merit particular attention because they have the potential to increase the vulnerability of the children and adults concerned (Baldwin and Carlisle 1994). It is useful to view them as experiences that are likely to be hazardous and stressful for all concerned if need is not addressed appropriately.

The notion of a transitional period refers to a critical stage where something important changes and a significant adjustment of individuals, circumstances and arrangements is required. This might, for example, be related to the child's age or development, to external arrangements and services, to family circumstances, or to a combination of some or all of these. Discovering disability, entering the education system, starting to live independently, and changing from children's to adult services are four examples of critical transition points experienced by disabled children and young people and those close to them. Typically, at one of these times, the territory is unfamiliar and a great deal of new knowledge, understanding and information has to be accessed, absorbed and applied if positive progress is to be made. Because significant outcomes hang on this, however, the stakes can feel very high indeed for all concerned. It is not difficult to see why a combination of such circumstances may induce stress. These examples are fairly predictable, and it is likely that such points in the lifecourse could present opportunities for useful and positive intervention by service providers. There are other less predictable but equally critical events in families' lives that also require significant reappraisal and adjustment and may destabilise existing supportive arrangements. These might include, for example, parental illness, death of a family member or parental separation and divorce.

Personal consequences for parents, disabled children and their siblings

When all of the experiences and circumstances that we have reviewed are taken together, it is not surprising that there can be substantial personal consequences for all the adults and children concerned. Although positive attitudes and experiences are apparent, the evidence suggests that there is a danger that those involved are coping with too great demands without adequate supports or resources to offset them.

In these circumstances, there can be an impact on the personal health and well-being of those who have the greatest responsibility for providing informal care (Russell 1991; Sloper 1999; Sloper and Turner 1993a). Parents of disabled children, particularly mothers, have been found to experience high levels of stress. Feeling tired or, in many cases, exhausted for a great deal of the time is a problem that many parents live with long-term.

We have already seen that there is evidence of an association between levels of parental stress and worries about money and material assets (Beresford et al. 1996). There is also evidence that paid employment for mothers of disabled children not only contributes to the household income but also is associated with lower levels of distress (Sloper et al. 1991). The factors that generate stress or promote personal well-being are complex, however, suggesting the need to be cautious about generalisation (Russell 1991). The experience of stress or well-being is likely to be linked to a range of interconnected factors, including the scale and timespan of any event or issue to be dealt with, the individual's personal resources and the way they view any situation or issue, the quality and level of the emotional and practical support they expect and receive, and additional significant problems or life events that come into play. Some research has sought to uncover the ways in which parents manage stressful circumstances by actively developing their own personal and characteristic coping strategies in order to create an equilibrium in their lives (Beresford 1994). However positive these strategies are, it has to be recognised that such are the pressures on these households that any balance they create can be rather fragile and upset easily by one of the unexpected events that are prone to occur in families' lives (Beresford 1994, 1995). Some of these events, such as hospital admission, may be related closely to the child's disability, but others, such as parental illness or divorce, may be experienced by many families, regardless of disability (Sloper and Turner 1993a). Also, because of limited resources and support services, the choices made by many families with disabled children about personal strategies for managing their lives may be within rather narrow confines. With a greater availability of resources, they could still put their own personal stamp on situations, but their scope and choice would be greater.

A great deal has been written about the impact of having a disabled child on marital or similar adult relationships. The situation is by no means clear, and there is some ambiguity in research findings. Overall, however, although some men and women report that their adult relationships are strengthened by the experience of having a disabled child, mothers of disabled children generally have an increased chance of becoming lone parents. For many, this will mean having a particularly onerous degree of responsibility for the upbringing and care of their sons or daughters in restricted financial circumstances (Baldwin and Carlisle 1994).

In considering the personal consequences for disabled and non-disabled children of the circumstances we have reviewed so far, a key issue has to be that substantial numbers are living on low incomes and, therefore, face many of the same restrictions commonly experienced by all children living at or near the poverty line. It is clear from the more general poverty studies how a lack of material resources insidiously affects almost all aspects of their lives and significantly erodes their choices, opportunities and well-being (Blackburn 1991; Gordon *et al.* 2000a; Graham 1993). These restrictions and exclusionary experiences may be magnified still further by both the extra demands and the limitations placed on disabled children and their families. Many other families with disabled children who are not living on the lowest incomes nevertheless also face significant human and material resource problems.

We have already referred to work that has highlighted the way in which a number of factors conspire to generate a gap between aspirations regarded as ordinary for disabled children compared with non-disabled children and young people (e.g. Hirst and Baldwin 1994). There is no doubt that many disabled children do not live what others would take for granted as ordinary lives and that many disabled children are excluded from experiences that may be regarded as significant for all children. A number of studies report that many parents are concerned about the limitations placed on both their disabled and their non-disabled children by a combination of circumstances. For example, Dobson and Middleton (1998) found that those parents in their study were acutely aware of their disabled children's isolation and restricted opportunities. They regarded them as children first and foremost and therefore sought experiences that they saw as being integral to any child's birthright and development. These were quite often difficult to come by and arranged only at some cost.

Other studies report that parents worry about not giving their non-disabled children enough time or attention and feel that the opportunities and activities of their non-disabled children are restricted by the necessity to organise many features of family life around the disabled child. These concerns are sometimes offset by an acknowledgement of outcomes that are seen to be positive such as siblings having a greater degree of maturity, understanding and a caring outlook (Glendinning 1983; Read 2000).

There has also been some research that seeks directly the views of siblings of disabled children (Atkinson and Crawforth 1995; Connors and Stalker 2003). As with parents, children record mixed reactions. Overall, most express positive attitudes towards their disabled brothers and sisters, but they also talk of being upset because of limitations placed on their lives. Unsurprisingly, a disproportionate amount of parental attention directed towards the needs of a disabled sibling, disrupted sleep and restrictions on family outings and leisure pursuits result in some children being jealous or angry. Some children in the studies by Atkinson and Crawforth (1995) and Connors and Stalker (2003) reported being teased or bullied at school because of their sibling's disability. Parents may find that extraordinary effort is often required on their part if their disabled and non-disabled children are not to miss out significantly on experiences and standards of living regarded as ordinary by their peers. This may prove an additional demand in a routine that is already exceptionally taxing.

Valued service provision

We turn now to some of the services that have been identified as valuable to disabled children and their families. In recent times, there have been a number of major policy initiatives designed to improve services to them. The Quality Protects programme set objectives to increase the use of services so that disabled children and their families could live as ordinary a life as possible (DH 2000b). In 2004, the Early Support Programme (ESP), which was intended to improve support to families with very young disabled children, began its pilot phase in 40 localities. The National Service Framework for Children, Young People and Maternity Services (NSF) was also launched in 2004 (DfES/DH 2004), with the aim of setting standards for services for all children, including those who are disabled, across the next decade. At this point, it is difficult to predict with any degree of certainty what will be the impact of initiatives such as the ESP and NSF. In this book, however, we use these initiatives as benchmarks for what children and families ought to be able to expect in the way of best practice and service provision.

Increasingly, it is seen as unacceptable to adopt an approach towards intervention that simply lives in hope that it may achieve what it sets out to do. From the mid 1990s, there was growing awareness that there had been very little research on the effectiveness of family support and community care services for disabled children and their households and few attempts to review them consistently (Beresford *et al.* 1996; Sloper 1999). Among other things, it has proved difficult to identify the effectiveness of particular services that are not isolated but are embedded within packages of support provided for diverse groups of children and households.

It is important to acknowledge, however, that a great deal of research has already has consistently identified children's and families' needs and preferences in relation to service provision (Mitchell and Sloper 2001; Sloper 1999). There is evidence of tried and tested approaches that can produce increased levels of parental satisfaction, enhance the rewarding aspects of bringing up the children concerned and provide a richer experience of growing up. Families identify the presence of appropriate services as a factor that makes a huge difference to their lives, and they often single out for mention a practitioner or provision that they rated highly (Haylock *et al.* 1993). Unfortunately, as we have seen, many parents caring for a disabled child at home lack vital services and both formal and informal supports (Baldwin and Carlisle 1994; Baxter *et al.* 1990; Beresford 1994, 1995; Chamba *et al.* 1999; Gordon *et al.* 2000b; Haylock *et al.* 1993).

A needs-led approach to assessment and integrated family service provision

There has been increasing recognition that disabled children and their families have diverse needs that cannot be met by uniform services and that a greater degree of flexibility is required in both assessment and provision (Appleton *et al.* 1997; Baldwin and Carlisle 1994; Ball 1998; Beresford 1994; DH 2000a, 2001a; Hall 1997; Russell 1988; Social Services Inspectorate 1998). The term 'assessment' is used in a variety of ways, and this can cause confusion. Sometimes, for example, it is used to refer to the process of arriving at a medical diagnosis or identifying impairment. The term may also refer to the process of identifying a much broader range of needs for personal and social support. Department for Education and Skills guidance (DfES 2003c, p.16) defines assessment as 'a process of gathering information about the health, education and social care needs of a child'. It goes on to point out that assessment should be seen as an ongoing process rather than one-off events and argues that this process should identify both those disabling social and physical barriers that inhibit the child's access to a good quality of life and what the support agencies can do to tackle them. The importance of assessment being supportive to the whole family is also emphasised. Although we recognise the importance of medical diagnosis for some children, in this chapter we adopt the broad focus indicated by the DfES. Any medical diagnosis and opinion, however, would be regarded as an important contribution to an holistic assessment of a child's needs.

We have seen earlier in this chapter that many disabled children have substantial and often complex needs for care and assistance – needs that are frequently met by their parents in their own homes. For a considerable time, the need to develop integrated or holistic systems of family support has been recognised (Russell 1991; Sloper 1999). Research and official reports highlight the importance of services being needs-led, flexible and focused on the family as a whole rather than solely on the disabled child (Appleton *et al.* 1997; DH 2000a; DH *et al.* 2000; Sloper and Turner 1992; Social Services Inspectorate 1998). It has been argued consistently that, particularly in the case of younger children, their own needs and those of the rest of the household are bound together inextricably. Although some services that are directed specifically at the disabled child may be seen to be helpful, it is sometimes equally beneficial to introduce provision that in one way or another simply creates the opportunity, time and space for members of the whole family to live a more ordinary life. Families' needs and circumstances vary to such an extent that if provision is to be effective, tailor-made packages are essential. Paying attention to the household as a unit is important, but it is also important to consider parents, the disabled children and their siblings as individuals with distinctive needs and rights. Services or opportunities offered to one individual may frequently have spin-offs for another in the household. For example, services that are seen as helpful and appropriate for their children tend to be regarded by parents as indirectly beneficial to themselves (Beresford 1994), and provision that alleviates parental stress has been shown to have positive benefits for the children's development and well-being (Sloper 1999). It is important to be aware that many parents are simply unlikely to use services that they regard as inappropriate for their child, even if others believe that making use of them might help the adults concerned.

In relation to child and family support services for disabled children, policy, research and practice have begun to adopt an outcome focus (DH 2001a; Rabiee *et al.* 2005). In simple terms, a range of desirable outcomes are identified for children and others in their families, and various arrangements are put in place with the aim of achieving them. There is growing emphasis on services at all levels being shaped by the outcomes that children and families have themselves identified as significant (Beresford *et al.* 2004; Cavet and Sloper 2004; Rabiee *et al.* 2005). The success of any intervention is judged on whether the outcomes are achieved satisfactorily. The arrangements made to achieve the outcomes may take the form of familiar or established service provision, but this is not inevitably the case. Sometimes other arrangements are put in place that are judged to bring about the same outcome. Flexibility is also seen to be increased by the fact that it is now possible for local authorities to make direct payments in cash to families, so that the families themselves may pay for whatever it has been agreed will help to achieve the outcome (see Chapter 4). The Practice Guidance for the Carers and Disabled Children Act 2000 (DH 2001a) offers a range of examples designed to illustrate the flexibility that is required to meet needs and achieve desirable outcomes.

There is already an established literature on valued approaches to working with families and particularly on ways of working in partnership with parents (Appleton and Minchom 1991; Cunningham 1983; Mittler and McConachie 1983). It has been argued that the most effective services aim, where possible, to support directly or indirectly parents' own personal styles and strategies for managing their lives (Appleton *et al.* 1997; Beresford 1994). This is not, of course, the same as assuming that every parent knows exactly what they would like or what might be best for their child at any point. They may never have had access to information on the full range of options and how they might be made to work for individual children and their families. If they have not had the chance for discussion either with other families or with sensitive and informed professionals, then they may simply opt for approaches and supports that they happen to know about, restricting themselves or their children unnecessarily. Given the opportunity, they may be only too happy to identify a range of desirable quality-of-life outcomes, despite the fact that these had hitherto been seen as beyond the reach of the children and adults in their households. Preferences also differ, and it is increasingly recognised that, like other families, those with a young disabled child have their own distinctive approaches to childrearing, lifestyle and coping strategies. Services that take the family's preferences and ways of living at least as a starting point are more likely to meet with success (Beresford 1994; Mukherjee, Beresford and Sloper 1999). In a context where so many factors are set to generate stress and create barriers to positive action, practitioners who support parents and children to regain a sense of direction and control over their own lives may help to accomplish something very significant.

There has been consistent emphasis on the need to negotiate carefully with parents and for professionals to regard them as partners contributing their own skill, knowledge and expertise (Appleton *et al.* 1997; Russell 1991; Stallard and Lenton 1992). Like other people, parents of disabled children tend to prefer to be taken seriously and treated with respect. It should also come as no surprise that empathy, warmth and good interpersonal skills rank high on the list of characteristics they value in the practitioners with whom they are involved (Russell 1991; Sloper and Turner 1992). Parents also report being able to form positive working relationships with professionals whom they believe genuinely to value and accept their child (Ballard *et al.* 1997). It may be important, however, to sound a cautionary note about approaching notions such as partnership uncritically. These often amount to little more than rhetoric, particularly when the essential power balance in professional–user relationships shifts very little. Service users may come to feel understandably cynical about ideas of partnership that do not appear to go beyond words.

As we have suggested, listening to parents does not and should not preclude listening to children. While it may be true that some parents find it unusual that a practitioner wishes to seek the disabled child's opinions, we have also seen that parents have positive regard for practitioners whom they believe value and appreciate their disabled children. Provided that the practitioner has some of the required skills, consults appropriately about the most effective means of communication and is sensitive to the feelings of the child, it is likely that many parents will welcome their child being involved and consulted. There is a range of tried and tested approaches to consulting with disabled children that can be employed by the practitioner who is able to be flexible enough to engage in the process (Beecher 1998; Beresford *et al.* 2004; NSPCC 2001; Rabiee *et al.* 2005).

In summary, good practice would therefore demand that *together with the children and adults concerned*, practitioners should:

- identify outcomes that are a priority for all family members and that help them to live more ordinary lives

- consider the needs that have to be met in their daily lives

- plan an individualised package of provision that addresses those needs and achieves the outcomes

- agree whether provision will be arranged directly by service providers or whether the family will receive direct payments to enable them to purchase the provision that they have been assessed as needing, or a mixture of the two

- monitor and review how the arrangements are working at agreed intervals and modify them as needs and circumstances change.

In addition to the Practice Guidance already discussed (DH 2001a), such a needs-led approach to assessment and provision is to be found in both the Policy Guidance Framework for Assessing Children in Need (DH *et al.* 2000) and the companion volume of Practice Guidance (DH 2000a), which contains detailed material on the way in which the framework should be applied to disabled children and their families. As we shall explain in detail in Chapter 4, under the Children Act 1989 disabled children are defined as 'children in need', and this assessment framework therefore applies to them. Chapter 4 also explains in detail the duties placed on local authorities in relation to these assessments. The local authority practitioner undertaking an assessment is required to look at any child in the context of the whole family and local community. The framework consists of three domains, and within each there are a number of dimensions to be explored.

1.   Domain A: child's developmental needs:

- health
- education
- emotional and behavioural development
- identity
- family and social relationships
- social presentation
- self-care skills.

2.   Domain B: parenting capacity:

- basic care
- ensuring safety
- stimulation
- guidance and boundaries
- stability.

3.   Domain C: family and environmental factors:

- family history and functioning
- housing
- employment
- income
- family's social integration
- community resources
- involving disabled children in the assessment process.

The Practice Guidance (DH 2000a) takes the view that practitioners need to start by assuming that disabled children have the same basic needs as all children, but because they are living with impairments some may require additional support, assistance and intervention. Considerable emphasis is placed upon social factors that restrict and disable. The guidance demands that the needs, capacities and opinions of all family members, including the disabled child, are taken into account. Those undertaking assessments are required to consider the direct impact of the child's impairment, the barriers that impede access to experiences that are regarded important in the lives of all children and their families, and ways of overcoming such barriers.

Because we know from research that many families with disabled children lack even basic information about their entitlements or about services that they may regard as helpful, practitioners responsible for assessment will need to ensure that the discussion has sufficient scope to enable the family to think through the range of needs and interventions that might be supportive to them. Practitioners who use the Framework for Assessment will need to find a way of gathering information that is comfortable for the family. There are many methods of doing this. For example, with a family's consent, the practitioner might ask them to talk in detail about what happens from morning until night (and, in some cases, through the night) over two or three days during a week and weekend. By doing this, the practitioner may begin to understand the pattern of the family's life and caring commitments in addition to the barriers they face in trying to do things that others often take for granted. Practitioners can also gain a sense of what families regard as really important, what strengths need reinforcing and supporting, the major problems they would like to see solved and the outcomes that they would like to achieve. In view of research findings on unmet needs, it might also be helpful for practitioners and service users to bear the following checklist in mind:

- Has the service users' eligibility for both general income maintenance and disability-related benefits been checked? Do they qualify for financial help from the Family Fund? Do they qualify for financial help related to hospital and other NHS costs, such as prescription, optical and dental charges?

- Do they need housing adaptations or assistance to apply to move to suitable public housing?

- Do they need aids and other equipment?

- Would parents and children benefit now or in the future from any of the range of short-term breaks, either outside or inside the home, for example someone providing assistance, support or care directly with the disabled child, a sitting-in service, a family link scheme, etc.?

- Would parents value help from homecare or domiciliary services to meet the disabled child's needs for care, assistance and supervision on an ongoing basis?

- Would parents value help with general household duties to relieve stress and, for example, to create more time to spend with children or meet the demands of direct caring?

- Does the disabled child have a reliable means of communication or is one being developed? Who understands the child best and how can their knowledge be used?

- Would other children in the family benefit from a service in their own right? What arrangements would help them to be able to do things that are important to them?

- Does the parent who has main responsibility for care wish to return to work now or in the future, and what arrangements would facilitate this?

Even if a practitioner does not approach the task of assessment for services in the way described, there is no reason why service users themselves should not adopt such a focus if they find it useful.

Following the implementation of the Children Act 2004 (see Chapter 4), there have been additional developments in relation to the assessment of children. At the time of writing, a Common Assessment Framework (CAF) for all children who are defined as having 'additional needs' has been prescribed for use across all children's services and is being piloted (DfES 2005). While it is stated that it is not the intention that the CAF should replace the Framework for the Assessment of Children in Need and their Families described above, the relationship between them will need some clarification. In the context of this rapidly changing policy environment, perhaps it is important to argue that although assessment frameworks and procedures may come and go, the basic core principles of decent, sound assessment remain the same.

Improving information

As we have seen, it is widely recognised that families with disabled children are not provided with crucial information at a time when they need it and in a form that they can make use of. A range of work has been undertaken to try to bring about improvements. It has been argued that if effective local registers of disabled children were better developed, they could be used not only as a database for planning purposes but also as a means to target information appropriately to those who need it (Association of Metropolitan Authorities 1994; DfES 2003c). As there have been considerable difficulties in many local authorities with establishing registers at all, the day when they could be employed universally as accurate and effective service-user information systems may be some way off.

Research has identified what families of disabled children regard as the key elements of effective information systems (Mitchell and Sloper 2000). The families wanted short, clear written guides to local services together with more in-depth information booklets geared to key periods in their children's lives or important issues such as benefit entitlements and disabling conditions. Parents wanted written information to be jargon-free and in different formats. They stressed, however, that this alone was not enough to ensure that they and their children would get what they needed from services. Families said that written information should still be accompanied by support from a facilitator or key worker. In a survey of more than 1000 parents of disabled children and other family members by the voluntary organisation Contact a Family, information for parents was seen as a priority. Participants suggested that it should be coordinated and delivered through written materials, drop-in centres, key workers and support groups (Contact a Family 2003). There now exists a range of written information sources for parents and children that attempt to respond to the need for clear and reliable information (e.g. Morris 1998d, 2003; Watson *et al.* 2004).

The parents in Mitchell and Sloper's (2000) study also drew attention to the potential future role of the Internet. A small amount of research has now been published on the potential of information and communication technologies and online information to meet families' needs (Blackburn and Read 2005; Soutter *et al.* 2004). It is helpful to locate any discussion of the potential of online services and information for families with disabled children in the context of broader debates about Internet access and use in the general population. General Household Survey data indicate that computer access is low among most types of financially disadvantaged households. For example, 16 per cent of households dependent on state benefits owned a computer compared with 45 per cent for the overall population (ONS 2002). We have already established that families with disabled children are vulnerable to living in poverty or at its margins, which suggests that some at least are likely to find themselves on the wrong side of the 'digital divide'.

Blackburn and Read's (2005) study of Internet access and use by 788 families with a disabled child found that a high proportion (75%) had previously used the Internet and that a substantial proportion (63%) of these were frequent users. In summary, they used the Internet for a range of purposes, some of which were related directly or indirectly to the care and upbringing of their disabled children. Other purposes were associated with the maintenance of a reasonable quality of life more generally. Not only did they obtain useful information and services, but also they used the Internet to keep in touch with family, friends and other people, do their shopping, pursue leisure activities, and so on. The findings suggest that the participants who used the Internet did so in relation to a range of issues that research has identified as important in the lives of families with disabled children. Despite these positive benefits, regular Internet users neverthe-less experienced a range of problems associated with technical issues and equipment and system design. In addition, lack of time owing to caring and other responsibilities was seen as a barrier to Internet use for more than half of the families who had online experience. The 'digital divide' among carers reported elsewhere (Blackburn, Read and Hughes 2005) also manifested itself clearly in this study, with non-Internet users tending to be the most socially disadvantaged. One-quarter of those who had never used the Internet identified cost, access to equipment and lack of skill as barriers to use.

In Soutter and colleagues' (2004) pilot research, skill was also identified as an important issue. Seventy-four families, each with a son with Duchenne muscular dystrophy, were provided with a personal computer with Internet connection. The project had a range of objectives, one of which was to provide ready access to a range of appropriate information and services. While the experience had many positive benefits for the individuals and families concerned, the researchers concluded that an unanticipated and important issue was that using information technology was not part of the everyday world of many of the families. To make full use of the Internet, parents and children were found to require much more training than had been anticipated.

Although some families may undoubtedly derive considerable benefits from online information and services, research indicates that the Internet may not currently be a suitable and reliable means of transmitting essential information to all, including some of those with the greatest needs for services and support. This makes it important to have a range of strategies for enabling the widest spectrum of families to access crucial information.

Care coordination and key working

In this section, we consider approaches to combating the difficulties that families experience in accessing services that are often fragmented, uncoordinated and difficult to navigate. As we have seen, following the Green Paper *Every Child Matters: Change for Children* (DfES 2003b), the Children Act 2004 was passed. The Act placed a duty on local authorities to put in place arrangements to promote cooperation between agencies that work with children and young people. It is planned that children's trusts will be introduced, which will bring together education, social services and health services for children within one organisational structure at a local level. Trusts are, at the time of writing, being piloted to introduce ways of developing joint service planning, commissioning and service delivery to children and their families. Russell (2003) argues that trusts offer an important opportunity to develop and evaluate new patterns of joint working and to model multi-agency approaches to identification, assessment, referral and tracking. Whatever aspirations there are for these new organisational arrangements, at the time of writing their exact shape and the outcomes resulting from them seem likely to be uncertain for some time to come.

There is already a substantial literature, however, on the importance of key agencies developing collaborative arrangements and practices that are variously termed 'interagency', 'multi-agency' and 'care coordination'. In addition, there is an overlapping literature on the related practice of key working, which explores the development of models for providing families with one named person within the services whom they may regard as their main point of contact. This literature may prove to be of some benefit as the new arrangements are put into place.

Care coordination

The importance of effective collaboration between the services and personnel involved in order to deliver a coherent service to disabled children and their families has long been recognised. Research and official reports show just how difficult this has proved to achieve (Appleton *et al.* 1997; Audit Commission 1994; Ball 1998; Hall 1997; Social Services Inspectorate 1994, 1998; Yerbury 1997). The lack of commitment to joint planning and development between agencies, geographical boundaries that are not coterminous, disputes over agencies' respective responsibilities, a lack of clarity about responsibility for disabled children in some health authorities, concerns about resources, underdeveloped mechanisms for interagency cooperation and inadequate management information systems are some of the issues that have been identified as creating barriers to the delivery of coordinated services to disabled children and their families. The need for the development of appropriate organisational, financial, managerial and practice mechanisms to overcome these problems and to ensure joint planning, joint commissioning and coordinated service delivery to meet needs effectively has been argued powerfully (Appleton *et al.* 1997; Audit Commission 1994; Ball 1998; Kirk and Glendinning 2004; Sloper *et al.* 1999; Social Services Inspectorate 1994, 1998; Townsley *et al.* 2003). In addition to creating collaborative strategic, budgetary and organisational arrangements, there need to be agreements between key agencies about who takes a lead operational role at particular points. Practitioners and managers with whom families have contact in one service will also need to ensure that they know their entitlements from other services and have realistic and reliable ways of accessing them. These links need to be made in a proactive way that will have an outcome for the family rather than simply being a token form of notification.

It is not enough for these matters to be left to the initiative of individual practitioners, as this makes the situation too fragile and unreliable for the children and families concerned. Clear agency and interagency agreements together with joint training and development not only are in the interests of the families but also provide a sound context in which the individual practitioner can operate. The process is undoubtedly easier and more effective in places where there are established procedures for interagency cooperation. A key recommendation of a major report by the Association of Metropolitan Authorities (1994) was that social services, health authorities and education authorities should make local cross-agency agreements and in turn take the lead role in brokering services required in the disabled child's early life.

Reports vary about the extent and quality of the development of care coordination nationally over recent years. Both Townsley *et al.* (2003) and Russell (2003) suggest that there have been significant attempts in many authorities to improve the situation, with many projects and initiatives being established with the purpose of improving joint working. In a national survey of 159 local authority Children with Disabilities Teams, however, only 35 (22%) reported having a care coordination scheme, a third of which were pilot projects (Greco and Sloper 2004). While health, education and social services were involved in setting up the majority of these schemes, contribution of all three agencies to funding the schemes was rare. Research on six multi-agency services working with disabled children with complex health needs and their families found that two-thirds of the service users who participated felt that this organisation had made a positive difference in their lives. Despite this, many still experienced significant problems over accessing some types of support and obtaining a coordinated response over certain services (Townsley *et al.* 2003).

Key working and advocacy

When we bear in mind the difficulties that parents and children have in obtaining comprehensive and reliable information, as well as accessing complex, fragmented and uncoordinated services, it is hardly surprising that research has emphasised repeatedly that one of the most valued provisions is the allocation of a particular worker to parents and their children (Appleton *et al.* 1997; Baxter *et al.* 1990; Beresford 1995; Chamba *et al.* 1999; Glendinning 1986; Haylock *et al.* 1993; Mukherjee *et al.* 1999; Shah 1997; Stallard and Lenton 1992). Families frequently refer to the impact that a capable and conscientious practitioner can have on their lives (Audit Commission 2003). Some research has identified the key worker as a critical element of successful care coordination (Sloper *et al.* 1999). The recommended roles for such practitioners vary but include the single point of contact for families, the provider of information and guidance, the mediator and facilitator with professionals, the coordinator of services, the care manager, the advocate and a source of personal support. These individuals are well placed not only to fill the information deficit so often described but also to act as a guide through the maze, to take some of the strain of negotiation from parents and to help them access services they need and want. Through being proactive, these practitioners may also be effective in tackling the problem that those families most in need are often least well placed to gain support. Finally, when appropriate, such practitioners may offer personal and emotional support through experiences that are upsetting, difficult or wearing.

One study defined a key worker as a named person who parents can approach for advice about any problem related to their disabled child. Key workers may be practitioners from a number of different agencies that have responsibility to collaborate with professionals from their own and other settings (Mukherjee *et al.* 1999). Research findings suggest that it is crucial for those practitioners identified as key workers to have a clear understanding of the task, to assume fully the role as defined and to have protected time to carry it out. Families reported particular features that made key working a beneficial and distinctive form of support:

- proactive contact by the key worker
- an open relationship
- an holistic, family-centred approach
- working across agency boundaries
- working with the family's strengths and ways of coping
- working and advocating for the family rather than the agency.

Research indicates that, nationally, only a minority of services have introduced systematic key working (Greco and Sloper 2004). A commitment to multi-agency working does not always lead to the development of key worker provision. In Townsley and colleagues' (2003) study of services where multi-agency working was established, only half of the families in their sample had access to a named person or key worker; in addition, they reported a lack of clarity about their role.

When we take into account the value placed on a key worker or consistently available named person, it is probably not surprising that the existence of specialist workers or teams is also associated with higher levels of service user satisfaction (Ball 1998). It is not only that such practitioners and managers develop essential expertise in relation to the children and their families, but also that they provide a clear point of contact and an avenue to other appropriate services for both service users and colleagues from other agencies.

In addition to key working, recent social and healthcare policy has placed an emphasis on the provision of advocacy for a range of groups of service users, including children (e.g. DH 2000a, 2001b). While practitioners, including key workers, may adopt an advocacy role from time to time, the independence of advocacy services from mainstream service provision is usually regarded as important (e.g. Henderson and Pochin 2001). This is to ensure that the advocate's accountability to the service user is clear and uncompromised. However, although good advocacy services may be highly valued by some who use them, they remain rather under-funded and thin on the ground.

Just as families appreciate workers who focus on their interests and advocate on their behalf, so too do individuals within those households. It may be positive and appropriate in some circumstances for disabled children to have their own advocate, particularly as they get older (Russell 1998). Many non-disabled children find that in the normal run of things, they have the chance to establish relationships and points of reference outside their immediate household. Fewer situations may occur naturally for the disabled child to do this, unless positive steps are taken to create the opportunity. Again, it is important to stress that this should not be taken as a criticism of the child's parents. If the arrangement is discussed and put into practice with sensitivity, it may be seen as providing both child and parents with something that many other children take for granted. In addition, as we have already reported, some young carers' projects continue to provide support, advocacy and diversion for non-disabled brothers and sisters (Dearden and Becker 2004; Frank 2002).

Interventions to enhance children's development

There is consistent evidence that many parents value and feel supported by provision aimed at aiding the child's development, either through work undertaken by professionals directly with the child or in collaboration with parents. Examples include opportunity groups and nursery classes, daycare, early-intervention or teaching programmes such as Portage, home teaching services and conductive education, speech and language therapy and physio-therapy (Cameron 1997; Hall 1997; Haylock et al. 1993; Read 1996). The provision of specialist equipment may also be seen as a means to enhance a child's development. Apart from the valued aims in terms of the child's development, some schemes may help to give parents confidence in themselves and their children. On occasion, contact with a centre or professional providing a specialist service gives parents and children access to valuable information, support and other benefits that are not linked directly to the primary purpose of the agency. It has been argued by some that because services that aim to enhance children's development are so valued by parents, it may be important to provide them even when appropriate methods of evaluating all aspects of their outcomes are not yet available (Hall 1997).

Some services developed specifically for disabled children are undoubtedly valued by some families, but there continues to be a debate about the degree to which some of the specialised or separate interventions are desirable or necessary. Some have warned against an emphasis on special teaching and therapy, particularly if it is founded on uncritical normalisation, because this may serve to undermine disabled children's sense of intrinsic worth by pressing them to aim for goals that are established as desirable with reference only to non-disabled children (Middleton 1999; Read 1998). It has also been argued that some specialist interventions may create an over-structured and contrived upbringing (Gregory 1991). Some families may see it as most enhancing for a child to be included in mainstream activities and facilities and regard it as a priority to have those practical and professional supports that make this possible.

In recent years, there has been growing recognition of the importance of trying to enable every child to have an effective means of communication. There has been concern about the numbers of disabled children who have never been given the opportunity to learn ways of letting others know about significant things that have happened to them or of expressing sometimes even the most basic preferences and choices (Beresford 1997; Kennedy 1992; Marchant and Page 1992; Russell 1998). There is now greater recognition of the value of systems of communication that can be used in addition or as an alternative to speech. Sometimes these are elaborated into a formal system such as Makaton, British sign language or Bliss. Sometimes approaches are tailor-made to particular children, their needs and abilities. The use of multiple systems and a variety of media can be extremely helpful for some children, and there is now a range of literature and accounts of innovatory projects to aid those parents and practitioners wishing to ensure that they are best informed (Beecher 1998; Burkhart 1993; NSPCC 2001; Russell 1998). Whatever the system, it is clear that enhanced opportunities for effective communication aid children's cognitive and social development and give them the chance to act upon their world rather than simply being acted upon by others. Because improved opportunities to communicate offer such significant possibilities for disabled children and young people, it is crucial that the means to achieve this are understood, taken seriously and employed by everyone in key service settings where the children and young people spend time. We shall give further consideration to the issue of communication in Chapter 6, which deals with the school-age years.

Assistance with financial and practical problems of daily living

Families benefit from practical assistance and financial support to relieve them of the additional personal and monetary costs associated with having a disabled child in the household. Their needs in relation to a range of aids, equipment,

transport and minor and major adaptations to the home should be est
part of a social or community care assessment. The law related to this
in Chapter 4. Although this book does not address benefit entitlement in detail, ..
is crucial to acknowledge its importance. The annual *Disability Rights Handbook*
(Disability Alliance 2005) includes an excellent guide to benefit entitlement and
to the applications that families may make to the Family Fund for cash grants to
offset the costs of certain items related to the care and upbringing of a disabled
child. Clear and straightforward information about benefits for disabled children
and their families can also be found on the website of the voluntary organisation
Contact a Family at www.cafamily.org.uk.

Short-term breaks, homecare and support workers

Schemes that offer parents and children a range of short-term breaks, formerly
known as 'respite care', are seen as valuable by many who use them (McConkey
and Adams 2000; MacDonald and Callery 2004; Prewett 1999; Robinson 1996;
Stalker 1991). It has been pointed out, however, that it should not be construed as
the primary or only service to be offered to children and their families; nor should
it be seen as a universal panacea (Ball 1998; Russell 1996). The government
identified the increase of short-term breaks and domiciliary services for disabled
children and their families as an objective of the Quality Protects programme,
indicating the importance of such services in the lives of disabled children and
those close to them.

The more established models of short-term break provision consist of residential units and family-link schemes. Some hospices also offer provision to
children with life-limiting or life-threatening conditions (Robinson and Jackson
1999). Domiciliary services consisting of workers going to family homes to
support disabled children are gaining favour but are a more recent development.

It is generally agreed that the need and demand for short-term break services
exceeds the supply (McConkey and Adams 2000; Prewett 1999). A survey of
services in England, Wales and Northern Ireland (Prewett 1999) reported that
there were 152 schemes, which were being used by 7521 children, representing
an 8 per cent increase since 1992. Despite the fact that many schemes have eligibility criteria that screen out those who are not regarded as being in most need,
nearly 90 per cent have waiting lists. Year-long waiting periods are not unusual,
and the numbers on the waiting lists are equal to half the number actually
receiving services (Prewett 1999). Consistently, research has raised concerns
about the under-representation of black and lone-parent households among
users of these services, despite having high levels of need (Ball 1998; Chamba *et
al.* 1999; Flynn 2002). Over ten years, there has been no overall improvement in

the take-up of short-term breaks by families from ethnic minority backgrounds (Flynn 2002). While there are examples of schemes that offer provision for children who have complex support needs (Prewett 2000), research reports that these children and their families have considerable difficulty finding suitable short-break services (Kirk and Glendinning 2004).

There may be many reasons why families do not use short-term break provision, and a lack of take-up should not be assumed to mean either that families do not want or need a break of some kind or that they do not need any other services. First, research on low take-up of short-term breaks indicates that substantial numbers of families do not have information about available schemes (Flynn 2002; Robinson 1996). We have already acknowledged that even when families have information, provision is generally in short supply. Consequently, families may not be able to obtain what they need at a point when it is most helpful to them. There is a general shortage of family-link placements, and children and young people who have challenging behaviour or profound and complex impairments or who require lifting are less likely to be placed in them. Disabled children from poor families and those from ethnic minority groups are also under-represented in family-based schemes (Robinson 1996; Stalker 1991). Compared with white families, a disproportionate number of families from ethnic minority backgrounds use institutional rather than family-based provision (Chamba *et al.* 1999; Flynn 2002). Some studies have shown that families on low incomes tend to be users of institutional care in the form of health service units or residential homes (McConkey and Adams 2000; Robinson 1996).

It is clear that attention needs to be given to the degree to which short-term break provision is sensitive to the social and cultural needs of potential users and whether the lack of information available to users has created a significant barrier to take-up (Chamba *et al.* 1999; Flynn 2002; Robinson 1996). In addition, it is crucial to acknowledge that what is acceptable and useful varies from household to household, from child to child and from time to time. It is perfectly legitimate for most parents to exercise their judgement that some things are suitable for their children but others are not. Although the importance of having diversity of provision has been emphasised repeatedly (Aldgate, Bradley and Hawley 1995; McConkey and Adams 2000; Robinson 1996; Russell 1996), the range of services that would allow families to choose something that really fits their needs and circumstances is simply not on offer in many areas. Some parents find the link with another family providing short-term family-based breaks immensely supportive. Some families feel that a good residential unit is most appropriate. Other parents do not find it acceptable to place their disabled child away from home (Beresford 1994; Russell 1996) and would prefer a regular sitting-in service, domiciliary support or a homecare worker to spend time with the disabled child at home or to take them out. In some circumstances, it may be advantageous to regard someone from outside the family as a child's or young person's personal assistant or enabler. They may undertake those tasks that the children cannot accomplish themselves in order to increase autonomy and enable access to new experiences. While the case has long since been made for the provision of such personal assistants for disabled adults (Morris 1993), it is regarded as a relatively new idea in services for disabled children. Some families may also appreciate a support worker who will on occasion concentrate on the needs of the non-disabled children in the family.

Whatever the arrangement, however, it is increasingly clear that parents as well as good professional practice demand that breaks outside the home and schemes involving support workers, personal assistants and homecare provision should be seen as a positive experience for both the disabled child and the rest of the family (Robinson 1996). Successful provision can offer a child an enjoyable and wider experience with people other than family members and sometimes, with support, the opportunity to do things that non-disabled children more often take for granted. It can also give a break to those who usually take most responsibility for care. Parents may find that they have the opportunity to spend time on other things that are important to them and can so easily be pushed aside or made difficult by the rigours of everyday caring.

Concluding remarks

In this chapter, we have drawn together some key themes from the research on the experiences and needs of disabled children and their families when they are living together at home for most of the time. We have also considered some of the approaches to service provision that either are tried, tested and valued or attempt to address deficits that research has identified repeatedly. We have also acknowledged the importance of researching and monitoring the outcomes of interventions that are intended to improve the quality of life of children and their families.

In the next chapter, we move on to offer a legal commentary on these overarching issues and explore how the law can be seen as a tool to enable good policy and practice in relation to disabled children and those close to them. We consider what disabled children and their families can expect of the law and whether it can help both service users and providers to create the opportunities that research indicates are essential for their well-being.

CHAPTER 4

The Law and Frequently Encountered Legal Obstacles

Introduction

Although all disabled children are unique, unfortunately the legal problems they and their carers face are not. Experience has shown that certain difficulties or issues of concern recur time and time again. Some problems arise at particular moments in the child's development, whereas some, such as poor communication between different agencies, can be ever present.

The purpose of this chapter is to provide an overview of the legal framework relevant to all disabled children and their families. In addition, we consider the legal principles that are relevant to the recurring themes and problems that have been identified as important in the previous chapter. We shall, therefore, review the following:

- what is meant by 'the law'
- the specific obligations and powers of local authorities for the provision of social services, education and housing
- the obligations and powers of the NHS
- the duties on the statutory agencies to cooperate with one another
- the problems that arise at transitional periods in the disabled child's development
- the disabled child's perspective
- the perspective of the disabled child's parents and siblings
- confidentiality and access to information
- the procedures for making representations and complaints.

Special note on terminology

In this edition, we seek to (among other things) highlight and incorporate the legal changes arising from the Children Act 2004. One of these changes involves, in England, the effective merger of local authority children's services' responsibilities with their education responsibilities and the creation of a new Children's Services Department[1] and in due course the creation of children's trusts, in which the NHS-specific functions are also incorporated.

This organisational change brings with it terminological difficulties for a book such as this. The main organisational reconfiguration does not apply in Wales, and in England the change affects only children: on reaching the age of 18 years, social-care responsibility for a disabled person shifts to the relevant adult social services department, creating yet another transition for the disabled child to negotiate.

On p.23, we express concern about the impact of continuous organisational upheaval in this field. We also suggest that, notwithstanding these changes, there will be no true merger of social care and education responsibilities within the new children's services departments. We believe that they will, in practice, continue to operate two budgets and have two workforces – one concerned with the social-care needs of children 'in need' and the other concerned with the educational provision for all school-age children. For this reason, in this book, we use the following terms when referring to local authority responsibilities:

- *Children social services*: the social services section of the local authority with responsibility for children.
- *Children education services*: the education section of the local authority with responsibility for school-age children.
- *Adult social services*: the social services section of the local authority with responsibility for adults.

What is meant by 'the law'

Rights-based law

As we have noted (see p.26), certain laws are of importance because of their basic human rights content. The clearest examples are of course the international covenants and conventions that have emerged from the United Nations (UN) and the Council of Europe. The UN treaties include, most importantly for our purposes, the UN Convention on the Rights of the Child (1989).[2] Although the UK has ratified this convention, it is, like most other UN treaties, not directly enforceable by aggrieved individuals. Its principal purpose is to act as an internationally agreed standard as to the basic rights of children. In addition, however, every four years the UK has to lodge a report with the UN explaining how the UK government is ensuring that the rights in the convention are being implemented.

British courts are not generally concerned with UN conventions of this type; such conventions are not part of UK domestic law but are merely international treaties. Judges will have regard to such conventions only if UK law is ambiguous or unclear. In such cases, when deciding how to interpret a provision, the courts endeavour to give it a construction that does not conflict with any treaty that the government may have signed.[3]

Unlike most UN covenants, the European Convention on Human Rights (ECHR) was drafted with the intention that it would be enforced by aggrieved individuals; to this end, the Council of Europe made provision for a court (the European Court of Human Rights) to oversee the enforcement of the ECHR. The ECHR has been incorporated into UK domestic law by the Human Rights Act 1998. Conventions that have effective enforcement procedures tend to concentrate on 'negative' rights.[4] Such rights are those that generally can be fulfilled by the relevant state refraining from acting in a particular way. Thus, the ECHR requires the state to refrain from killing people (Article 2), torturing people (Article 3), enslaving people (Article 4), unlawfully imprisoning people (Article 5), and so on. The ECHR does not, however, protect many of the positive rights found in other 'free-standing' treaties. Examples of such positive rights include the right to 'adequate food, clothing and housing and to the continuous improvement of living conditions';[5] the right 'to rest, and leisure and to engage in play';[6] and the right of disabled people to 'vocational training, rehabilitation and resettlement'.[7]

The ECHR was originally signed in 1950 and during the intervening period many of its apparently 'negative' provisions have, upon analysis by the court, been shown to contain 'positive' characteristics. Thus, although Article 3 merely asserts that 'no one shall be subjected to torture or to inhuman or degrading treatment or punishment', the court has held that this obliges states to:

- have laws and procedures that protect individuals from abuse[8]
- ensure that it does not single out a group of people for grossly different treatment on the basis of race or other grounds[9]
- conduct independent investigations when ill-treatment in a public institution appears to have occurred.[10]

Likewise, the requirement in Article 8 of 'respect' for individuals' private and family life and home has been interpreted as requiring positive measures by the state. It must, for instance, take reasonable steps to prevent people from being harassed[11] or abused.[12] This may mean passing laws to criminalise such behaviour and enforcing these laws, by, for instance, prosecuting people who breach them. Other positive measures required by the ECHR may include facilitating access by service users[13] or their carers[14] to social services files and ensuring that community-care policies do not result in the unnecessary institutionalisation of disabled people.[15]

The courts have now begun to grapple with some of the more profound forms of discrimination experienced by disabled people. In *Botta* v. *Italy* [1998],[16] the courts took tentative steps to articulate in the language of human rights law aspects of what has come to be termed the 'social model of disability' (see p.00). Likewise, in *Price* v. *UK* [2001][17] and a number of UK judgments, the courts have sought to entrench the concept of 'dignity' within the human rights law discourse – for instance, in relation to the way disabled people are 'manually handled'[18] and the treatment of disabled people in hospitals[19] and care homes.[20] In *Price* v. *UK*, Judge Greve expressed the proposition in the following terms:

> In a civilised country like the United Kingdom, society considers it not only appropriate but a basic humane concern to try to ameliorate and compensate for the disabilities faced by a [disabled person]… In my opinion, these compensatory measures come to form part of the disabled person's bodily integrity.

The Human Rights Act 1998 is not the only statute that contains broad civil liberty provisions. In the context of disabled children, the Children Act 1989 itself is of particular relevance. Part I of the Act lists certain guiding principles that apply when a decision materially affecting a child is to be made:

1. The 'best interests principle', namely that the paramount consideration is always the child's best interests, for which the Act provides at Section 1(4) a checklist of factors to be borne in mind.

2. The 'delay principle', namely that in general delay in making decisions is detrimental to the child's interests.

3. The 'no order' principle, namely that if faced with a choice of making a court order affecting the interests of a child, or making no order, then no order should be made, unless it can be shown that the making of an order is better for the child.

We see in other domestic legislation statements of general human rights principles, for instance in the Race Relations Act 1976, Section 71,[21] which obliges public authorities to promote (among other things) equality of opportunity and good relations between people of different racial groups. Likewise, the Disability Discrimination Act 1995 obliges (in certain situations) employers, service providers and the owners of premises to take steps to ensure that they do not discriminate against disabled people. In relation to public bodies, this duty has been reinforced by the Disability Discrimination Act 2005, which (among other things) introduces a new duty on public bodies to promote equality of opportunity for disabled people.[22]

The hierarchy of the law: statutes, regulations and guidance

From the perspective of public authorities, the body of law of primary relevance to disabled children is legislation approved by Parliament.[23] At its simplest, one can express such law as a straightforward hierarchy. At the top of the scale, we have primary statutes, such as the Children Act 1989, the Education Act 1996 and the NHS Act 1977. In general, statutes create the basic structure of the public body's obligations, but like a skeleton they need to be fleshed out with detail, and this is done by subordinate legislation – commonly labelled regulations, orders and rules (Box 4.1). Subordinate legislation is 'law', since it is promulgated by Parliament (although the actual process is generally routine).

Lawyers do not generally regard government guidance as having the force of law. However, such guidance is something to which a public officer must have regard when reaching a decision, for instance when deciding whether a service should be provided to a disabled child. Thus, if it can be shown that in taking a decision relevant guidance was ignored or not followed, then a court may be prepared to cancel the decision and order the authority to consider the matter again, having regard to the relevant guidance. Therefore, it is frequently asserted by lawyers that government guidance does not have to be followed 'slavishly' but is something that a decision-maker must bear in mind when making a decision.

In general, Department of Health and Welsh Assembly social services guidance is labelled 'practice guidance'. This guidance advises authorities how they should go about implementing a legislative obligation or other govern-mental initiative. Such guidance is essentially practical and need not be followed to the letter when for sound reasons good practice dictates another approach. Examples of practice guidance include the Department of Health's publication *Assessing Children in Need and their Families* (DH 2000a) and the practice guidance issued under the Carers and Disabled Children Act 2000. Non-social services guidance such as education and housing guidance generally has the same status as practice guidance, for instance the guidance issued to housing departments concerning disabled facility grants (see p.271).

This analysis of general guidance has one slight refinement in relation to what is known as social services 'policy guidance'. Policy guidance must be followed in all but the most exceptional situations: it is guidance that tells author-

Box 4.1 The law and guidance: its relative importance

Statutes

> Children Act 1989
> Disability Discrimination Act 1995
> Education Act 1996
> Human Rights Act 1998

Regulations, orders and rules

> Review of Children's Cases Regulations 1991
> Education (Special Educational Needs) Regulations 1994
> Representation Procedure (Children) Regulations 1991

Guidance

Policy guidance – what social services must do

> Volume 6 of the Children Act Guidance, 'Children with Disabilities' (1991)
> Framework for the Assessment of Children and their Families (2000)

Codes of practice

> Code of Practice on the Identification and Assessment of Special
> Educational Needs 1994

Practice guidance – suggests what should be done, in general

> Assessing Children in Need and Their Families (2000)
> Carers and Disabled Children Act 2000 (2001)

---

ities what they must do in order to implement a statutory provision. Policy guidance is issued under Section 7(1) of the Local Authority Social Services Act 1970; its binding nature derives from the wording of the section. In *R* v. *Islington LBC ex p. Rixon* [1996],[24] the court explained the effect of such guidance in the following terms:

> Parliament in enacting s.7(1) did not intend local authorities to whom ministerial guidance was given to be free, having considered it, to take it or leave it... Parliament by s.7(1) has required local authorities to follow the path charted by the Secretary of State's guidance, with liberty to deviate from it where the local authority judges on admissible grounds that there *is* good reason to do so, but without freedom to take a substantially different course.

Examples of policy guidance of relevance to disabled children include the guidance volumes issued under the Children Act 1989, for instance Vol. 6, *Children with Disabilities*[25] and the *Framework for the Assessment of Children in Need and their Families.*[26]

Central government may also issue guidance in the form of a code of practice; such guidance has more weight than ordinary practice guidance. Authorities are required to have regard to such guidance, and the ombudsman and judges pay it especial regard when making decisions. The most relevant code of practice in relation to disabled children concerns the Special Educational Needs Code of Practice (see p.151).

The general obligations and powers of the statutory agencies

A number of statutory agencies have specific responsibilities for disabled children and their families. Most notably, these include children's social services and children's education services, the NHS, housing departments and the Department of Work and Pensions.

Although, as we have seen, legislation spells out with varying degrees of precision the powers and duties of these agencies, they must also (for reasons of administrative efficiency, if no other) adopt local policies in order to facilitate the implementation of these obligations in their particular geographic areas. However, in framing these local policies, agencies cannot decide to not follow or to ignore the statutory responsibility in question. However, many disabled children and their families experience severe problems because local professionals and policy-makers fail to properly appreciate the relevant legal opportunities and duties that exist. Practising lawyers frequently come across cases where families have been told that a service is simply not available. Typically, this might be expressed thus:

- 'We don't do carers' assessments in this local authority.'

- 'Our authority no longer provides respite care', or 'We don't provide respite care at the weekends' or '...in the evenings', and so on.

- 'Although your child needs a day-centre place, due to cutbacks we cannot provide this.'

- 'Our department doesn't believe that residential placements are appropriate for disabled children.'

All of these statements are unlawful. Statutory agencies, like everyone else, must obey the law; they cannot pick and choose what laws they will comply with and then ignore the rest. This is known in legal parlance as 'fettering' their discretion or duty. If the law states that local authorities must carry out a Carers Act assessment when certain criteria have been satisfied (see p.264), then the local authority has no choice over the matter. If an authority has a power to provide a particular service, then it cannot decide for reasons of dogma or resource constraints that it will never provide it. If an authority has a duty to provide a service and has decided that a disabled child needs that service, then in most cases it must provide that service, regardless of whether it has budgetary problems.

Although this much is clear, statutory agencies do make comments such as those listed above – frequently out of ignorance, for instance because they have followed this practice for many years, without challenge by service users. This practice is then so oft repeated that it becomes part of the culture of that agency. There are good reasons why service users do not challenge practices that run counter to their interests. Service users are often bereft of information and support, extremely busy and, not infrequently, exhausted. A combination of such factors can make people unassertive. When, however, someone has the temerity to seek the forbidden service, the request is often met with the same incomprehension that greeted the young child's comments in the 'Emperor's New Clothes'. In such situations, the service is usually obtainable only by making early complaint and taking the request to a level at which the agency's general policy is capable of review (we review the procedures for making complaints at p.255).

The specific obligations of local authorities

Social services obligations

As we discuss below, the responsibilities of the various agencies (health, education, housing, etc.) may vary as a child grows older, such that the child and his or her parents have to negotiate many transitions. Throughout, however, children's social services have the core responsibility of ensuring that these transitions run smoothly. Children's social services are, in effect, the safety-net service: they should always be available, even if they are not actually providing a service, and be ready to step in if, for whatever reason, one of the other agencies fails to deliver.

The most obvious and arguably the most fundamental obligation of social services to disabled children and their families is the duty to provide a social-worker service. In addition, however, social services have a duty to:

- prepare strategic plans in order to meet the needs of disabled children
- maintain registers of disabled children
- assess individual disabled children and their carers and, where appropriate, to provide a range of services to meet their needs
- provide information about services that may be available.

Definition of child in need

These duties listed above are owed not to all children in the local authority's area but to those 'in need'. Section 17(10) of the Children Act 1989 defines a child as being 'in need' if:

- he is unlikely to achieve or maintain, or to have the opportunity of achieving or maintaining, a reasonable standard of health or development without the provision for him of services by a local authority; or,

- his health or development is likely to be significantly impaired, or further impaired, without the provision for him of such services; or,

- he is disabled.

Section 17(11) of the Act then defines a disabled child as being:

blind, deaf or dumb or suffers from mental disorder of any kind or is substantially and permanently handicapped by illness, injury or congenital deformity or such other disability as may be prescribed; and in this Part – 'development' means physical, intellectual, emotional, social or behavioural development; and 'health' means physical or mental health.

As we have already observed (see p.32), children with hyperactive and attention deficit disorders (sometimes referred to as attention deficit/hyperactivity disorder (ADHD) and attention deficit disorder (ADD)) should, if professionally diagnosed as having such a disorder, be considered to be within the definition. Even if there is no such diagnosis, such children would fall within the two definitions above, taken from the Children Act 1989. The same would be the case for a child diagnosed as having a milder form of Asperger's syndrome.

A social welfare service

A major innovation of the National Assistance Act 1948 was its recognition of the importance of a social welfare service, which would provide 'advice and support as may be needed for people in their own homes or elsewhere'.[27] The Act, in effect, identified the need of disabled people for social workers to act as 'brokers' by dealing with all the various agencies that might be able or obliged to provide services. The social-work service duty owed to disabled children and their families is now contained in the Children Act 1989 at Section 17 and in Part 1 of its Second Schedule.[28] This places a duty on local authorities to provide (among other things) advice, guidance and counselling services.[29] In addition to the general support and assistance provided by social workers, there are now many specific obligations, including the duty to plan and carry out assessments (considered below).

As we have noted, research has shown that access to a named social worker or key worker is a service highly valued by families. All too often, however, disabled children have no named social worker responsible for ensuring that their care needs are monitored and satisfied by the provision of properly coordinated services.

Although a failure to assign a social worker may be due to staff shortages within the local authority, any prolonged failure should be challenged. A precedent letter to this effect is given on p.275. If this fails to result in a satisfactory response, then it will generally be appropriate to instigate the review procedures (see p.241).

Advocates

Advocates are people who help disabled people and their families communicate their wishes and feelings in various contexts. In certain situations, for instance when a complaint is being made about social services, the law provides disabled children with a statutory right to an advocate (see p.244). In other situations, although the law does not accord advocates any particular legal status, good practice presupposes their existence; for instance, the practice guidance Assessing Children in Need and their Families (2000)[30] states at Para. 3.18: 'some families would like friends, advocates or relatives to support them during assessments and this should be facilitated'.

Social services should be able to direct disabled children and their parents to such advocates when requested. Advocacy services are required to be independent of the local authority and generally to provide short-term assistance (sometimes labelled 'crisis' or complaints advocacy) or longer-term support (sometimes labelled 'citizen advocacy').[31]

The duty to plan and keep registers

The Children Act 1989 requires local authorities to plan their services with the object of safeguarding and promoting the interests of disabled children in their area.[32] Authorities must produce children's services plans[33] that spell out their priorities and procedures for joint working with the statutory and voluntary agencies that have responsibilities towards children in need. We consider the definition of this phrase in detail on p.74, but by Section 17 of the Children Act 1989 all disabled children are deemed to be children in need. These plans will be modified as a result of regulations to be made under Section 17 of the Children Act 2004 and in due course will be termed 'children and young people's plans'.[34] In addition, Section 12 of the 2004 Act provides for the creation of a more substantial information database, potentially in relation to all children in need rather than only disabled children.

As part of the children's social services planning and monitoring obligations, they are required to keep a register of children with disabilities.[35] The register is considered in detail on p.55.

The social services assessment and service provision obligations

In addition to providing advice, counselling, guidance and other personal support services for disabled children and their families, social services have specific assessment and service provision obligations in relation to individuals.

The Children Act 1989 rationalised childcare law and introduced much needed reform of the process by which vulnerable children were protected. In relation to disabled children, it could, however, be argued that the reform created greater complexity, since the 1989 Act provided for new rights and duties without repealing much of the pre-existing legislation. As a consequence, disabled children and those close to them have rights to child and family support services under both the Children Act and community care regimes. Legally, this means they have a right to:

- be assessed under both the Children Act 1989 and community care legislation
- receive services under the Children Act 1989, Section 17, and the community care legislation, for instance under NHS Act 1977, Schedule 8.

It is no simple matter to explain the inter-relationship between these various statutes, but in practice the problems are less daunting and can be summarised as follows.

Assessments

Under the Children Act 1989, Section 17, local authorities are required to assess the support and services required by children in need and, where necessary, to provide services and support to meet the needs identified. As noted on p.74, all disabled children come within this definition of 'child in need'.

Under a separate set of statutes known as the community care legislation, disabled people have a right to support services from social services departments. Although the obligation under some of these Acts arises only in respect of adults, i.e. people over the age of 18 years, that is not invariably the case; some of the duties are owed to disabled people of any age, for instance under NHS Act 1977,

Schedule 8. However, since the assessment process under the community care regime is broadly the same as that under the Children Act 1989, good practice dictates that disabled children should be assessed according to the Children Act regime.

There is nothing magical or obscure about an assessment; it is, no more, no less, an information-gathering exercise, the aim of which is to ascertain the support needs of the disabled child and his or her family. Once an assessment has taken place, the next stage is to decide what services, if any, should be provided in order to meet the identified needs. We consider on p.49 what research and good practice tell us about the importance of the assessment process; on p.251, we consider precisely what the law requires to be addressed in an assessment.

Services resulting from an assessment

The object at law of an assessment is to identify what social support services may be needed by the disabled child and his or her carers. The range of potential services that can be provided are specified in various Acts, most importantly the Chronically Sick and Disabled Persons Act 1970 and the Children Act 1989.

The services that can be provided under the 1970 Act are specific, e.g. home help, day-centre placement, home adaptations, etc., whereas those provided under the Children Act 1989 are very wide-ranging, being virtually anything that could 'safeguard and promote' the welfare of the disabled child. In practice, it is generally irrelevant whether a particular service is made available under the 1989 or the 1970 Act, as long as the service is provided. The child and his or her parents may consider the statutory basis for the provision of a particular service as unimportant – and so it is in the vast majority of situations. In a few cases, however, the question is not academic – most commonly when the local authority is failing to provide or seeking to withdraw or curtail a service. The reason for this is that the obligation under the 1970 Act is considered to be more binding on the local authority than the obligation under the Children Act.[36] As a general rule of thumb, however, if a service could be provided to the disabled child under the 1970 or 1989 Act, then it will in fact be provided under the 1970 Act.[37] Thus, the only services provided to disabled children by social services under the Children Act 1989 are those services that cannot be provided under the 1970 Act,[38] for instance residential accommodation.

Residential accommodation

Where the assessment reveals that the disabled child requires the provision by social services of residential accommodation, this accommodation will almost invariably be provided under Part III of the Children Act 1989.[39] The accommodation can be provided under either Section 20 or Section 17 of the 1989 Act; the distinction between these two provisions is considered on p.219.

One of the most common situations in which a residential care under the 1989 Act is provided for a disabled child is in the form of respite care, where, in order to give the child and/or the family a break, short-term residential care is provided. When this occurs, the residential accommodation is provided under the 1989 Act. The provision of residential accommodation by social services depart-ments is considered in detail in Chapter 8. It should be noted, however, that local authorities have the power to provide accommodation to both the disabled child and the parents under the 1989 Act[40] in appropriate cases (see p.195).

Non-residential services

As noted, local authorities are able to provide, under the Children Act 1989, disabled children with almost any service they deem appropriate, provided it is considered necessary in order to 'safeguard and promote'[41] the child's welfare. Although the range of services available under the 1970 Act is more limited, it is still a substantial list, including such things as home adaptations, recreational activities, help in the form of practical assistance within the home, and so on. The range of services available under the 1970 Act is considered in greater detail on p.258.

Where the assessment concludes that other non-residential services are required (i.e. services not available under the 1970 Act, for instance advice, coun-selling, residential care, etc.), then these services will be made available almost invariably under the Children Act 1989.

Social services duties towards carers

As a result of three separate acts – the Carers (Recognition and Services) Act 1995, the Carers and Disabled Children Act 2000 and the Carers (Equal Oppor-tunities) Act 2004 – social services have specific responsibilities for parents and other people who are providing or intending to provide regular and substantial unpaid care for a disabled child. The social services obligation under these acts is detailed on p.258, but can be summarised as follows:

- The 1995 Act assesses the sustainability of the caring situation – the carer's 'ability to provide and continue to provide care'. If the assessment suggests that the caring role is not sustainable, then the local authority is obliged to take action to rectify this situation, normally by making services available to support the disabled child (for instance, under the Children Act 1989 or the Chronically Sick and Disabled Persons Act 1970; see above).

- The 2000 Act, in so far as it applies to parent carers, makes provision for them to be provided with direct payments – in lieu of services[42] – or respite care vouchers (see p.265).

- The principal impact of the 2004 Act is to require social services when undertaking an assessment under either the 1995 or the 2000 Act to have specific regard to the carer's work, education, training and leisure aspirations.

The social services duty to 'inform'

Para. 1 of Schedule 2 of the Children Act 1989 requires social services to identify the extent to which there are children in need in their area and to publicise the availability of services. This duty is considered in Volume 6 of the Children Act 1989 Guidance (Children with Disabilities), which makes the following observations:

> 3.6 …SSDs [social services departments] should build on their existing links with community groups, voluntary organisations and ethnic minority groups to involve them in planning services and as a sounding board when formulating policies. The publicity required must include information about services provided both by the SSD and, to the extent they consider it appropriate, about such provision by others (e.g. voluntary organisations). Publicity should be clearly presented and accessible to all groups in the community, taking account of linguistic and cultural factors and the needs of people with communication difficulties. SSDs should take reasonable steps to ensure that all those who might benefit from such services receive the relevant information.

Section 1 of the Carers (Equal Opportunities) Act 2004 additionally requires social services departments to inform parent carers of their rights to an assessment under the Carers (Recognition and Services) Act 1995 and the Carers and Disabled Children Act 2000.

The power of social services to charge for services

Local authorities are entitled to charge for the services they provide under the Children Act 1989 and the Chronically Sick and Disabled Persons Act 1970, although in practice very few local authorities do charge for non-residential care services provided under these Acts.

The rules relating to the assessment of charges for residential and non-residential charges are considered in detail on p.268. In essence, however, the local authority may impose such charge as it considers reasonable, but if the parents are in receipt of income support or any element of child tax credit (other than the family element) or working tax credit or of an income-based jobseeker's allowance, then no charge may be made. The parents' income is relevant only when the disabled child is under the age of 16 years. The amount of a charge in relation to services provided to a young person aged between 16 and 17 years is assessed on that young person's income alone.

The specific obligations of children and adult education services

Although education is of course a 'lifelong commitment', in practice the specific education obligations of local authorities generally arise at specific phases of a disabled child's development. The duty to provide general and special needs education is first engaged in the child's early and school-age years and is considered accordingly on p.133. The obligation in relation to further and higher education generally arises during the young person's transition into adulthood and is considered on p.188.

The specific obligations of housing authorities

Without the provision of appropriate accommodation, other efforts to promote the quality of life of a disabled child may be of no avail. As the practice guidance notes, 'when houses are well adapted for a particular child, the family's life can be transformed'.[43] Housing authorities have duties to process disabled facilities grants for adaptations; these are reviewed on p.27, while the obligation of the authorities to accommodate homeless people is considered on p.195. In addition, social services authorities have powers to provide accommodation for disabled children under the Children Act 1989; this function is considered on p.195.

The NHS's obligations to disabled children

The obligations of the NHS towards disabled children are substantial. At birth, a hospital's acute paediatric service may be involved, and thence services such as health visitors, speech and language therapists and physiotherapists may be required. These general duties, including the obligation of family general practitioners (GPs), are outlined on p.123. The obligation of the NHS to provide continuing care, short breaks/respite care and longer-term residential care is considered on p.126.

Cooperation among the statutory agencies

The Children Acts of 1989 and 2004, in common with the community care legislation,[44] look to children's social services to fulfil a central coordination role in ensuring that services are made available to meet the care needs of disabled children.

Section 27 of the 1989 Act provides children's social services with significant powers to require the cooperation of other authorities in relation to a specific child, whereas the 2004 Act provides a wide-ranging power to promote the well-being of children in the authority's area generally. Section 27 enables a children's services department to request the help of another authority, for instance a housing department or NHS body, when it believes that this assistance could safeguard or promote the interests of a child for whom they have responsibilities. It will be seen that a request for assistance obliges the other authority not only to consider the request and to respond constructively but also to comply with it unless it would unduly prejudice the discharge of its functions; that is, any prejudice caused to the organisation by taking action is not excessive. Thus, the mere fact that providing assistance would prejudice its activities is insufficient. Section 27 cannot, however, be used by children's social services as a mechanism for shifting responsibilities to another authority.[45]

A broad generic power to require cooperation is to be found in Section 10 of the Children Act 2004 (Section 25 in Wales). It enables children's social services to request a wide range of other authorities; for example, in addition to housing departments and NHS bodies, it also includes the police service, probation services, youth offending teams, learning and skills councils and their funded institutions. These bodies must cooperate when so requested, so as to improve the general 'well-being of children in the authority's area' in relation to:

- their physical and mental health and emotional well-being
- their protection from harm and neglect
- their education, training and recreation
- the contribution made by them to society
- their social and economic well-being.

The good practice implications of the Section 27 duty to cooperate are amplified in the Children Act 1989 guidance[46] in the following terms:

Care management arrangements also take account of the multiple service providers which will be required to meet the majority of special needs. The approach aims to encourage the identification of the full range of services which may be needed. The SSD will have overall responsibility for the coordination of the services required. However, the day to day management and provision of these services may rest elsewhere. Packages of support can be put together using the statutory and the voluntary and independent sectors thereby making use of whatever pattern of provision has been developed within the context of a particular SSD.

Frequently, it is difficult if not impossible to say with precision which particular statutory agency is responsible for providing a particular service, or, put another way, which agency is at fault in any given situation. The experience of practising lawyers is that agencies frequently end up blaming one another and suggesting that it is to the other that complaint should be made. As Lord Laming observed in his Victoria Climbié Inquiry Report,[47] all too often the delivery of children's services is:

> too unpredictable and the co-operation between staff of the key agencies relies too heavily on personal inclination. The need to work across ever-changing geographical boundaries has created the danger that too much time is being spent on the bureaucratic aspects of inter-agency working and too little on actually helping children and families in need.

There are a large number of other statutory provisions that require agencies to cooperate in this field, including in relation to health services,[48] housing services[49] and education services.[50] Where delay is caused by an interagency dispute, it is generally appropriate for a complaint to be made against each authority primarily on the basis that they have failed to 'work together' in violation of their specific statutory obligations; see p.241 which considers complaints process. The ombudsman has repeatedly criticised authorities for allowing disabled children and their families to suffer while the authorities squabbled over their respective obligations. One such finding concerned the failure of the NHS and children's social services to cooperate. The local ombudsman considered that the NHS involvement had been 'reluctant, if not unhelpful', and, in consequence, the service user became caught in the cross-fire. The ombudsman nevertheless held that since children's social services had accepted that a need existed, social services should have 'grasped the nettle' and secured the provision before entering into protracted negotiations with the NHS on liability for the care costs.[51]

In many cases, the failure of 'joint-working' is an internal rather than an inter-agency failure. Adult social services and children's services departments, including education, are always part of the same authority, and in many cases so too is the housing department, i.e. in unitary authorities, metropolitan boroughs and London boroughs. Frequently, disabled children and their parents are told by the education section of a local authority that a particular need is the responsibility of the social services section and that the family should, therefore, make a formal approach to that particular unit. This is manifestly unprofessional practice, since there should be internal liaison by which the various sections coordinate their support. A request made to a local authority for help should trigger obligations in all sections of that authority; indeed, in many cases, the law requires the local authority to be proactive, not waiting for a request but providing support once there is an 'appearance of need'.[52]

Transitional periods in a disabled child's lifecourse

As we have emphasised (see p.45), negotiating transitions is one of the key problems faced by disabled children and their families. For example, new requirements brought about by a child growing older or by changes in other circumstances mean that he or she has to move from a familiar service or professional and find out about and access new services. These transitions not only are from one agency to another (typically from the health service to children's social services, to children's education services, to the welfare benefits agency, to the Department for Work and Pensions and then to a housing authority) but also may be transitions within agencies, typically from a children's services team to an adult social services team, from a hospital health team to a GP, and so on. In addition, there will inevitably be turnover among healthcare, social-care and education staff, with not infrequent transitions from one officer to another. This being so, commitments made by an individual worker may have value only if that worker remains or puts the commitment in writing as part of a formal agreement or plan.

Legislative recognition of these difficulties exists in relation to a child's transition into adulthood; this stage is considered in detail in Chapter 7. If a transition is not managed properly and results in difficulties, it will be clear evidence of a joint working failure, and, where appropriate, this should form the substance of any complaint (see p.241).

The disabled child's perspective

Since the end of the Second World War, the law has moved gradually from the perspective of the state doing things to/for disabled children and their families to the state enabling and empowering disabled children and their families to participate as fully as possible in ordinary social life. Today, social services and education statutes specifically recognise the importance of involving disabled children in the decision-making process and in doing so reflect the fundamental requirements of the UN Convention for the Rights of the Child, not least (in this context) Article 123, which recognises that children have a right to be involved in decisions about their care. Although such explicit references are absent from statutes dealing with health, housing and social security, this does not mean that these agencies have no equivalent duty. All agencies have a general obligation to take account of the wishes and feelings of a disabled child, and a failure in this regard will frequently constitute maladministration[53] and/or a breach of a professional code of practice.

Children's social services

Section 1(3) of the Children Act 1989 gives as an overriding principle that in the making of any decision concerning the welfare of a child, regard shall be had to 'the ascertainable wishes and feelings of the child concerned (considered in the light of his age and understanding)'. This has now been reinforced by Section 53 of the Children Act 2004, which inserts into the 1989 Act a new Section 17 (4A), which provides that:

> Before determining what (if any) services to provide for a particular child in need in the exercise of functions conferred on them by this section, a local authority shall, so far as is reasonably practicable and consistent with the child's welfare –
>
> (a)   ascertain the child's wishes and feelings regarding the provision of those services; and
>
> (b)   give due consideration (having regard to his age and understanding) to such wishes and feelings of the child as they have been able to ascertain.

The formal guidance under the Children Act 1989 requires children's social services to 'develop clear assessment procedures for children in need...which take account of the child's and family's needs and preferences, racial and ethnic origins, their culture, religion and any special needs relating to the circumstances of individual families'.[54] The guidance continues (at Para. 6.6):

> Children and young people should be given the chance to exercise choice and their views should be taken seriously if they are unhappy about the arrangements made for them. Plans should be explained, discussed and, if necessary, reassessed in the light of the child's views...With young children, the social worker should make efforts to communicate with the child to discover his real feelings. All children need to be given information and appropriate explanations so that they are in a position to develop views and make choices.

And at Para. 6.7:

> If the child has complex needs or communication difficulties arrangements must be made to establish his views. Decisions may be made incorrectly about children with disabilities because of ignorance about the true implications of the disability and the child's potential for growth and development... Even children

with severe learning disabilities or very limited expressive language can communicate preferences if they are asked in the right way by people who understand their needs and have the relevant skills to listen to them. No assumptions should be made about 'categories' of children with disabilities who cannot share in decision-making or give consent to or refuse examination, assessment or treatment.

The importance of involving children in the assessment process is emphasised in the policy guidance Framework for the Assessment of Children in Need and their Families,[55] which at Para. 3.41 stresses:

> ...direct work with children is an essential part of assessment, as well as recognising their rights to be involved and consulted about matters which affect their lives. This applies to all children, including disabled children. Communicating with some disabled children requires more preparation, sometimes more time and on occasions specialist expertise, and consultation with those closest to the child. For example, for children with communication difficulties it may be necessary to use alternatives to speech such as signs, symbols, facial expression, eye pointing, objects of reference or drawing.[56]

In a similar vein, the guidance accompanying the NHS and Community Care Act 1990 requires that both the disabled person

> ...and normally, with his or her agreement, any carers should be involved throughout the assessment and care management process. They should feel that the process is aimed at meeting their wishes. Where a user is unable to participate actively it is even more important that he or she should be helped to understand what is involved and the intended outcome.[57]

The High Court has stressed the importance of assessments taking into account the disabled person's wishes, feelings and preferences and has suggested that the following should be investigated in difficult cases:[58]

> 133. In a case where the disabled person is, by reason of their disability, prevented, whether completely or in part, from communicating their wishes and feelings it will be necessary for the assessors to facilitate the ascertainment of the person's wishes and feelings, so far as they may be deduced, by whatever means, including seeking and receiving advice – advice, not instructions – from appropriate interested persons...involved in the care of the disabled person.

> 134. Good practice...suggests...that:

> (i) A rough 'dictionary' should be drawn up, stating what the closest carers...understand by the various non verbal communications, based on their intimate long term experience of the person. Thus with familiarisation and 'interpretation' the carers can accustom themselves

to the variety of feelings and modes of expression and learn to recognise what is being communicated.

(ii)   Where the relatives are present with the carers and an occasion of 'interpretation' arises, great weight must be accorded to the relatives' 'translation'.

(iii) As I commented in Re S (2003)[59] 'the devoted parent who...has spent years caring for a disabled child is likely to be much better able than any social worker, however skilled, or any judge, however compassionate, to "read" his child, to understand his personality and to interpret the wishes and feelings which he lacks the ability to express.'

(iv)   That said, in the final analysis the task of deciding whether, in truth, there is a refusal or fear or other negative reaction to being lifted must...fall on the carer, for the duty to act within the framework given by the employer falls upon the employee. Were the patient not incapacitated, there could be no suggestion that the relative's views are other than a factor to be considered. Because of the lack of capacity and the extraordinary circumstances in a case such as this, the views of the relatives are of very great importance, but they are not determinative.

A failure to properly involve a disabled child in his or her assessment, even if there are profound communication problems, may well result in a court holding the procedure unlawful.[60] The case of R (CD) v. Anglesey County Council [2004][61] illustrates this point well. This case concerned a 15-year-old wheelchair-user with quadriplegic cerebral palsy who was registered as blind and had moderate learning disabilities. Her mother was unwell and felt unable to care for her full-time, and so she had spent considerable time with foster parents. The local authority sought to bring this fostering arrangement to an end despite her having developed a very strong bond with these carers. The judge was highly critical of the authority's actions, commenting:[62]

I cannot recollect a case in which, otherwise than in relation to secure accommodation, it has been considered seriously arguable that a 15 year old child should be required to reside at an establishment to an extent substantially contrary to her or his wishes and feelings. In this case...C's wishes and feelings have not even been satisfactorily reported by the local authority. That seems to me, by itself, to go a substantial way towards establishing a breach of section 20(6) the Act of 1989. Of course a 15 year old who does not suffer substantial disabilities and who is directed to stay at a location to which she or he has strong objection can...vote with her or his feet. C can do no such thing; but it would, for obvious reasons, be wrong to pay any less respect to her wishes and feelings in consequence. In particular it should be noted that her wishes and feelings are not in any way capricious. They are based upon the natural wish of any teenager not to be singled out at school as having home circumstances with unique deficits and upon the related feature, namely her wish to continue partly to live with Mr and Mrs R.

Education

The Special Educational Needs Code of Practice[63] stresses the importance of involving the child in any assessment or planned intervention in his or her life, stating that as a matter of principle 'children have a right to be heard. They should be encouraged to participate in decision-making about provision to meet their special educational needs.' The guidance continues at Para. 3.2:

> Children and young people with special educational needs have a unique knowledge of their own needs and circumstances and their own views about what sort of help they would like to help them make the most of their education. They should, where possible, participate in all the decision-making processes that occur in education...

NHS services

The statutory duties placed upon health bodies are expressed in broad and general terms, such that there is no specific requirement that health professionals involve disabled children when choices need to be made about their healthcare needs and the services that may be available to them.

We emphasise throughout this book the crucial importance of maximising the disabled child's ability to communicate; on p.125 we argue that since this amounts to a fundamental human right, it places a substantial obligation on the NHS to ensure that the child's wishes and feelings are taken into account.

The issue of user involvement is also a matter of relevance to the common law and professional ethics. If the child is mentally competent,[64] the doctor is unable to do anything that is invasive or intrusive in the absence of the child's specific consent, unless sanctioned by the court or permitted by the Mental Health Act 1983. The Children Act 1989 guidance makes this point clear, stating: '[The ability of disabled children] to give consent or refusal to any action including examination, assessment or treatment is only limited by the general conditions regarding sufficient understanding which apply to other children under the Children Act 1989.'[65]

The NHS, like all local authority departments, is subject to the 2004 guidance The National Service Framework for Children, Young People and

Maternity Services, as discussed on p.48.[66] The Core Standards volume requires that 'children and young people and families receive high quality services which are coordinated around their individual and family needs and take account of their views' (Standard 3), which means 'seeing services through the eyes of the child and family, and planning and delivering services according to their needs'.[67] This in turn requires that 'particular efforts should be made to ensure that children and young people who are often excluded from participation activities are supported in giving their views'.[68]

The National Service Framework gives specific advice on how these general principles should be taken forward. Thus, the volume of guidance concerning primary care[69] requires that:

> Every child, young person and parent should be actively involved in decisions about the child's health and well-being, facilitated by appropriate information. Formal working arrangements are in place for the provision of link workers, advocates to support children and young people, interpreters and/or support workers for children in special circumstances and children and families from minority ethnic groups, to represent their needs during individual consultations with PCPs [primary care providers]. Children and young people are offered choices wherever possible, for example, in the location of care or treatment, treatment options or the gender of the professional that they see.

The volume concerning Hospital Services[70] contains the following Standard:

> Children and young people should receive care that is integrated and coordinated around their particular needs, and the needs of their family. They, and their parents, should be treated with respect, and should be given support and information to enable them to understand and cope with the illness or injury, and the treatment needed. They should be encouraged to be active partners in decisions about their health and care, and, where possible, be able to exercise choice.

> Children, young people and their parents will participate in designing NHS and social care services that are readily accessible, respectful, empowering, follow best practice in obtaining consent and provide effective response to their needs.

This Standard is amplified at Para. 3.16 as follows:

> Staff working with children and young people should have training in the necessary communication skills to enable them to work effectively with children, young people and parents, and to support them to be active partners in decision making. Ideally, this should include:

>> How to listen to and communicate with children, young people, parents and carers, and the need to understand the extent and the limits of children's comprehension at various stages of development.

Recognition of the role of parents in looking after their children in hospital.

Providing information that is factual, objective, and non-directive, about a child's condition, likely prognosis, treatment options, and likely outcomes.

Giving bad news in a sensitive non-hurried fashion, with time offered for further consultation away from the ward environment.

Enabling a child and family to exercise choice, taking account of age and competence to understand the implications.

In relation to the children with complex health needs, there is a further volume of guidance to the NSF concerning disabled children:[71]

Disabled children want staff to listen to them, ask them for their ideas, take notice of what they say and give them choices. Children can contribute unique and essential knowledge during decision-making. Parents of disabled children also want to be involved in decisions about the services and treatments their children receive. Involvement of children and their parents in planning services results in the provision of more appropriate services.

However, disabled children are less actively involved in decision-making than children who are not disabled. Therefore, professionals should ensure that disabled children, especially children with high communication needs, are not excluded from the decision-making process. In particular, professionals should consider the needs of children who rely on communication equipment or who use non-verbal communication such as sign language.

The perspective of parents and siblings

The difficulties experienced in meeting the needs of disabled children frequently have a profound and negative impact on the lives of other household members. It is, therefore, essential that account is taken of this impact, not only as an aid to ensuring that the disabled child's needs are satisfied but also to enable the child's parents and siblings to have as full and normal a life as possible.

Children's social services, children's education services and the health service all have responsibilities in relation to the parents of disabled children. 'Partnership with parents' is a central theme of the Children Act 1989, which has implications for the way in which social services staff are expected to work. The formal guidance asserts that partnership includes an appreciation that 'the family has a unique and special knowledge of a child and can therefore contribute significantly to that child's health and development – albeit often in partnership with a range of service providers'.[72] The guidance continues at Para. 6.4:

Equally partnership and consultation with parents and children on the basis of careful joint planning and agreement is the guiding principle for the provision of services whether within the family home or where children are provided with accommodation under voluntary arrangements. Such arrangements are intended to assist the parent and enhance, not undermine, the parent's authority and control.

Questions continue to be raised concerning the extent to which many authorities actually engage in such partnership working. In *R (J)* v. *Caerphilly CBC* [2005],[75] the judge reiterated criticisms he had made in the past[74] concerning 'The "mindset" and "culture" of local authorities who exclude families from the decision-making process, merely "sharing" the decision with them after it has been taken…'.

The practice guidance Assessing Children in Need and their Families[75] notes that 'services should seek to build on parents' strengths, and since parents cope in very different ways an approach sensitive to individual difference is necessary' and that the 'siblings of disabled children have often been invisible to professional eyes'.

In addition to the obligation of social services to work in partnership with parents are the duties owed to parents as carers by virtue of the Carers (Recognition and Services) Act 1995, the Carers and Disabled Children Act 2000 and the Carers (Equal Opportunities) Act 2004. These Acts, which are considered in detail on p.264, oblige social services departments to (among other things) carry out an assessment of the ability of carers with a view to ascertaining what additional services may be required by the household and the aspirations of carers to work or access education, training and leisure activities.

The Special Educational Needs Code of Practice[76] states that it is 'essential that all professionals (schools, LEAs [local education authorities] and other agencies) actively seek to work with parents and value the contribution they make'. The guidance continues by emphasising the importance of ensuring that assessments take account of the wishes, feelings and knowledge of parents at all stages and that:

> It is vitally important that schools welcome and encourage parents to participate from the outset and throughout their child's educational career at the school. Schools need to regularly review their policies to ensure that they encourage active partnership with parents and do not present barriers to participation. Schools should seek to actively work with their local parent partnership service.

The responsibility of the NHS to pay proper regard to the views and needs of parent carers is described in general terms in The National Service Framework for Children, Young People and Maternity Services guidance,[77] both in the Core

Standards guidance and the more specific volumes concerning primary care,[78] hospital services[79] and children with complex health needs.[80] Standard 2 of the Core Standards[81] Supporting Parenting provides:

> Parents or carers are enabled to receive the information, services and support that will help them to care for their children and equip them with the skills they need to ensure that their children have optimum life chances and are healthy and safe.

Guidance issued under the Carers (Recognition and Services) Act 1995[82] drew to the attention of NHS staff and, in particular, primary care staff (including GPs and community nurses through their contact with users and carers) that they were in a good position to notice signs of stress, difficulty or rapidly deteriorating health, particularly in carers. It advised such staff that the provisions of the Act would assist them:

> ...to meet the medical and nursing needs of their patients who are carers. When making a referral for a user's assessment they should be able to inform the carer that they may also have a right to request an assessment and will be well-placed to encourage patients whom they consider will benefit most to take up the opportunity. Social services departments should make sure that primary care staff have relevant information about social services criteria and know who to contact to make referral.

In recent years, there has been a growing awareness of the needs of siblings and the importance of services being responsive to them. The Children Act 1989 guidance reminds children's social services that the 'needs of brothers and sisters should not be overlooked and they should be provided for as part of a package of services for the disabled child. They may however be children in need in their own right and require separate assessment.'[83]

Research suggests that the siblings of disabled children are frequently 'young carers', 'carrying out significant caring tasks and assuming a level of responsibility for another person, which would usually be taken on by an adult'.[84] Accordingly, the Children Act 1989[85] makes provision not only for disabled children but also for other 'children in need'. Guidance[86] issued by the Social Services Inspectorate refers to and accepts research that has demonstrated that

> many young people carry out a level of caring responsibilities which prevents them from enjoying normal social opportunities and from achieving full school attendance. Many young carers with significant caring responsibilities should therefore be seen as 'children in need'. Once a young person is accepted as a 'child in need' the social services department is able to make a wide range of services available to that person (and his family) to safeguard and promote his or her welfare.[87]

The Carers (Recognition and Services) Act 1995 also obliges social services authorities to make provision for 'young carers'; this duty is considered on p.264.

Confidentiality and access to information

Personal information about disabled children and their families held by professionals and agencies is subject to a legal duty of confidence and normally should not be disclosed without the consent of the subject.[88] This duty of confidence applies to children as well as to adults, provided that if they are under the age of 16 years 'they have the ability to understand the choices and their consequences'.[89] The Framework for the Assessment of Children in Need and their Families Policy Guidance (2000) provides a brief overview of the obligations of social services departments in relation to the law of confidentiality as well as an abbreviated checklist in relation to their duties under the Data Protection Act 1998.[90]

The Data Protection Act 1998 guidance issued by the Department of Health[91] makes clear that where a person under the age of 18 years seeks access to their records, the authority must decide whether or not the person has 'sufficient understanding to do so', which means asking the question 'Does he or she understand the nature of the request?'. If the requisite capacity exists, then the request for access should be complied with. If, however, insufficient understanding exists, the request may be made by a person with parental responsibility who can make the request on the child's behalf. Disclosure to parents in such cases should occur only after the authority has satisfied itself that:

- the child lacks capacity to make a valid application, or has capacity and has authorised the parent to make the application; and
- (where the child does not have capacity) the request made by the parent on the child's behalf is in that child's interest.

This reflects the common law position, as propounded by the House of Lords in *Gillick* v. *West Norfolk and Wisbech AHA* [1985],[92] that the parents' right to make decisions on their child's behalf ends when the child achieves sufficient intelligence and understanding to make his or her own decision.

The duty on public bodies to 'maintain confidences' is not, however, an absolute one; for instance, it is displaced if the protection of a child requires it. It is also important to appreciate that the duty exists to protect the interests of the disabled person, not those of the local authority. Public bodies should always analyse precisely why they are asserting confidentiality and ask themselves whether this does indeed promote the disabled person's best interest or whether confidentiality is being claimed in order to protect themselves rather than the disabled person. In its guidance on protecting vulnerable adults, *No Secrets* LAC (2000)7, the Department of Health emphasises this point at Para. 5.8, stating:

> Principles of confidentiality designed to safeguard and promote the interests of service users and patients should not be confused with those designed to protect the management interests of an organisation. These have a legitimate role but must never be allowed to conflict with the interests of service users and parents.

Department of Health practice guidance requires that advocates are given access to relevant information concerning the person for whom they advocate and are enabled to consult with appropriate individuals in order to establish the best interests of that person.[93] The local government ombudsman has also suggested that confidentiality should not be used as a reason for not disclosing relevant information in such cases. In criticising a council for not sharing information with the parents of a 24-year-old man with serious learning difficulties, the ombudsman commented:

> I accept that this would not be regular practice when the Council is looking after an adult: the privacy of the individual demands that the parents be kept at some distance. But [the user] had such a high level of dependency that the Council should have been willing to reconsider its approach to parental involvement in this case.[94]

Even where the Data Protection Act 1998 makes no provision for documents to be made available to the disabled child or the parents, the public body retains a discretion to disclose the information.[95] In other words, even if an individual has no right to insist on seeing a particular document or piece of information, the public body has a discretion to allow that access.

Such a situation arose in the Court of Appeal case of *R (S)* v. *Plymouth CC* [2002],[96] where the mother sought access to parts of her 27-year-old son's social services and health files. Her son lacked sufficient mental capacity to agree to her seeing the papers, and so the court had to decide whether it was in his best interests that his mother had sight of them. The court considered the approach that should be adopted in such cases, and concluded:

> The simple answer to this case is that, both at common law and under the Human Rights Act, a balance must be struck between the public and private interests in maintaining the confidentiality of this information and the public and private interests in permitting, indeed requiring, its disclosure for certain purposes. There is no evidence…that the local authority had made any attempt to strike that balance. They began from the proposition that they had no power to disclose the information at all. They then modified this to 'no power without a very good reason'… The local authority no longer seek to justify that stance. The

more difficult question is how that balance is to be struck in the light of the disclosure which they now concede.

In view of the particular facts of the case and undertakings given by the mother's lawyers, the court concluded that she should see the relevant parts of the files.

A precedent letter seeking access to information is shown on p.282. If a dispute arises concerning access to information, then the usual response would be for a complaint to be made (see p.241). The Data Protection Act 1998, however, provides for a procedure by which disputes can be resolved by either the Information Commissioner[97] or the courts; the choice of remedy is up to the applicant.

Procedures for making representations and complaints

Many disabled children and their parents have nothing but praise for the help that they receive from the statutory agencies. Not uncommonly, however, problems do arise. Although these problems may often be resolved informally, statutory procedures exist to ensure that persisting problems are dealt with expeditiously.

Complaints procedures

In most cases, the appropriate procedure will be for a local complaint to be made and then dealt with under the local authority or NHS complaints procedures. These are considered in detail on p.241. Evidence suggests that for many people, the process of complaining about the NHS and the support available to complainants is poor, with a major problem being the defensive or dismissive way in which some complaints are handled.[98]

If the complaints process does not resolve the problem, it is possible to then refer the matter to the ombudsman or for a judicial review. Both of these procedures are outlined below. Where there is a possibility of a judicial review, expert assistance should be sought at an early stage, as the procedure is complex and subject to strict time limits.[99]

Where the disabled child lacks sufficient mental capacity to articulate a complaint,[100] a parent or 'friend' may do so on the child's behalf. This is also the case with complaints to the ombudsman and in court proceedings, such as judicial reviews.

Local government ombudsman procedures

The Commissioners for Local Administration in England and Wales (the formal title for the local government ombudsmen) investigate complaints from members of the public who claim to have sustained injustice in consequence of mal-administration in connection with action taken by or on behalf of an authority. Maladministration is unacceptable, although not necessarily unlawful, behaviour by a public body. It is concerned with the manner in which decisions by the authority are reached and the manner in which they are or are not implemented and has been held to include such matters as 'bias, neglect, inattention, delay, incompetence, ineptitude, perversity, turpitude, arbitrariness and so on'.[101]

Complaints must, in general, be made within 12 months from the date on which the person first had notice of the matters alleged in the complaint. The local ombudsman cannot investigate a complaint unless it has first been drawn to the attention of the local authority and that authority has been afforded an opportunity to investigate and reply to the complaint. In practice, this means that the ombudsman will expect the complainant to have gone through the formal complaints procedure locally.

The local ombudsman has a comprehensive website (www.lgo.org.uk), which provides full details of the complaints procedures, the application forms and selected extracts from past investigation reports.

Health Service Ombudsman

The Health Service Commissioner, generally called the Health Service Ombudsman, has wide powers to investigate complaints concerning GPs, trusts and health authorities, including clinical practice. As with the local ombudsman, the Health Service Ombudsman cannot, in general, consider a complaint until the relevant NHS complaints procedures have been exhausted.

Complaints should be made within one year of the date when the action complained about occurred. Complaints must concern issues of mal-administration. The ombudsman's website is at www.ombudsman.org.uk.

Judicial review

Judicial review is a procedure by which the High Court reviews the lawfulness of decisions made by public bodies, such as the departments of state, local authori-ties and NHS bodies.

Public bodies must act 'reasonably'; what is 'reasonable' depends on the nature of the decision and the context in which it is to be made. It will invariably require that, in reaching a decision, all relevant matters are considered, all irrelevant matters are disregarded and the body applies the relevant law correctly. In certain situations, 'reasonableness' may require that before making a decision, consultation must take place with the people who are likely to be affected. Likewise, 'reasonableness' may require that a particular decision-making procedure must be followed, if affected parties have a 'legitimate expectation' that this will occur. Even if a public body adheres to all of these principles, its ultimate decision generally will be capable of judicial challenge only if the decision bears no sensible relationship to the material facts on which it was based (if it, in essence, 'defies logic').

Judicial review is not available where an equally convenient, expeditious and effective remedy exists. In general, therefore, an applicant should first utilise the complaints procedures.

If it is contemplated that a legal challenge will be taken by way of a judicial review, then it is essential that contact be made with a lawyer specialising in this field at a very early stage (in general, proceedings must be issued, at the very latest, within three months of the date when the decision being challenged was taken). Judicial review proceedings are complex and relatively expensive, although legal aid is available to assist with the costs if the applicant has insufficient resources. Frequently, the applicant, and, accordingly, the person whose 'resources' are assessed, will be the disabled child – albeit that the proceedings will be issued on his or her behalf by the parent or some other 'litigation friend'.

Notes

1 S.18 Children Act 2004.

2 Copies of all UN treaties can be accessed from the UN website at www.un.org. The University of Minnesota also has an excellent website for all human rights documents, including non-UN treaties, at www1.umn.edu/humanrts/treaties.htm.

3 That is, a government is unlikely to enact laws that conflict with undertakings it has given at the international level; see *R* v. *Secretary of State for the Home Department, ex p. Brind* [1991] 1 AC 696.

4 For a detailed analysis of the impact of the ECHR on domestic law in this field, see Clements, L. and Read, J. (2003) *Disabled People and European Human Rights*. Bristol: Policy Press.

5 Article 11 UN International Covenant on Economic, Social and Cultural Rights 1966.

6 Article 32 UN Convention on the Rights of the Child 1989.

7 Article 15 Revised European Social Charter of the Council of Europe 1996.

8 *A* v. *UK* [1998] 27 EHRR 611.

9 *Patel* v. *UK* (*the East Africans case*) [1973] 3 EHRR 76.

10 *Assevov* v. *Bulgaria* [1999] 28 EHRR 652.

11 *Osman* v. *UK* [1998] 29 EHRR 245; see also *A* v. *UK* [1998] 100/1997/884/1096 23 September 1998, where the court held that 'the obligation...under...the Convention to secure to everyone within their jurisdiction the rights and freedoms defined in the Convention...requires States to take measures designed to ensure that individuals within their jurisdiction are not subjected to torture or inhuman or degrading treatment or punishment, including such ill-treatment administered by private individuals. Children and other vulnerable individuals, in particular, are entitled to State protection, in the form of effective deterrence, against such serious breaches of personal integrity.

12 *X and Y* v. *Netherlands* [1985] 8 EHRR 235.

13 *Gaskin* v. *UK* [1989] 12 EHRR 36.

14 *R (S)* v. *Plymouth City Council* [2002] 5 CCLR 251.

15 See, for instance, *R* v. *Southwark LBC ex p. Khana and Karim* [2001] 4 CCLR 267 and *Olmstead* v. *LC* [1999] 527 US 581.

16 153/1996/772/973 24 February 1998; 26 EHRR 241.

17 *The Times* 13 August: 34 EHRR 1285.

18 *R (A and B)* v. *East Sussex County Council* [2003] EWHC 167; [2003] 6 CCLR 194; accessible at www.bailii.org/ew/cases/EWHC/Admin/2003/167.html.

19 *R (Burke)* v. *General Medical Council and Disability Rights Commission (Interested Party)* [2004] EWHC 1879 (Admin) *The Times* 6 August. A full copy of the judgment can be accessed at www.courtservice.gov.uk/judgmentsfiles/j2775/burke-v-gmc.htm.

20 In this context, see the comments made by Baroness Hale of Richmond in the Paul Sieghart Memorial Lecture: What Can the Human Rights Act do for My Mental Health?, accessible at www.bihr.org/transcript_hale.doc.

21 As amended by s.2 Race Relations (Amendment) Act 2000.

22 S.3 Disability Discrimination Act 2005, which amends s.49 Disability Discrimination Act 1995 by inserting the new general duty to promote equality (as s.49A of the 1995 Act).

23 As opposed to the 'common law', which was created on a case-by-case basis by judges.

24 1 CCLR 119, at 123; [1996] *The Times* 17 April. For a fuller account of the legal effect of such guidance, see Clements, L. (2004) *Community Care and the Law*, 3rd edn. London: Legal Action Group, Para. 1029.

25 The Children Act 1989 Guidance and Regulations, Vol. 6: *Children with Disabilities* (1991). London: HMSO. Indeed, all the volumes of guidance issued under the Children Act 1989 are expressed as being 'policy guidance'.

26 In England, The Stationery Office (2000); in Wales, The Stationery Office (2001).

27 S.29 National Assistance Act 1948 and Appendix 2 LAC (93)10, Para. 2(1)(a).

28 This duty is reinforced by s.6(6) Local Authority Social Services Act 1970, which requires the local authority to provide 'adequate staff' in order to assist the director of social services.

29 Para. 8(a), Part 1 Schedule 2 Children Act 1989.

30 See also Para. 38 Department of Health's *Care Management and Assessment: Practitioner's Guide*, which stresses the importance of advocates 'taking a full part in decision-making'.

31 Citizen advocacy is a form of advocacy where 'an ordinary citizen develops a relationship with another person who risks social exclusion or other unfair treatment because of a handicap. As the relationship develops, the advocate chooses ways to understand, respond to, and represent the other person's interests as if they were the advocate's own'; see Sang, B. and O'Brien, J. (1984) *Advocacy: The United Kingdom and American Experiences*. King's Fund Project paper no. 51. London: King's Fund, p.27.

32 S.17 and Para. 1 of Schedule 2.

33 Children Act 1989 Schedule 2 Part I Para. 1A. Copies of these plans should be available free of charge from local social services departments.

34 At the time of writing, the outcome of the government's consultation on the form and content of children and young people's plans is awaited; see www.standards.dfes.gov.uk/la/planrat/?version=1.

35 Para. 2 of Schedule 2; see also Para. 4.2, Vol. 6 of the Children Act Guidance (Children with Disabilities).

36 For a detailed discussion of this question, see Clements, L. (2004) *Community Care and the Law*, 3rd edn. London: Legal Action Group, Para 1.5 *et seq.* and Para 18.18 et seq.

37 *R* v. *Bexley LBC ex p. B* [1995] 3 CCLR 15.

38 Ibid.

39 Residential accommodation for disabled adults is generally provided by social services under s.21 National Assistance Act 1948. Before its amendment by the Children Act, s.21 services were also available to disabled children. Disabled children who have been detained under s.3 Mental Health Act 1983 may be entitled to residential accommodation under s.117 of the 1983 Act. Consideration of this provision is outside the scope of this text; for an analysis, see Clements, L. (2004) *Community Care and the Law*, 3rd edn. London: xxx, Para. 7.143.

40 *R* v. *Barnet ex p. G (and others)* [2003] UKHL 57, [2003] 3 WLR 1194.

41 S.17(1) Children Act 1989.

42 That is, services that the child has been assessed as needing under the Children Act 1989 or the Chronically Sick and Disabled Persons Act 1970.

43 Assessing Children in Need and their Families: Department of Health Practice Guidance (2000), Para. 3.115.

44 s.47(3) NHS and Community Care Act 1990 obliges the social services department to seek help from the NHS or housing department if a health or housing need is identified.

45 R v. Northavon DC ex p. Smith [1994] 3 All ER 313, HL.

46 Vol. 6 of the Children Act Guidance, Children with Disabilities, Para. 5.9.

47 Lord Laming (2003) The Victoria Climbié Inquiry: Report of an Inquiry. London: The Stationery Office, January 2003 CM 5730 Para. 17.90.

48 See, for instance, s.22 NHS Act 1977 and s.26 Health Act 1999.

49 See, for instance, s.213(1) Housing Act 1996.

50 See, for instance, s.5 and s.6 Disabled Persons (Services, Consultation and Representation) Act 1986.

51 Complaint 96/C/3868 against Calderdale MBC.

52 R v. Gloucestershire County Council ex p. RADAR [1995] 1 CCLR 476.

53 See p.241, where these remedies are considered.

54 Para. 5.1 The Children Act 1989 Guidance and Regulations, Vol. 6, Children with Disabilities (1991). London: HMSO; see p.251, where this duty is considered in greater detail.

55 (2000). London: The Stationery Office; also available at www.dh.gov.uk/assetRoot/04/ 01/44/ 30/04014430.pdf.

56 See also the practice guidance Assessing Children in Need and their Families (2000). London: Department of Health. Para. 3. 128 et seq., which refers to the fact that there may be surprise among others that the child be involved in the process.

57 Para. 3.16 Community Care in the Next Decade and Beyond Policy Guidance (1990). London: HMSO; see p.251, where this duty is considered in greater detail.

58 R (A and B) v. East Sussex County Council [2003] EWHC 167; [2003] 6 CCLR 194; www.bailii.org/ ew/cases/EWHC/Admin/2003/167.html.

59 [2003] 1 FLR 292 at 306 (Para. [49]).

60 R v. North Yorkshire CC ex p. Hargreaves [1994] 1 CCLR 105.

61 [2004] EWHC 1635 (Admin) 16 July 2004.

62 Ibid. Para. 61.

63 Department for Education and Skills (2001) and Welsh Assembly (2004); see, in particular, Chapter 3: Pupil Participation.

64 As defined by the House of Lords in Gillick v. West Norfolk and Wisbech Area Health Authority [1985] 3 All ER 402.

65 Para. 6.7 The Children Act 1989 Guidance and Regulations, Vol. 6, Children with Disabilities (1991). London: HMSO.

66 Department of Health (October 2004).

67 Para. 3.1, p.90.

68 Para. 3.3, p.91.

69 The National Service Framework for Children, Young People and Maternity Services: Primary Care, p.19. Department of Health (October 2004).

70 Getting the Right Start: National Service Framework for Children Standard for Hospital Services. Hospital Standard Part One: Child-Centred Services, p.13. Department of Health (October 2004).

71 Disabled Children and Young People and those with Complex Health Needs National Service Framework for Children, Young People and Maternity Services, Para. 5.10. Department of Health (October 2004).

72 Para. 6.1 The Children Act 1989 Guidance and Regulations, Vol. 6, Children with Disabilities (1991). London: HMSO.

73 [2005] EWHC 586 (Admin) at Para. 30.

74 *Re G (Care: Challenge to Local Authority's Decision)* [2003] EWHC 551 (Fam), [2003] 2 FLR 42, at Paras [2]-[3] and [57].

75 Department of Health (2000), Para. 3.104 *et seq.*

76 Op. cit. Para. 2.10 *et seq.*

77 Department of Health (October 2004).

78 The National Service Framework for Children, Young People and Maternity Services: Primary Care; see, for instance, p.14: the 'importance of supporting parents before birth and, subsequently, through all stages of the child's life'. Department of Health (October 2004).

79 Getting the Right Start: National Service Framework for Children Standard for Hospital Services. Hospital Standard Part One: Child-Centred Services; see, for instance, p.9: the right of parents to be 'treated with respect, and should be given support and information to enable them to understand and cope with the illness or injury, and the treatment needed. They should be encouraged to be active partners in decisions about their health and care, and, where possible, be able to exercise choice.' Department of Health (October 2004).

80 Disabled Children and Young People and those with Complex Health Needs National Service Framework for Children, Young People and Maternity Services; see, for instance, p.25: the 'need for parent/carers to have effective support, help with complex nursing care in the home and opportunities for short term breaks from caring'. Department of Health (October 2004).

81 The National Service Framework for Children, Young People and Maternity Services: Core Standards, p.64. Department of Health (October 2004).

82 Para. 30 LAC (96)7.

83 Ibid. Para. 6.4.

84 SSI guidance letter 28.4.95; CI (95)12.

85 s.17(10).

86 SSI guidance letter 28.4.95; CI (95)12.

87 s.17(1) Children Act 1989; see p.257, where this duty is considered in greater detail.

88 Para. 3.47, *Framework for the Assessment of Children in Need and their Families, Policy Guidance* 2000. London: The Stationery Office.

89 Ibid. Para. 3.48.

90 Ibid. Para. 3.46 *et seq.* and at Appendix E.

91 The volume of Guidance Data Protection Act 1998 – Guidance to Social Services Accompanying Circular LASSL (2000)2 at Para. 5.8 *et seq.* Guidance in Wales has been issued as Data Protection Act 1998 – Guidance to Social Services, June 2000, and is almost identical. Guidance to the NHS has been issued as HSC 2000/009 Data Protection Act 1998: Protection and Use of Patient Information, March 2000, with follow-up guidance in June 2003 as Guidance for Access to Health Records Requests under the Data Protection Act.

92 [1986] AC 112, [1985] 3 WLR 830, [1985] 3 All ER 402.

93 *Care Management and Assessment Practitioners Guide* (1991). London: HMSO, Para. 3.28.

94 Local Government Ombudsman complaint no. 97/C/4618 against Cheshire (1999).

95 *R v. Mid Glamorgan FHSA ex p. Martin* [1994] BMLR.

96 [2002] 5 CCLR 251, [2002] 1 FLR 1177.

97 See www.informationcommissioner.gov.uk.

98 See Phelps, L. and Williams, A. (2005) *The Pain of Complaining: CAB/ICAS Evidence of NHS Complaints Procedure.* London: Citizens Advice.

99 For detailed consideration of this issue, see Clements, L. (2004) *Community Care and the Law,* 3rd edn. London: Legal Action Group. Para. 19.121.

100 The legal definition of 'mental capacity' is considered on p.197.

101 For a fuller account, see Clements, L. (2004) *Community Care and the Law,* 3rd edn. London: Legal Action Group, Para. 19.101.

CHAPTER 5

The Early Years

Introduction

In this chapter, we concentrate on some aspects of the experiences and needs of parents and their young disabled children that are associated with the early years. In doing so, we revisit some of the themes already established in Chapters 3 and 4. Here, however, we consider the importance of these issues as parents become aware of a child's impairment and begin, together with their child, to establish their own way of living with disability. In this chapter, we concentrate mainly on the pre-school years, but we are aware that in some families the early stages of living with disability occur later in the child's life.

Recent government guidance identifies four barriers that parents and children routinely face at this time:

- a lack of sensitivity at the time of diagnosis
- inconsistent patterns of service provision
- lack of coordination between multiple service providers
- exclusion from mainstream and community services and facilities.

DfES (2003c, p.5)

Such is the impact and significance of these early times that they are frequently remembered in sharp relief by those involved, particularly parents (Scope 2003). Not only does this early period have a particular importance of its own, but also it can be seen as a time when the foundations may be laid for attitudes, behaviours and ways of living that become established and enduring. One way of characterising the very early years is to view this time as the first of a number of critical transitional periods in the lives of children and their families. We should not underestimate the consequences of attempting to deal with a situation that is both new and very complex in practical and emotional terms.

In this chapter we consider the following:

- Families' experience of the early years:
  - discovering disability
  - establishing a way of living with disability
  - isolation and lack of support and information.
- Valued and effective approaches to meeting the needs of children and their families:
  - accessing useful information
  - accessing family support services
  - services to aid children's development
  - daycare, playgroups, nursery education and short-term breaks
  - accessing education.
- The law that is relevant to the early years.

Families' experience of the early years

Discovering disability

To some disabled people, particularly, perhaps, those who have lived with impairment all their lives, the notion of 'discovering disability' may seem curious. If living with impairment is an ordinary part of your life, then the idea that it is being discovered by others may in some way be seen to place your experience in the province of the unknown and to deny its authenticity. Even those who regard living with impairment as an ordinary part of their everyday lives may nevertheless feel that the disabling barriers that they face should never be seen as ordinary, unremarkable or acceptable. In this part of the chapter, we explore what happens to parents at the time when their child is identified as being disabled and the experiences of those parents and their children as they begin to discover the nature of the restrictions and barriers that there are to be faced.

Research has indicated consistently that the process of discovering that they have a disabled child, whether at birth or later, is experienced as exceptionally stressful by substantial numbers of parents (Audit Commission 1994; Scope 2003; SCOVO 1989a). Although some men and women may not experience shock or distress, there are very many reasons why others may feel desperate when they discover that they are the parents of a child they were not expecting. Individual reactions are diverse and complex, and it is important that we do not make predictions based on generalised assumptions about what someone will feel or want to do in this situation.

Since negative perceptions about disability are so prevalent in the population as a whole, however, it is reasonable to assume that many parents of disabled children initially approach the experience with at least some of the attitudes that they may later come to modify or even wholeheartedly reject. Later, many parents report that as a result of getting to know their children and finding themselves involved in a loving, caregiving relationship with them, they not only become close to their particular child but also adopt changed views about some aspects of disability generally (Goodey 1991; MacHeath 1992; Murray and Penman 1996; Read 2000; Traustadottir 1991). This is not, of course, to suggest that some do not continue to wish that their children were without their impairments.

It is crucial to recognise the distress that many parents experience when their child is identified as being disabled, but it is also important to be aware of the impact that discussions about this issue can have on disabled children and young people themselves. If the prevailing attitude is that parents need to be helped to cope with something that is unequivocally tragic, then disabled children may feel devalued and undermined.

In addition to their perceptions of disability and their personal reaction to having a disabled child, some parents may be unsure whether they can cope with what they think will be demanded of them. They may not wish their lives to change in ways that they assume will happen.

Depending on the child's condition, parents may also be desperately concerned about the child's health or survival. They may be very unfamiliar with the impairments or medical condition and understandably anxious about the immediate and longer-term implications. For some children and their families, the early stages may be characterised by a health or medical focus. They may find themselves spending a great deal of time with substantial numbers of unfamiliar health-service and other professionals and feel that their lives are on hold until they see the outcome of various investigations. Recent practice guidance from the Department for Education and Skills (DfES) illustrates this issue with reference to the experience of the family of a 13-month-old baby with a 'combination of dis-abilities'. Over a nine-month period, the family attended a total of 315 service-based appointments in 12 different locations (DfES 2003c, p.5).

It is not only the fact of finding themselves parents of a disabled child that is reported by many parents as the cause of the initial distress and disorientation. Parents also find the response of some professionals and their organisations to be a major problem. Many studies have discovered high rates of dissatisfaction among parents about the services they receive at the crucial time when they are discovering that they have a disabled child.

In relation to the diagnosis or identification of a specific condition, concern is expressed about both the nature of the information that they were given and the manner and circumstances in which it was delivered (Green and Murton 1996; Scope 2003; SCOVO 1989a; Sloper and Turner 1993b). A number of studies have also highlighted that in many cases, parents are the first to suspect that there is something unexpected or unusual about a child's development, and that their anxiety may be exacerbated by professionals who do not appear to be taking their concerns seriously (Audit Commission 1994; Hall 1997; Quine and Pahl 1986).

Apart from the concerns that these findings raise about the standards of practice that families should be able to expect from service providers at this time, it is important to acknowledge the enduring sense of hurt and injustice that remains with many parents who believe that they and their child received less than they deserved at such an important turning point in their lives (Scope 2003; Statham and Read 1998).

Beresford *et al.* (1996) reviewed the research on the process whereby families learn that their children are disabled. They report that professionals sometimes argue that parental dissatisfaction should be seen as part of the inevitable personal reaction to the news that they are being given rather than a reliable indicator of the quality of services. Beresford *et al.* refute this, pointing to studies that indicate that when services are shaped by research findings on practice that is valued by parents, the process of disclosure is evaluated as being much more positive and effective (e.g. Cunningham, Morgan and McGucken 1984).

In considering the unsatisfactory aspects of the experience, Beresford *et al.* (1996) draw attention to studies that have found that professionals are sometimes more negative than parents about the impact of a disabled child within a family and also have lower expectations of the child's progress. Professionals can be uncomfortable about giving what they regard as 'bad news', and this can appear to the parents to be an overly negative attitude towards the child. Beresford and colleagues also point to some professionals' lack of communication and counselling skills as factors that make for difficulties. Finally, they highlight the lack of consistent policies within and between services to ensure clear, coordinated and guaranteed procedures at this critical point.

Some studies and service users' accounts have indicated that the process of identification of disability and the encounters with professionals and organisations that accompany it can be particularly difficult for some parents and children from ethnic minority communities (Baxter *et al.* 1990; Shah, 1997; Sheik 1986). Services responsive to their needs, including culturally sensitive forms of counselling, may be very thin on the ground. It can be very difficult indeed for those who do not have English as a mother tongue to gain access to essential information and other supports, either verbally or in writing. It has also been argued that predominantly white European professionals often hold quite damaging and generalised assumptions about the lifestyles of service users from ethnic minority communities and that this affects the quality and nature of the provision they are offered at this crucial time (among others). As we have already suggested, some professionals may be unfamiliar with impairing conditions that affect predominantly ethnic minority populations (Ahmad and Atkin 1996; Dyson 1992, 1998).

Establishing a way of living with disability

Despite the problems that many parents experience around the time of the identification of the child's impairments, the evidence is that the majority adjust to their new situation and find a way of living that both accommodates the needs of their disabled child and manages all the things that go along with having a son or daughter growing up with disability. We have already suggested that it would be a mistake to assume that families characterise their children as burdens to be shouldered. Many radically alter their stance on disability through getting to know their own disabled child. As we have seen in Chapter 3, however, many establish a positive way of living against the odds and cope with very many stressful situations in isolation.

Without denying the positive and supportive experiences that some families have, all the available evidence suggests that we should view the early years as a potentially hazardous time for young disabled children and those close to them. The taxing level of activity demanded of parents may frequently be accompanied at this early stage by understandable anxiety about the child's health, the outcomes of medical interventions and key decisions about, for example, nursery or primary school placement and other services. The impact of the extra costs of disabled living combined with reduced income may also bite quite early (Dobson and Middleton 1998). As we have seen already, money worries can be a major cause of stress.

Some issues and experiences that have a great impact during the early period may continue to have an ongoing significance in the lives of the children and their families. We have identified some of these ongoing features in Chapter 3. In the early days, however, children and parents may be encountering these things for the first time and in a situation where both the idea and the experience of living with disability are new. Given the right support during this period, however, families may be helped to establish with confidence a preferred way of living that stands them in good stead for the future as well as the present.

Families of young children who are still establishing their own way of living and growing up with disability need flexible support from professional services or elsewhere. Given the growing numbers of disabled children who are living with complex impairments, many parents have to learn new, sometimes highly technical skills as they begin to care for their child at home (Kirk and Glendinning 2004). Any family with a new child, whether disabled or not, may need to test different approaches to care and living arrangements in order to see what works for them. Given the unfamiliarity and complexities of the situation in relation to many disabled children, it is important that parents and other family members have the opportunity, time and support to try things, change their minds and adjust arrangements until they are the best fit for everyone concerned.

Families may need to test things out to see what works for them, but it is also important to recognise that needs can change quite significantly within a relatively short period in the lives of any young child, their parents and their brothers and sisters. Similarly, a specific factor or event – for example, a young disabled child becoming ill and spending time in hospital – may have an unanticipated impact. As a result, the profile of the practical, financial and personal needs of all family members can alter quite dramatically. If parents and children are not given the opportunity to review the changing needs and preferences of different members of the household, some arrangements may become an established way of life simply by default, whatever those concerned might wish.

One example of this is the way in which mothers of disabled children may become locked into being the main provider of care in the home over a protracted period, without ever having the choice of employment outside (Baldwin and Glendinning 1983; Beresford 1995; Read 2000). Some mothers of pre-school disabled children may not find it unusual to be at home and may feel strongly, as do many others, that they wish to give the majority of their time and attention to their son or daughter during their early years. The mother of the disabled child may not anticipate, however, that without the provision of appropriate services, this pattern is likely to persist long after the pre-school years are over. With time, the mother of a non-disabled child can reasonably expect that the two of them will have an increasing degree of independence from each other and the mother may consider taking paid employment outside the home, and so on. Not only are the practical arrangements that allow this to happen less easily available for young disabled children and their mothers, but also disabled children's needs for care, attention and support may well increase as they get older. Even if this state of affairs does not concern the mother at the start, as time goes on the situation may be so well established that she may feel that there is little to be done about it. Research has indicated that one-third of parents, the majority being mothers, who are looking after their disabled children full-time would prefer to have the opportunity to go out to work (Beresford 1995); some would undoubtedly wish to return to paid employment soon after the birth of a child. Studies have also indicated how difficult it is for parents with disabled children to manage jobs outside the home (Kagan et al. 1998).

Isolation and lack of support and information

Research studies and official reports have repeatedly revealed substantial numbers of families of pre-school disabled children who feel isolated, unsupported and ill-informed (Audit Commission 1994; Baxter *et al.* 1990; Haylock *et al.* 1993; Sloper and Turner 1992; Stallard and Lenton 1992). Studies report parents' experience of being very anxious as they struggle to cope with a new situation without the information and support that would enable them to deal with the present situation and plan for the future (Stallard and Lenton 1992). Individual families from all social backgrounds can experience these problems, but those on low incomes, those from ethnic minority populations and those caring for children severely affected by impairment are particularly vulnerable to high levels of unmet need (Baxter *et al.* 1990; Chamba *et al.* 1999; Sloper and Turner 1992). Baxter *et al.* (1990, p.60) describe the isolated circumstances of many black and ethnic minority parents with pre-school children with learning disabilities as 'particularly bleak'.

As we have seen in Chapter 3, families of disabled children of all ages experience difficulties in accessing crucial information. Throughout the early years, the provision of information and advice is vital, and there are critical times, such as the point of diagnosis and the transition to nursery or primary school, when it is particularly important to ensure that families are well served in this respect (Appleton *et al.* 1997; Baldwin and Carlisle 1994). Unfortunately, the available evidence points to families with pre-school children lacking very basic information about essential services and financial benefits (Appleton *et al.* 1997; Audit Commission 1994; Baxter *et al.* 1990; DfES 2003c; Haylock *et al.* 1993; Robinson and Stalker 1993; Sloper and Turner 1992; Stallard and Lenton 1992). Studies of families' experiences frequently paint a picture of parents of young disabled children searching for crucial information for themselves in the face of complex and fragmented organisational systems. They have to be extremely active and persistent in order to find things out and often come across important information by chance. Those whose opportunities are already more restricted because of poverty, stressful life events or ethnic minority status are likely to experience greater barriers to accessing information (Baxter *et al.* 1990; Sloper and Turner 1992).

As we have also seen in Chapter 3, official reports and research findings have frequently concluded that services for disabled children and their families are uncoordinated and fragmented with the ever-present danger that the service user falls through the gaps or experiences enormous frustration in trying to access essential provision. The research on families' experiences of trying to obtain helpful services during the pre-school years indicates that many have to struggle to make headway and that outcomes of their efforts are at best uncertain

(Appleton *et al.* 1997; Baxter *et al.* 1990; DfES 2003c; Goodey 1991; Haylock *et al.* 1993; Sloper and Turner 1992; Stallard and Lenton 1992). Frequency of contact with professionals and service organisations gives no guarantee that needs are met (Sloper and Turner 1992), and in some cases the encounters are experienced as frustrating and unhelpful. While this may be the situation for parents and children for many years to come, we need to be aware of the impact on parents and their children who may be facing these barriers for the first time.

Valued and effective approaches to meeting the needs of children and their families

A recognition of the need to improve services for children and their families in the early years has resulted in a number of guides to good practice, including *Together from the Start* (DfES 2003c), *Right from the Start* (Scope 2003), *Working with Families Affected by a Disability or Health Condition from Pregnancy to Pre-School* (Contact a Family 2004) and the *National Service Framework for Children, Young People and Maternity Services* (DfES and DH 2004).

When disability is identified

The delivery of information at the time when parents are first finding out that they have a disabled child is crucial, as are the manner and circumstances of the delivery. This applies to both initial and subsequent contacts between families and professionals. A number of writers and organisations have proposed procedures and practices designed to offset some of the major difficulties and build on positive experiences that parents have identified (Beresford *et al.* 1996; Cunningham 1994; DfES 2003c; Scope 2003; SCOVO 1989b). A number of key points emerge from this and other related work:

- Parents' fears and worries should never be dismissed or treated lightly.
- Practitioners should share information as soon as possible, preferably in an ongoing way, even if they are uncertain about a diagnosis or the outcome of an assessment.
- Information about a child's condition, its implications and any proposed medical or other interventions needs to be clear and straightforward.
- Information needs to be realistic and honest without overemphasising the negatives.

- Parents need enough time and encouragement to take in important information, go over it and ask questions in initial and subsequent meetings.

- One-off information sessions are unsatisfactory for people who feel upset or disoriented.

- Important information should be shared as it becomes available.

- Parents should be given information that is important or upsetting in private, preferably in the presence of a partner, friend or relative.

- Usually, the child should be present or nearby when parents are given significant information.

- Professionals should refer directly to the child by name, and attention should be given to the child's level of understanding and to appropriate ways of explaining and discussing issues with them.

- The main information that parents are given verbally should also be put in writing for them in a clear form, possibly a 'parent-held record', so that they can refer to it and show it to other people who need to know.

- Parents should be given the name of a contact person to whom they can refer for clarification of matters that occur to them between appointments or meetings.

- Arrangements for discussion of important matters should reflect the needs of all significant family members with care being taken, for example, not to exclude fathers from future involvement.

- Professionals who show warmth and seem to understand parents' concerns are valued.

- Initial appropriate information about services is regarded by families as important, as is contact with a key person who will help them access information and support at an appropriate point.

- Contact with support groups or networks, including those made up of other families with disabled children, may be a positive option for some families.

- It should be regarded as a basic minimum standard for written information to be provided in minority languages and for interpreting services to be available for those people who need them.

Coordinated follow-up information and services

In Chapter 3, we discussed the range of information and ways of accessing it that research has found to be useful to parents and their children (Blackburn and Read 2005; Contact a Family 2003; Mitchell and Sloper 2000). Reliable information in an accessible and usable form enables families to make informed choices and to gain an important degree of control over their lives. In the early years, this might include information on:

- the child's impairment or medical condition and its likely impact
- the range of services available locally in the public, voluntary and private sectors; how to contact and access different types of support; and the duties and responsibilities of different agencies
- provision for children with special educational needs and procedures for accessing education
- choices about therapeutic or other interventions designed to enhance a child's development
- national voluntary organisations, helplines and websites
- names, postal and email addresses and telephone numbers of all agencies and professionals with whom they may need to be in regular contact.

In the demanding situation in which families find themselves, it has to be recognised that many still rely on informal sources of information such as other parents whom they happen to meet at a place that is offering a service to their children. One of the bonuses that parents associate with having access to specialist facilities such as opportunity groups and early intervention schemes is that they find out invaluable information that is unrelated to the primary purpose of the particular service (Haylock *et al.* 1993). While it has long been recognised that many parents of disabled children are uniquely qualified to help each other (Kerr and McIntosh 2000), the support and information that they receive in this way should nevertheless be in addition to that which they have a right to expect from service professionals. Some families may find that a helpful source of support and information comes through joining a support group or organisation designed to serve the needs of families with disabled children. These take many forms, including small local groups, national or international organisations, groups bringing together families whose children have particular impairments or conditions, and organisations that focus on specific issues such as education. Some provide the opportunity for parent-to-parent and family support on an individual basis or in groups, some organise leisure activities, and others mainly provide information and guidance. Only a minority of families report that they belong to any such voluntary organisation (Beresford 1995). It is helpful to recognise, however, that some who may not wish to join or become actively involved may nevertheless appreciate having contact from time to time in order to gain information as and when they need it.

In Chapter 3, we discussed the importance of a coordinated approach to services and information. All available evidence points to the fact that during the early years, if families are to avoid the problems of accessing crucial information and services that were identified earlier in this chapter, there needs to be better joint planning and care coordination between organisations with different responsibilities (DfES 2003c). The process of accessing appropriate information and services is undoubtedly easier and more effective in places where there are established procedures for interagency cooperation (Sloper *et al.* 1999; Townsley *et al.* 2003) or where several essential services can be accessed in one place, at a one-stop shop (DfES 2003c).

As we have seen already, the process of interagency collaboration has always proved difficult, and there have been many attempts to find ways of solving this intractable set of problems. In the mid 1990s, a report by the Association of Metropolitan Authorities (1994) emphasised the importance of making local cross-agency agreements between social services, health authorities and education authorities, with each in turn taking the lead role to broker the services required in the disabled child's early life. Appleton *et al.* (1997) describe a system in which an assessment and care management model was developed for pre-school disabled children and their families in a particular authority. Care coordinators undertook interagency work to develop care plans for the children concerned. In recent years, a number of models have been proposed and piloted in an effort to make effective interagency collaboration and care coordination a more standard approach at all levels (DfES 2003c; Sloper *et al.* 1999). There are encouraging examples of good practice, but it is clear that in many areas comparable organisational arrangements have not been put into operation (Audit Commission 2003; Greco and Sloper 2004; Kirk and Glendinning 2004).

Regardless of whether there is a developed system of care coordination in their area, in the early days parents and their disabled children undoubtedly need allies on the ground. When we take into account the new, taxing and isolating circumstances of many families, the complexity of services they need to understand and the dearth of usable information available to them, it is hardly surprising that key workers, link workers and care coordinators of some description are frequently regarded as practitioners who can really make a difference. Practitioners linked specifically to particular families may provide a clear point of reference, a first port of call and a conduit for information. Key workers may be employed by any of the agencies with responsibilities in relation to disabled children and their families, but it has been argued that it can make sense for them to be located in the agency that has the largest role in supporting the family at a particular time (DfES 2003c). It is not unlikely that the understanding practitioner who acts as a guide through the maze in these difficult times may also become the person to whom the family feels able to turn for more personal discussions. There is clear evidence that people in this key role are valued by the families concerned (Appleton *et al.* 1997; Audit Commission 1994, 2003; Chamba *et al.* 1999; Glendinning 1986; Haylock *et al.* 1993; Mukherjee *et al.* 1999; Stallard and Lenton 1992).

We have seen how at the outset, health and medical services are the main points of contact for some families. Some studies have revealed that only a small proportion of those with disabled pre-school children have contact with social workers (Haylock *et al.* 1993). Despite this, it is important to emphasise that the provision of family support services is the responsibility of local authority children's social services. This underlines how important it is for practitioners working for one agency – say, the health service – to see it as their responsibility to put a family in touch with another service that may have a duty to make provision for them. The pivotal role of the health visitor in this respect has been emphasised (Contact a Family 2004).

The DfES (2003c) argues for a fully integrated approach to assessment and service planning and delivery in the early years, and attention is being drawn to the positive future role of children's trusts following the implementation of the Children Act 2004 (DfES 2003c; Russell 2003). The DfES (2003c) practice guidance proposes that professionals from different agencies should work together to undertake a coordinated assessment and produce a Family Service Plan. It is suggested that the process should aim to have the following outcomes:

- define the nature of the child's disability and impact on the family
- assess the level and type of service needed and agree the nature of the equipment, medical care, therapy, information and practical advice required
- agree how, where, when and by whom professional support will be provided
- agree how often the family will be visited in the home and by whom
- agree how and when the appropriateness of the care/support package will be reviewed
- agree how, when and by whom the child's development will be monitored
- agree who will undertake the role of the key worker.

DfES (2003c, p.18)

For some families, this level of coordination and planning may be particularly critical in the early years. For example, if the parents of a child who is dependent on technology such as a ventilator are to care for the child safely and confidently at home, there needs to be effective planning and preparation by both the hospital and the community-based health and local authority children's services. The parents will need to be assured that the guidance, support and equipment that they need will be available to them as they learn to take care of their child outside the hospital environment.

In Chapter 3, we considered the importance of child and family support services. We outlined a flexible approach to assessment and service delivery that focused on organising services and other interventions that enable identified needs to be met and important outcomes to be achieved. Such a flexible approach is particularly valuable at a time when families of young children are still establishing their own way of living with disability. They may take some time to find out what really helps them, particularly if the situation is not stable.

In Chapter 3, we also considered what research tells us about families' needs for child and family support services, and we outlined a range of valued services to meet those needs. In addition to care coordination and key working, these services included interventions to enhance children's development, assistance with financial and practical problems of daily living, and the provision of homecare, support workers and short-term breaks. All of these are important for the child and the family in the early years. In this section, however, we shall focus on three groups of provision for the pre-school child: services that aid the child's development; playgroups, nursery education, daycare and short-term breaks; and support to access primary education.

Services to aid children's development

There is consistent evidence that parents of young disabled children appreciate and feel supported by services that are designed to aid their children's development, whether through work that professionals undertake directly with the child or indirectly through their parents. These services may be found in the public, voluntary and private sectors and may be mainstream or specialised. Examples include opportunity groups, playgroups and nursery classes, early intervention and teaching programmes such as Portage, home teaching, conductive education, speech and language therapy and physiotherapy (Cameron 1997; Hall 1997; Haylock et al. 1993; Read 1996). It has also been shown that programmes that are effective in helping parents to deal with commonly reported difficulties such as challenging behaviour or broken sleep patterns are also valued (Beresford et al. 1996; Quine 1993). While the long-term impact of some programmes on the development of the children concerned remains unproven, it has been argued that the direct and indirect benefits on parents and children, particularly in the short term, warrant their continuing provision (Hall 1997).

Some concern has been expressed about the fact that some systems designed for disabled children may place undue demands upon already over-burdened families, over-professionalise parenting or render the child's upbringing too stilted and unusual (Appleton and Minchom 1991; Gregory 1991). Some have also questioned whether an undue focus on constantly trying to change or 'improve' children may be undermining to their self-esteem and identity (Middleton 1999). Perhaps the point to be made here is that services of this kind should aim to enhance the positive and individual aspects of the parent–child relationship as well as the child's upbringing more generally, rather than detract from it or place extra pressure on the adults and children concerned. As in other families, many families with disabled children eventually find an equilibrium between the things that, ideally, they would like to do with and for their children and what they can all manage or tolerate at a particular time. Many families also create a successful balance between encouraging their children's cognitive, motor and speech and language development to an appropriate level, while being perfectly accepting of their impairments and consequent requirements for aids, adaptations, effective communication systems and other assistance. In other words, as is the case with many other families, parents of young disabled children walk a fine line between encouraging a child to develop while accepting them for whom and what they are.

There is a further issue to be raised. It need not be assumed that all interventions that assist a disabled child's development are those that have the 'special' label attached to them. Mainstream facilities may prove enhancing for both the children and their parents (Newton 1995; Sebba and Sachdev 1997). Although current policy emphasises the importance of all mainstream services and facilities adopting an inclusive approach in relation to disabled children and their families (DfES 2003c), parents may nevertheless find that this does not always happen in areas where they live. Consequently, arrangements regarded as unusual in a particular locality may have to be made, and even argued or fought for, to enable their disabled child to participate in mainstream provision.

Daycare, playgroups, nursery education and short-term breaks

Good daycare or nursery provision, whether specialist or mainstream, can serve at least two purposes in the lives of disabled children and their families. As with other pre-school children, it can offer the disabled child the chance to learn and socialise in an enjoyable setting outside the home. Access to appropriate and affordable provision will also be one of the main factors that determine whether a mother can choose to work outside the home (Beresford 1995; Russell 2003). Apart from the chance to increase the household income, having the opportunity of going to work outside the home is one of the factors known to reduce the stress and enhance the well-being of some mothers (Sloper 1999; Sloper et al. 1991).

There is a considerable shortage of affordable and appropriate daycare for disabled children (Russell 2003; Kagan et al. 1998). In some areas, the concern to ensure that young disabled children have access to mainstream facilities has been a political and operational priority, while in others less has been achieved in this respect. Parents report that few nurseries and childminders have accessible buildings and the appropriate training and expertise needed for children with complex needs (Kagan et al. 1998). Beresford et al. (1996) report that despite having some obvious benefits for child and family, childminders are often reluctant to take disabled children and that specialist training that might encourage them to do so is available in very few places. Some voluntary-sector organisations offer daycare, and in some areas local authorities have purchased places for disabled children in the private sector. Surveys of independent daycare providers have shown that the majority are willing to offer places to children with impairments and 'special needs' (Cameron and Statham 1997). The special-needs referral system set up in the 1990s in most counties of Wales was reported to be a positive way of ensuring that children with learning disabilities gained access to the right sort of support and to appropriate playgroups (Statham 1996). Funded by the Welsh Office and local social services departments, the scheme provided coordinators to find places in local playgroups for children with learning disabilities, to arrange for any special equipment and extra helpers needed, and to give support to parents and staff. However, although the scheme was regarded widely as successful and non-stigmatising, there often proved to be too few places to meet demand.

In Chapter 3, we stressed the important part that flexible short-term breaks in the home and elsewhere can play in offering a positive form of separation for disabled children, their parents and their brothers and sisters. We have also acknowledged that the informal childcare arrangements on which many parents of young children depend are less available for those with disabled children. Russell (1996) stresses that parents want short-term break arrangements that are age-appropriate; many of those with very young children regard domiciliary based services provided in the child's own home as the age-appropriate option.

We have already discussed the way in which mothers can, almost by default, become their children's full-time carers throughout their lives. If women and their sons and daughters are gradually to have choice about the degree of independence they have from each other in the early days as well as at a future time, practitioners may need to be extremely proactive in searching for and offering safe and enhancing daycare, playgroups and short-term break opportunities for the child.

Accessing education

We deal with access to the school system mainly in the next chapter, but we recognise that some parents of pre-school disabled children will begin the process of identification and assessment of their special educational needs quite early in order to facilitate their access to services that they need. Some of these children will go to mainstream nursery schools, but others may be placed in the nursery departments of special schools.

The process through which a pre-school child's educational needs are identified and provision allocated is described in the legal commentary later in this chapter. It is not difficult to see why this process should be regarded as potentially stressful for the service user. Another critical transitional point in the child's life has been reached, and the decisions made are crucial to present and future well-being. The procedures involved are likely to be new and quite daunting to many parents of young disabled children. They may not know any other parents going through the same process. They may also be unfamiliar with the range of educational provision that can be made available to disabled children, and they may not have had the opportunity, for example, to think through the pros and cons of mainstream or special schooling, let alone the range of options within those two broad categories. While the law requires assessment that is needs-led rather than provision-led, the likelihood is that in some authorities families are steered predominantly towards the educational facilities already available within the locality. The information that would help parents to familiarise themselves with what is a whole new territory and make confident and informed choices in their children's best interests may not be available to many in a form that they can use. Clearly, a child's transition into the education system provides an important point where a care coordinator or key worker can supply a valuable service to the young child and the parents (Appleton *et al.* 1997). The local education authority is required to provide a named officer to be the point of contact for parents and to give them guidance on all matters related to the assessment of special educational needs. Parents may also welcome independent advice and guidance. The local education authority is obliged to make arrangements for provision called parent partnership services (PPSs). These exist to provide independent advice and support to parents whose children have special educational needs. PPSs can put parents in touch with an independent parental supporter, who can offer support

ı, attend meetings with them, and so on. A comprehensive guide
ᶠ accessing special education is provided by Wright and Ruebain
ion, advice can be obtained from the Independent Panel for
௵ɑɪ Education Advice (IPSEA), the Advisory Centre for Education (ACE), the
National Autistic Society (NAS) and the National Deaf Children Society (NDCS).
Contact a Family (www.cafamily.org.uk) has produced a clear online guide to
education for parents of disabled children. This includes a section on pre-school
options and the procedures that families and professionals need to understand.

LEGAL COMMENTARY
Introduction

Disabled children and their parents testify that if they are to avoid social exclusion
and ensure that they receive appropriate services, they need to acquire an
enormous range of skills and knowledge. This becomes important as soon as they
embark on the process of establishing a way of living with disability. As we have
seen, they are frequently left to do this without sufficient support and information.

Once the statutory agencies are aware that a child has a physical and/or intellectual impairment, it is likely that a number of professionals will appear and seek
to confirm the diagnosis. As we have seen from research, it is not uncommon for
children and their families to undergo serial assessments that result in little that is
tangible in the way of ongoing service provision. As soon as a condition or
impairment has been identified or diagnosed, service professionals may fade
away without any support or significant information being provided for the
family. All too often, nothing further is done until a crisis develops. In the legal
arena, therefore, disabled children and their parents need to acquire:

- a detailed knowledge of the responsibilities of the various statutory
  authorities and what one has the right to expect from them
- the ability to plan ahead and to anticipate the next obstacle that the
  legal system will require to be traversed.

As we have outlined above, good practice dictates that help should be readily
available throughout the disabled child's life and, most importantly, that this
contact is established in a positive way from the outset. In this section, we
consider the legal obligations that are of particular relevance in the early years
and, in doing so, highlight the role of the NHS, since it will frequently be the
health service that is the first statutory service provider to make contact with a
disabled child and his or her parents. At this stage, the family may well be

unaware of even the most basic of organisational and professional matters, such as:

- the role of social workers

- the divisions between the responsibilities of the NHS trust and the primary-care teams (or even what an NHS trust is or what the term 'primary care' means)

- who has responsibility for coordinating care arrangements upon discharge from hospital, e.g. liaising with the GP to ensure continuity of healthcare

- who is responsible for the performance of health visitors, community nurses, GPs, social workers, etc.

- who arranges transport to and from a hospital or clinic if it is some distance from the family home.

Although we highlight the important role that the health services should play in the life of a young disabled child, this is not intended to imply that during these years children's social services are entitled to take a backseat. The local authority's legal responsibilities that were outlined in the previous chapter apply as much in the early years as at any other time in the lifecourse of the child.

Before seeking to clarify the legal situation in relation to these specific issues, it is necessary to consider the general obligation of the health service to provide specific healthcare treatments and services.

The NHS and hospital services

Inpatient treatment

Parents of young disabled children will necessarily be anxious to ensure that their child receives the best possible health and medical care, but the legal obligations on health authorities to provide specific healthcare treatments are limited.

The National Health Services Act 1977 (Sections 1 and 13) places only a general and indeterminate obligation on health authorities to promote a comprehensive health service in their area. This does not of itself mean that a particular service must be made available for a particular child. Their general discretion is, however, constrained by three factors:

- The authority must aim towards the provision of a 'comprehensive service', so that if it decides not to make available any services in a particular discipline (or grossly inadequate services) the court may intervene on behalf of an aggrieved child or parent. For example, in *R* v. *North and East Devon Health Authority ex p. Coughlan* [1999],[1] it was held unlawful for a health authority to decide not to provide health services for patients who had a need for substantial but non-specialist nursing care, on the basis that the local authority could make provision for such people in nursing homes. The health ombudsman reached a similar conclusion in a complaint against Leeds Health Authority.[2]

- NHS bodies must take into account and generally follow guidance issued by the Department of Health, Welsh Assembly or the NHS Executive. On p.70 we review briefly the effect of such guidance. By way of example, however, in R v. *North Derbyshire Health Authority ex p. Fisher* [1998],[3] the court ruled that the respondent authority had failed, without good reason, to follow government guidance Executive Letter EL(95)97 concerning the prescription of beta-interferon drugs to people with multiple sclerosis and accordingly held that its actions were unlawful.

- The fundamental requirements of the Human Rights Act 1998 (Section 6) requires NHS bodies (among others) to uphold the rights of individuals under the European Convention on Human Rights. This, therefore, places upon such organisations a positive duty to protect life (Article 2) and to ensure that patients do not suffer degrading treatment (Article 3) and that proper respect is shown for their private and family life (Article 8).

In general, however, the courts are reluctant to interfere with the decisions of doctors and health authorities with regard to what treatments should be provided and what treatments are inappropriate. In R v. *Cambridge Health Authority ex p. B* [1995],[4] for instance, the issue concerned 'the life of a young patient'. The child's father challenged the health authority's decision that because of its cost and its poor prospects of success, it would not fund any further chemotherapy treatment for his daughter. The Court of Appeal rejected the father's application, stating:

> Difficult and agonising judgements have to be made as to how a limited budget is best allocated to the maximum advantage of the maximum number of patients. That is not a judgement which the court can make... It is not something that a health authority...can be fairly criticised for not advancing before the court.

The decision does not mean, however, that courts will not scrutinise very carefully questions that engage fundamental human rights. In the above case, the court heard evidence of the lengths to which the health authority had gone to weigh up the likelihood of the treatment being successful and the adverse effects of the treatment and that the health authority had consulted with the family. It concluded that the decision was taken on an individual basis and supported by respected professional opinion. In such cases, where the key consideration is expertise that the court does not possess, even with the enactment of the Human Rights Act 1998, the courts will inevitably hesitate to substitute its opinions. The situation will, however, be otherwise where the issue concerns questions of law or logic.

The Human Rights Act will, however, impose a positive obligation on all NHS bodies to justify any decision not to provide treatment, where the consequence could be the earlier death of the child (Article 2) or increased suffering (Article 3) or discrimination (Article 14). Thus, by way of example, a decision to restrict funding on kidney dialysis machines could certainly lead to deaths and increased suffering. Accordingly, if challenged, that decision would be scrutinised carefully by the court. Relevant factors in this analysis would include the cost of such equipment, the extent of the health bodies' resources, the other calls upon those resources, and the regard that was taken of government guidance and of individual patients suffering from kidney failure. If, however, the authority had decided that it would not offer dialysis to children with a particular condition, for instance Down syndrome, then this would be discriminatory action (contrary to Article 14 and, indeed, Part III of the Disability Discrimination Act 1995; see p.157). It would be extremely difficult for such a decision to be justified, unless of course there are particular medical reasons why a person with Down syndrome is less likely to benefit from such treatment than a person without that condition.

Hospital discharge planning

The volume of the *National Service Framework for Children, Young People and Maternity Services* (DfES and DH 2004, p.13) dealing with hospital services and the general guidance *Discharge from Hospital: Pathway, Process and Practice* (DH 2003) (referred to below as the 'Hospital Services NSF' and the 'pathway guidance', respectively) spell out what patients and their families are entitled to expect from the NHS during the hospital discharge process.

The pathway guidance states that 'the engagement and active participation of individuals and their carers as equal partners is central to the delivery of care and in the planning of a successful discharge' (Para. 1.4). It further stresses the importance of patients and their carers being 'kept fully informed by regular reviews and updates of the care plan'.[5] This awareness is not restricted to older people: Para. 4.1 notes that young people may also be carers and 'should be offered a carer's assessment if they are under 16 years of age, when the adult receives a community care assessment'.

The guidance acknowledges that carers have often considered themselves marginalised by discharge arrangements, particularly with patients being sent home too early (Para. 4.1), leaving their carers to cope with unacceptable caring situations[6] and advises at Para. 4.3:

> The need of the carer should be under constant review to take account of their personal health and social care needs as well as the caring role they are under-taking. The assessment and review process should consider the need for a short-term break from caring.
>
> Patients may also have responsibilities such as being the parent of young children or as a carer of someone who has a disability and who is unable to live independently. It is important to identify whether an adult has dependent children and to ensure that arrangements are in place for their care during the period of admission. If the child is the carer of an adult with a chronic illness or disability, the child's own needs for support must be addressed. It is vital that every effort is made to ensure that the family has sufficient services to ensure that children are not left with unacceptable caring responsibilities that affect their welfare, education or development. In addition, patients can also be carers, and it is important to ensure that if they are caring for someone that they have the right services upon discharge, to ensure that they can look after their own needs, as well as the person they are caring for.

Later in this legal commentary (p.122), we consider further NHS and local authority responsibilities towards carers in addition to those that apply during the hospital discharge process. Guidance on the process by which disabled children are discharged from hospital has been provided in the Hospital Services NSF (see p.48), which emphasises at Para. 3.30 that 'hospital stays should be kept to a minimum through the coordinated delivery of care'. It continues:

> Planning for discharge, and the prevention of unnecessary readmission, should be the norm for all children and young people. Where the hospital episode has been simple, discharge planning need not be elaborate, but should at least include a letter to the GP (copied to the patient) and a briefing for the patient and their parent about likely after effects, any follow-on treatment needed, any continuing drug therapy, and the implications for school attendance, together with a contact point in case of difficulty or confusion. Where applicable, the role of the social worker in discharge needs to be effectively linked in. Where needs are more complex, detailed planning may be required, for example, for equipment or to ensure that rehabilitation programmes can be continued at home, or that social care needs are addressed.

The NSF identifies at Para. 3.32 newborns from neonatal intensive care units as requiring particular attention in view of their high risk of readmission to hospital and the need in such cases for properly coordinated care plans that pay attention to vision, hearing and developmental progress, as well as the coordinated input of services such as genetics'.

Role of the hospital social worker

While the hospital and the primary-care team (GP, community nurse, health visitor, etc.) have much of the responsibility for ensuring that the above obligations are met, the hospital social worker's role is also pivotal. The social worker may be hospital-based, but he or she will be an employee of the local authority social services department. In respect of the social worker's role in discharge planning, the Children Act 1989 Guidance notes at Para. 13.11:[7]

> Where a child's stay in hospital is prolonged, the hospital social worker may have an important role to play. Chronic illness places enormous strain on a family's emotional and financial reserves. Counselling, practical and financial support (for example, for hospital visits, baby-sitting, etc.) during and immediately after hospitalisation will do much to avoid longer term problems. SSDs will need to work closely with health services including GPs and health visitors to support families when the child returns home.

Primarily, then, the social worker's responsibility is to ensure that the obligations of children's social services towards the disabled child and the family are fulfilled. Most importantly, the social worker needs to ensure that both the disabled child's and the carers' care needs are assessed properly and services are provided to enable them to live as independent a life as possible at home. In addition, however, the hospital social worker will frequently need to act both as an advocate for the family and as a general facilitator, explaining how the system operates and assisting with arrangements such as transport, overnight parents' accommodation and duties to carers.

Transport and other social support services when a child receives hospital treatment

If travel arrangements are difficult, the hospital should arrange for the transport of the disabled child to and from hospital, by ambulance or hospital taxi as the case may be. The Hospital Services NSF volume (see p.48) specifically identifies the importance of children and their families receiving timely, relevant and effective support concerning (among other things) the availability of:

- financial support, including, for example, for families whose child is in hospital at a distance from home
- help with childcare arrangements for siblings

- help with transport and travel to tertiary or other referral centres, for example through hospital transport schemes.

A disabled child and his or her parents are entitled to receive help with the cost of fares and other expenses if they are on a low income:

- The travel costs to and from hospital for the child and his or her parent (if needed as an escort) will be covered by the hospital scheme if the parent is in receipt of income support or income-based jobseeker's allowances. In certain situations, those in receipt of other financial support because they are on a low income – for instance, certain recipients of disabled person's working tax credit and/or child tax credit – will also qualify.

- If, however, the cost is merely that of the parents or siblings wishing to visit the disabled child who is already in hospital, then the visitors' costs may be covered:

  o by a community care grant from the social fund, i.e. from the benefits agency; or failing this,

  o social services have the power to make a payment to cover the cost using their powers under Section 17 of the Children Act 1989; or failing this,

  o many hospitals have a charitable fund that may be able to provide limited assistance to help with such costs; again, the social worker should be able to assist the family in accessing such funds.

Hospital and social services duties to carers and siblings

We have already discussed what carers have a right to expect during the hospital discharge process. There are additional NHS and local authority duties to carers while a child is in hospital. The hospital should make arrangements, particularly in relation to young disabled children, for the parents or carers to remain overnight with them during inpatient stays. The government has stressed that in such cases they should not be charged for the use of such facilities.[8]

The Hospital Services NSF volume[9] elaborates upon this requirement, stating:

5.1 Hospital care of children and young people should be provided in buildings that are accessible, safe, suitable, and baby, child and family-friendly... Outpatient, A&E and day care facilities need to be accessible for all children, with facilities for wheelchairs and buggies, accessible car parking, clear sign posting, and low reception counters.

5.2 Facilities should also cater for parents and siblings, with suitable provision for overnight stay. These must include access to meals and relaxation, and must respect parents' privacy.

A social worker (usually based in a hospital) will be responsible for ensuring that the carers are offered an assessment of their needs, under the Carers (Recognition and Services) Act 1995. The legal rights of carers under the Carers Act legislation are considered separately (see p.264), but their needs and the impact of their caring responsibilities on their ability to cope must be considered during the discharge planning process. Guidance in the form of LAC (96)7 (p.16) explains this duty in the following terms:

> The [1995] Act covers those carers who are about to take on substantial and regular caring tasks for someone who has just become, or is becoming, disabled through accident or physical or mental ill health. Local and health authorities will need to ensure that hospital discharge procedures take account of the provisions of the Act and that carers are involved once discharge planning starts.

Health services in the community

While surgery and other forms of acute medical treatment are normally provided in general or specialist hospitals (i.e. acute NHS trusts), many of the other NHS responsibilities for healthcare are delivered by primary-care health workers, such as GPs, district nurses and other specialists working in the community. The types of service provided may include:

- physiotherapy
- speech and language therapy
- occupational therapy
- other early-intervention rehabilitation programmes, e.g. conductive education
- short-break/respite care in a community hospital or clinic
- general community nursing care
- a health visitor service provided in the disabled child's own home community
- paediatric and incontinence advice services (usually clinic-based).

In addition, the child's GP will also provide primary-care services. As we have already noted (see p.48), research shows that parents of young disabled children value particularly highly those services that are designed to enhance their child's development.

In general, the disabled child and his or her family can look to their social worker and their GP to help them access any of the services they believe they need. GPs are required by their contract to provide all necessary and appropriate medical services to their patients, including the referral of patients for other services under the National Health Services Act 1977.[10] Since the 1977 Act covers services provided by social services,[11] it follows that GPs are obliged to help patients, including disabled children and their families, gain access to services provided by other branches of the NHS and put them in touch with social services.

The obligation includes helping the family obtain a second opinion (i.e. from another consultant) concerning their child's medical condition. Families may find that consultation with a different specialist or other health professional sometimes results in a new or refined diagnosis being given and the possibility of a different medical or therapeutic intervention. The experience of practising lawyers is that there is frequently a reluctance to agree to a second opinion being obtained. If a reasonable request for a second medical opinion is refused, then consideration should be given to instigating the formal complaints procedures (see p.241).

Primary care staff and carers

We have already considered the duties towards carers when a child is receiving a hospital-based service. NHS primary care staff also have responsibilities towards carers. The importance of good collaborative working practices between social services and the NHS is emphasised in policy guidance issued on the Carers (Recognition and Services) Act 1995, as LAC (96)7. This stresses the role of the health services in supporting carers as well as the disabled people for whom they care:

> 30. Primary care staff, including GPs and community nurses through their contact with users and carers, are in a good position to notice signs of stress, difficulty or rapidly deteriorating health particularly in carers. The provisions of the Act will help primary care staff to meet the medical and nursing needs of their patients who are carers. When making a referral for a user's assessment they should be able to inform the carer that they may also have a right to request an assessment and will be well-placed to encourage patients whom they consider will benefit most to take up the opportunity. Social services departments should make sure that primary care staff have relevant information about social services criteria and know who to contact to make a referral. GPs, nurses and other members of multi-disciplinary teams may be able to assist in an assessment of a carer's ability to provide and continue to provide care.

Speech and language therapy

As we have noted elsewhere (p.34), research shows that it is crucial that all the statutory service providers cooperate in order to enhance the disabled child's ability to communicate. The obligation in relation to the provision of speech and language therapy or other equipment and assistance aimed at enhancing disabled children's communication is a shared obligation between the health and education services. Not infrequently, therefore, both agencies look to the other to fulfil their obligations; in consequence, the interests of the child suffer (see p.81 concerning the duty on agencies to cooperate). While we consider the obligation of the education authority to provide speech and language therapy (p.154), the primary duty for these services is owed by the NHS; this is particularly so in the early years. However, for a child with a statement of special educational needs that provides for speech and language therapy, in the vast majority of cases the obligation rests with the children's education service. Indeed, in *R* v. *London Borough Harrow ex p. M* [1997],[12] the High Court held that in such cases the obligation on the education service was 'absolute and non-delegable'.

Section 3 of the NHS Act 1977 makes specific reference to the obligation on the health service to provide facilities for 'young children' and, accordingly, health authorities must commission an adequate range of children's healthcare services, including language and speech therapists (e.g. DH 1997).

These specialists are generally employed by NHS trusts and frequently based in child health clinics. If the healthcare need has not already been picked up by the trust, then a reference should be made for assistance via both the GP and children's social services. In particular, when carrying out an assessment of the child's needs, social services should refer the speech/communication need to the relevant NHS body (see p.251) and ask for a positive input into the care plan. If this is delayed or the therapy assistance is inadequate, then the appropriate response generally will be the use of the complaints procedures (see precedent letter on p.279).

The widespread failure of the health services, children's education services and social services to ascertain the wishes and feelings of children with profound impairments is well documented (see p.34). In this respect, the Department of Health (1998a, Paras 10.3–10.4) has noted that in many assessments the section headed 'Child's view' was typically 'left blank or the social worker made comments such as "she is unable to verbally communicate therefore her view is not available"' and that many young disabled people did not have access to a communication system that suited their needs.

All too frequently, this occurs due to a thoughtlessness or lack of knowledge that has been reinforced by a shortage of therapists. As we have noted above, the general discretion of the NHS as to what services it funds is constrained by several factors, one of which being the requirements of the Human Rights Act 1998. Article 8 of the European Convention on Human Rights requires the state to show respect for everyone's private life, which may require 'the adoption of measures designed to secure respect for private life even in the sphere of the relations of individuals between themselves'.[13] Such an obligation demands at the very least that the NHS takes determined and ongoing steps to ensure that disabled children have access to therapies that improve their ability to communicate. The Department of Health (2000, Para. 3.125) appears to accept such a proposition in that it quotes with approval the assertion made by Morris (1998c, p.20) that 'disabled children have the human right to take part in play and leisure activities and to freely express themselves'.

The NSF Core Standards guidance (see p.48) gives emphasis to the importance of such provision, stating on p.22 that a key marker of good practice will be that therapy services will be 'available for all children and young people who require them, and systems are in place to minimise waiting times for access to these services'.[14]

Respite care and short breaks

Frequently, the care service that the household seeks is a short break (sometimes called respite care), whereby the carers can take a break from their responsibilities in caring for the disabled child and the child can have a break from his or her parents. The local authority's responsibility for making such arrangements is considered on p.262. Where, however, the disabled child's impairments are substantial and/or complex, it may be the NHS that has this responsibility, and, indeed, it may be that the NHS alone has the facilities to provide the necessary care. Unfortunately, NHS bodies are sometimes reluctant to provide respite care, and the family then becomes embroiled in a dispute between health and social services as to who should provide the care. In such cases, if the NHS is slow in making such assistance available (or refuses), then a complaint may be appropriate. A possible precedent letter in this respect is given on p.279. The NHS duties in relation to short-break care are also considered on p.192.

Children's social services

Although research has reported that families with young disabled children frequently have no contact with children's social services, it is often vital that contact is established at the earliest opportunity. We have seen how the services that the local authority can provide may make a difference to the quality of life of all family members and enable them to establish a positive and preferred way of living. If no contact has been made, then a formal request for assistance should generally be made by the family. Where there is no immediate need for care services, then the approach may be for nothing more than registration on the register of children with disabilities. Contact in such cases may be made by writing a formal letter – see, for example, the precedent letter on p.127.

Despite the research findings and government guidance emphasising social services' key networking role in relation to disabled children, practising lawyers find that an early approach of this kind sometimes results in an unhelpful response, such as:

- 'Why have you approached us?'
- 'What service do you think we ought to be providing?'
- 'Since your need is concerned primarily with your child's health [or education, etc., as the case may be], you should contact that agency directly.'

The first two of these statements disclose a clear failure by the authority to appreciate its planning and networking role as well as expectations on the way assessments should be carried out. Children's social services should have procedures in place to ensure that parents are put in touch with the appropriate statutory and voluntary agencies so that a support network can be constructed that maximises the potential of disabled children and their families to have as full and normal a social life as possible. Assessments should also be needs-led rather than determined by existing provision.

The third statement is unacceptable because it conflicts with good practice guidance (concerning, among other things, the register of children with disabilities) and suggests that this is an authority that sees its responsibilities in a very narrow sense. It does not matter which agency is approached first. All the relevant agencies have a common responsibility to 'initiate discussions with the parents about services or procedures which might be beneficial to the child and family' and this assistance 'should include an explanation of what other agencies can provide, as well as information about the register'.[15]

The family has a right to receive a full service from whichever agency it approaches. It will generally not know who is responsible for what and who the key personalities are in the various authorities. Standard 3 of the NSF Core Standards guidance states that children and their families have the right to 'receive high quality services which are co-ordinated around their individual and family needs and take account of their views'.[16] It is, however, generally the primary responsibility of social services to open these doors and to facilitate the provision of services by all these agencies. It is for this reason that powerful obligations exist under Section 27 of the Children Act 1989 and Section 10 of the

Children Act 2004 that enable children's services departments to bring pressure on other authorities and agencies to ensure that they all fulfil their responsibilities to disabled children (see p.81).

The register of children with disabilities

As part of their duty to safeguard and promote the interests of disabled children,[17] children's social services are obliged to keep a register of children with disabilities. Volume 6 of The Children Act Guidance: Children with Disabilities makes the following comments on the role of registers:[18]

> 4.2 There is no duty on parents to agree to registration (which is a voluntary procedure) and services are not dependent upon registration. Registration can contribute positively to coherent planning of service provision for children with disabilities under the Children Act.

> 4.3 SSDs...will need to liaise with their education and health counterparts to achieve an understanding of disability which permits early identification, which facilitates joint working; which encourages parents to agree to registration and which is meaningful in terms of planning services for the children in question and children in general. The creation of a joint register of children with disabilities between health, education and social services would greatly facilitate collaboration in identification and a coordinated provision of services under the Act.

> 4.4 Whichever agency is the first to identify a child as having a disability whether it is the LEA, SSD or child health services they should initiate discussions with the parents about services or procedures which might be beneficial to the child and family. This should include an explanation of what other agencies can provide and information about the register. The registration of children with disabilities will be effective and productive only if parents and children are regarded as partners in the assessment process and as experts in their own right, from whom professionals may have much to learn.

As we have noted above (see p.55), there is considerable scope for the imaginative use of registers, for instance not only as a database to facilitate planning but also as a means to target information appropriately to those who need it.

General advice and information

As part of their obligation to safeguard and promote the interests of disabled children, social workers must provide appropriate advice, guidance and counselling.[19]

Frequently, advice on some matters will be more appropriately obtained from other agencies, such as a Citizens Advice Bureau, law centre or solicitor with a legal aid contract to provide welfare and general benefits advice. However, children's social services do have a crucial networking role in this regard and, in particular, in relation to such matters as social security benefits, self-help user groups and general advice.

Social security benefits

A detailed analysis of the entitlement of disabled children and their families to social security benefits is beyond the scope of this book. For comprehensive (annually updated) details of entitlements, see *Disability Rights Handbook* (London: Disability Alliance).

As we have noted, research has shown that accessing social security benefits is a major cause of tension and distress among disabled children and their parents. Accordingly, the practice guidance reminds social services of their duty in such cases to explain what benefits are available and to 'ensure that families are receiving the benefits to which they are entitled and are referred, if appropriate, to the Family Fund Trust'.[20] The Family Fund Trust is a charity financed by the government whose object is to ease the stress on families who care for severely disabled children under the age of 16 years. The fund provides information and grants.

Advice on self-help user groups

We have already noted the research results that have found that 'many families welcome introductions to support groups as a means of reducing social isolation, and gaining useful information and valued support' (DH 2000, Para. 3.124). It is one of the functions of children's social services to support the social integration of disabled children and their families by (among other things) ensuring that those families who express an interest in being put in touch with such a support group are so assisted.

Employment rights: general

When a disabled child is born, the parents will need advice on a multitude of matters about which they are unlikely to have had any previous experience, for instance their general employment rights as well as their short-term right to time off work in order to care for their child or to be with their child in hospital.

As a general principle, the parents have the same right to work in common with all other parents. The practice guidance to the Carers and Disabled Children Act 2000 stresses this at Para. 36:

People with parental responsibility for disabled children will also benefit from joining or re-joining the workforce. Such carers often face difficulties re-entering the workforce because of lack of suitable child-care services. Many parents of disabled children would like to return to work and, if they were able to do so, would benefit socially and emotionally as well as financially.

Section 2 of the Carers (Equal Opportunities) Act 2004 requires that in any carers assessment (see p.265), consideration must be given to whether (among other things) the carer works or wishes to work. Commenting upon this provision, the Minister for Health has stressed that it is the government's intention that this provision applies to all carers.[21]

Employment rights: emergency leave

Under Section 57A of the Employment Relations Act 1996, an employee is entitled to take a reasonable amount of time off work:

- to provide assistance on an occasion when a dependant falls ill, gives birth or is injured or assaulted

- to make arrangements for the provision of care for a dependant who is ill or injured

- in consequence of the death of a dependant

- because of the unexpected disruption or termination of arrangements for the care of a dependant

- to deal with an incident with his or her child that occurs unexpectedly in a period during which an educational establishment that the child attends is responsible for the child.

There is a general obligation upon those who take such time off work to tell the employer the reason for the absence as soon as practicable and how long the absence is likely to last.[22] In relation to the situations detailed in the three sections above, the event that requires the carer to take time off need not be 'unexpected'. Any time off work claimed as a result of this statutory provision is to be taken as unpaid leave.

Employment: flexible working rights

Parents with children under the age of six years, or disabled children under the age of 18 years, who have worked for their employer for at least 26 weeks, have the right to apply for flexible working arrangements.[23] Employers have a statutory duty to consider such requests seriously and will be able to refuse only when there is a clear business reason or where the employee has made an application for flexible working in the past 12 months. In order to exercise this right, the employee needs to make the initial written application to the employer. An employee can request a change to the hours they work, a change to the times they work, or to work from home. Since any changes will be permanent, it is important to consider the future implications carefully. This may include any drop in salary and the impact that any reduction in hours may have on state benefits, such as Working Tax Credit.

The government has indicated that it is proposing to extend flexible working rights to include other carers.[24]

Children's social services assessments

As we have already noted (see p.76), the object of a social services assessment is to gather information concerning the disabled child's situation, so that a decision can be made about how best to help, both in the short term and in order to facilitate planning for the longer term. Guidance issued to social services emphasises:[25]

- Assessments should be of a situation rather than of a specific person, or for a particular service. For disabled children in particular, there is a risk that assessments may be focused around assessing the child's problems or assessing the child for specific services, rather than assessing the child's overall situation and needs.

- Services for disabled children are often fragmented between different agencies. Different perspectives, values and professional languages can complicate working together across agency and discipline boundaries. Young disabled children often come sequentially to the attention of health workers, followed by children's education services and then children's social services.

- In general, however, the social services assessment obligation in relation to a disabled child will become more substantial as he or she grows older and as the social handicap caused by the impairment becomes more acute.

A detailed analysis of the assessment duties is considered in greater detail on p.251.

The provision of services

The Children Act 1989 and the Chronically Sick and Disabled Persons Act 1970 require local authorities to make available an array of services in order to safeguard and promote the interests of disabled children. The potential range of these services is considered in greater detail on p.257; in the context of disabled children in their early years, these may include:[26]

- social, cultural, or recreational activities
- respite/short-break care (and see p.262, where the value of home-based respite care is emphasised)
- counselling
- home help, which may include laundry facilities
- travel assistance
- assistance to enable the disabled child and his or her family to have a holiday.

The Children Act 1989 emphasises that services may be provided to other family members if necessary in order to safeguard and promote the welfare of the disabled child. An example of this given in good practice guidance arises where the parents of a child with multiple disabilities find attendance at a local clinic impossible without daycare arrangements for the child's siblings. In such a situation, the guidance advises that it is the responsibility of the social services department to make such arrangements.[27]

Direct payments in lieu of services

People with parental responsibility for a disabled child have the right to receive the cash equivalent of the services that their child is assessed as requiring.[28] This right is subject to certain formalities, not least that the direct payment is spent on purchasing services to meet the child's assessed needs. Guidance on the direct payments scheme has been issued in both England[29] and Wales[30] and provides detailed advice on such matters as the quantification of the amount to be paid and the situations when a local authority is under a duty to make such payments and the conditions that attach to such payments. Direct payments have great potential flexibility and are considered further on p.261.

The children's social services coordination role

The NSF Core Standards guidance (see p.48) notes that 'for children, young people and parents, one of the greatest sources of frustration is the lack of integration between different services within an organisation or between organisations'.[31] The various duties on social services and the NHS to work together are considered on p.81. However, in relation to the NHS, and in particular its outpatient care functions, this has been reinforced by specific guidance that requires social services departments to:

liaise closely with their child health services counterparts not only to encourage their parents to share in recording their child's development and health care needs, but also to ensure that where children in need are identified parents and child can contribute to decisions on the type of care and support provided to the family.[32]

Thus, if for any reason there is a problem accessing any such community-based healthcare and the GP has failed to act as the facilitator, the social worker has a responsibility to help resolve the impasse. The social services authority has, for this purpose, considerable joint working powers (see p.81).

The role of children's education services

Although a number of agencies have responsibilities in relation to the provision of education for children, including local education authorities, school governing bodies, the Department for Education and Skills, the school's adjudicator and special educational needs and disability tribunal, it is the local education authority (LEA) that is charged with primary strategic responsibility. In this regard, the LEA has a duty to secure sufficient schools for children in its area and has a variety of other duties, contained in a multitude of Acts of Parliament and in regulations and guidance, to meet the varying needs of children, including disabled children. However, the primary source for the legal framework for disabled children is contained within Part 4 of the Education Act 1996, as amended by the Special Educational Needs and Disability Act 2001.

Part 4 establishes a framework for determining and providing for children who are identified as having 'special educational needs'. As the majority of such needs will be met in schools, the detail of these arrangements will be set out in Chapter 6 of this book. However, in general, if a child is to receive a 'statement' (see Chapter 6), it is often useful for the process to be commenced as early as possible, and the law does permit that assessments that may lead to 'statements' may be commenced at any time.

The Code of Practice on Special Educational Needs gives the following specific guidance in relation to children in their early years (DfES 2001, Para. 4.6):

Practitioners should work closely with all parents to listen to their views so as to build on children's previous experiences, knowledge, understanding and skills, and provide opportunities to develop in six areas of learning:

personal, social and emotional development

communication, language and literacy

mathematical development

knowledge and understanding of the world

physical development

creative development.

The Code of Practice advises that there should be a graduated response to special educational needs. This commences with what is termed 'Early Years Action' and, if necessary, moves to a more intensive response termed 'Early Years Action Plus' and finally, if necessary, through to a statutory assessment of special educational needs (although this step-by-step approach is not required in every case).

Early Years Action and Early Years Action Plus are similar to School Action and School Action Plus, which are considered in Chapter 6. They mark stages wherein, in turn, additional or different provision beyond that which is ordinarily available is required. Broadly, Early Years Action (described beginning at Para. 4.20 of the Code of Practice) arises when an early education practitioner who works day to day with a child or the special educational needs coordinator (SENCo) identifies a child with special educational needs and devises interventions that are additional to or different from those provided as part of the settings usual curriculum offer and strategies. Early Years Action Plus (described at Para. 4.29 of the Code of Practice) is characterised by the involvement of external support services that can help early education settings with advice on new individual education plans (IEPs)[33] and targets, provide more specialist assessments, give advice on the use of new or specialist strategies or materials and provide support for particular activities.

Then, if further or additional provision is required, the child may be the subject of a statutory assessment process, which is considered in Chapter 6.

Educational responsibilities of health and social services

If a primary care trust (or local health board in Wales) or a hospital is involved in the provision of healthcare for a child who is under the age of five years, and it believes that the child 'probably has' special educational needs, then it must undertake the following (by virtue of Section 332 of the Education Act 1996):

- advise the child's parents of its opinion and that it (i.e. the health authority or NHS trust) is obliged to notify the LEA[34] of this fact

- after discussing the matter with the parents, the health authority or NHS trust must then bring the child's special educational needs to the attention of the LEA.

The Code of Practice emphasises the importance of such an early liaison between health and education, noting at Para. 4.37 that 'for children under five very early contact with child health services will be important in order to ensure that there is no physical cause for the difficulty in question (such as a hearing or visual impairment) or to secure advice on the possible cause and the effective management of difficult behaviour'.

Notes

1 *The Times* 20 July 2999; 2 CCLR 285.

2 See Health Service Commissioner Second Report for Session 1993–94, case no. E62/93–94. London: HMSO; and in particular Clements, L.J. (2000) 'Legal Action.' In *Community Care and the Law,* 2nd edn. London: LAG.

3 [1998] 1 CCLR 150.

4 [1995] 2 All ER 129 CA.

5 Para. 1.2. Para. 4.5.1 provides a detailed 'carer's checklist' of relevant factors to be considered.

6 Carers England (2002) *Hospital Discharge Practice Briefing.* London: Carers UK. This reported that 43 per cent of carers considered they were not given adequate support when the person they were caring for returned home. See also Mather, J. *et al.* (2000) *Carers 2000.* London: Office of National Statistics.

7 The Children Act 1989: Guidance and Regulations, Vol. 6, *Children with Disabilities* (1991). London: HMSO.

8 Para. 3.4.

9 Para. 4.9, Welfare of Children and Young People in Hospital. HSG (91)1.

10 Regulation 15(5)(b) National Health Service (General Medical Services Contracts) Regulations 2004 SI no. 291 (as amended).

11 At Schedule 8.

12 *R* v. *Harrow LBC ex p. M* [1997] ELR 62.

13 *Botta* v. *Italy* [1998] 26 EHRR 241.

14 The National Service Framework for Children, Young People and Maternity Services: Primary Care, p.22. Department of Health (October 2004).

15 The Children Act 1989: Guidance and Regulations, Vol. 6, *Children with Disabilities.* London: HMSO, Para. 4.4.

16 The National Service Framework for Children, Young People and Maternity Services: Core Standards, p.88. Department of Health (October 2004).

17 S.17 and Para. 1 of Schedule 2 Children Act 1989.

18 Para. 2 of Schedule 2: The Children Act 1989: Guidance and Regulations, Vol. 6, *Children with Disabilities.* London: HMSO. See also Para. 4.2.

19 Schedule 2, Para. 8(a) Children Act 1989.

20 S.17(1) and Para. 8(a) Schedule 2 Part I Children Act 1989. See also DH (2000, Para. 3.121).

21 The Parliamentary Under-Secretary of State for Health (Dr Stephen Ladyman). Standing Committee C 10 March 2004, column no. 7.

22 S.57A (2) Employment Rights Act 1996.

23   S.47 Employment Act 2002 (which amended the Employment Rights Act 1996 primarily by way of the insertion of a new Part 8A to that Act). See also the Department of Trade and Industry (DTI) (2003) guidance *Flexible Working: The Right to Request and the Duty to Consider*, accessible at www.dti.gov.uk/er/individual/flexwork-pl520.pdf.

24   For details, see www.dti.gov.uk/er/workandfamilies.htm.

25   *Policy Guidance Framework for the Assessment of Children and their Families* (2000). London: The Stationery Office, Paras 3.20 and 3.23.

26   Schedule 2 Para. 8(a) Children Act 1989.

27   The Children Act 1989: Guidance and Regulations, Vol. 6, *Children with Disabilities*. London: HMSO, Para. 10.3.

28   S.17A Children Act 1989 (inserted by s.6 Carers and Disabled Children Act 2000).

29   Direct Payments Guidance Community Care, Services for Carers and Children's Services (Direct Payments) Guidance England 2003, accessible at www.dh.gov.uk/assetRoot/04/06/92/62/04069262.pdf.

30   Direct Payments Guidance Community Care, Services for Carers and Children's Services (Direct Payments) Guidance Wales 2004, accessible at www.wales.nhs.uk/documents/direct-payment-policy-e-merge.pdf.

31   The National Service Framework for Children, Young People and Maternity Services: Core Standards, p.22. Department of Health (October 2004).

32   The Children Act 1989: Guidance and Regulations, Vol. 6, *Children with Disabilities*. London: HMSO, Para. 10.3.

33   Code of Practice Para. 4.27. These identify things such as set short-term targets for the child, the teaching strategies and the provision to be put in place, when the plan is to be reviewed, and the outcome of the action taken.

34   That is, the children's services department; see p.67.

CHAPTER 6

The School Years

Introduction

In this chapter we will consider the experience of disabled children and those close to them during the school-age years. Many of the issues that become significant during this period will already have been evident in some form in the early years. As time goes on, at least some of these experiences are likely to become integrated into an established way of living. Some of the issues may have less impact simply because families are familiar with them and have found a way of coping. Over time or at specific points, other issues can become magnified or assume a greater significance. As we have already suggested, the experience of having a very young disabled child in the family has a number of distinctive aspects that marks it out from that of families with only non-disabled children. Nevertheless, families with very young disabled children have a significant amount in common with families with other young dependent children. As many children get older, however, the divergence in needs, opportunities and lifestyles between disabled and non-disabled children and their respective families may become increasingly marked.

In this chapter, we focus on:

- increasing autonomy and choice for the growing disabled child
- getting a decent education
- leisure and social life
- the personal, material and practical needs of individuals and families.

It is important to recognise that all of these areas are interrelated and that success in making headway in one area may well depend on offering relief or support in another. For example, parents may wish to meet the sometimes conflicting needs of their disabled and non-disabled children to develop leisure interests, friendships and social activities. Their ability to do so may be affected by the size of the family income, whether they own a car, the level of family support services that they have been offered, including sitting-in provision and short-term breaks, and so on. As researchers, policy-makers and practitioners have recognised, this makes it crucial to consider flexible packages or menus of services that take into account the needs of all individuals in the households and families concerned (Ball 1998; Beresford *et al.* 1996; DH 2001a; Russell 1996; Social Services Inspectorate 1998). In addition, the significance of key themes raised in Chapter 3 can be seen again. The coordination, organisation and delivery of services, families' access to information and their ability to negotiate the service maze successfully, the availability of advocates or key workers, etc. all have a bearing on the choices that growing children and their families have about the way they live their lives.

Increasing autonomy and choice for the disabled child

While the question of growing independence and individual identity is an issue of importance for children of all ages, it becomes increasingly significant as the child matures. Notwithstanding the diversity of such experience among non-disabled children, there is a general expectation that as they grow they will gradually broaden their horizons to include within their social world a greater number of people and situations in addition to their parents, their immediate family and home. Within varying limits, they will take a greater degree of responsibility for themselves and their actions. They are also likely to be able to make their voices heard more.

We suggested in earlier chapters that it has been recognised increasingly that too little attention has been paid to these aspects of disabled children's development and that there is a corresponding need to create opportunities that enable disabled children to have comparable aspirations and experiences to those of their non-disabled peers. We also recognised that the means and routes to achieving the experience may need to be very different. The notion that disabled children should have independence is not new, but in the past this has sometimes been limited to the idea of individual skill acquisition on the part of the disabled child. It may undoubtedly be regarded as positive to acquire useful skills or enhance, for example, individual motor and cognitive development, but there has been a strong challenge to the assumption that autonomy, choice and having a say about your life should be the preserve only of those who can achieve certain levels of functional independence (Morris 1993).

Because of their need for support and assistance and sometimes because of difficulties in communication, disabled schoolchildren have a far greater chance than their non-disabled peers of having someone make decisions on their behalf, of not being consulted about major questions that affect them and of having a more restricted and confining social and personal life (Beecher 1998; Beresford 1997; Noyes 1999; ONS 2004; Russell 1998). The process of being heard in your own right accords value to the things that you think and feel, gives others information to act on, and can make a vital contribution to growing maturity.

Concern over this has resulted in a growing body of work that emphasises disabled children as individuals in their own right, seeks to give voice to their experiences and preferences, and helps them and their families to find practical ways of moving forward. Perhaps the most important thing to stress is the variety of approaches that are necessary and desirable if individual disabled children are to be consulted effectively and enabled appropriately to increase the degree of autonomy and choice that they can have in their lives. Within the growing body of practice and research that focuses on these aspects of children's experience and potential, there are many examples of good practice that can be adapted or developed to fit the needs and circumstances of particular children or the settings of practitioners wishing to provide a more responsive service (e.g. Beecher 1998; Beresford 1997; Chailey Young People's Group 1998; Leighton Project 1998; Marchant and Page 1992; Minkes *et al.* 1994; Mitchell and Sloper 2003; Morris 1998d; Rabiee *et al.* 2005; Russell 1998; Ward 1997).

It is evident and very basic that if disabled children are to develop the possibility of expressing opinions, needs and preferences, then they, like others, must have a way of communicating. For some children this is straightforward, but for others it presents a major barrier in their lives. The past few years have seen an increasing emphasis on the importance of finding methods of communication that work effectively for every child and an acceptance that for children with complex impairments this can often entail the use of multiple systems and approaches. The contribution of skilled specialists such as speech and language therapists as well as the cooperation and commitment of everyone in a child's environment are essential if children are to be encouraged and enabled in this most central area of their development.

It is accepted widely that we need to think broadly and creatively about developing environments and people in them that are receptive to the variety of ways in which children make their observations and preferences known and that maximise and extend the possibilities for their doing so. As well as speech and formal communication systems such as Makaton, British Sign Language and Bliss, it is important that we regard, for example, body language, facial expression and 'pointing' with the head and eyes as legitimate ways of communicating that can be central to a child's development and well-being. In addition, recent years have opened up the possible use of a range of more high-tech communication aids such as computers and voice synthesisers, sometimes in combination with more low-tech approaches. Some children's initiatives and responses are so fine-grained or difficult for the untutored eye to appreciate that they will need and benefit from someone acting as their individual enabler or interpreter at least some of the time. In practice, this often turns out to be someone who lives or works closely with the child. As part of creating a receptive environment, it is important that this knowledge about individual children's ways of communicating is shared in detail with those who come into contact with them, so that possibilities for meaningful expression are extended and margin for error in understanding reduced. It is clear, however, that systems of communication are effective only if people in the child's environment believe that it is important to make use of them. As Russell (1998, p.23) suggests, 'In some instances, disabled children may not be heard because it is assumed they will have nothing to say.'

If we assume a willingness to hear, see and understand what disabled children may wish to convey, including their evaluation of any services they receive, then there is a variety of approaches that can aid the process once a system of communication is becoming established. Beecher (1998) and Russell (1998) provide helpful overviews of key research, approaches to practice and projects in action. Again, the importance of having available a range of approaches cannot be stressed too strongly. It is impossible to generalise about meeting the individual needs of disabled children, but there are key issues and suggestions that appear repeatedly in the literature concerned with ways to extend disabled children's opportunities to act on their worlds. For example, the importance has been stressed of having a range of age-appropriate and child-centred media available for exchange of information and opinion. Children may show what they wish to convey through play, use of pictures, stories, art, music and drama, as well as direct verbal and non-verbal conversations. Advocacy, self-advocacy and other forms of representation also offer opportunities for some individuals and groups. Buddying and other peer-support arrangements between different combinations of disabled and non-disabled children, either one to one or in groups, have proved helpful. Such initiatives can provide a supportive framework for children to spread their wings, learn from the experience of others and develop their own ideas. They may also provide a structured way of making new friendships or social networks in addition to those generated by family. In some services, key workers and enablers may ensure that work related to individual children's needs is coordinated and that their experience is heard in whatever form is appropriate.

It would seem a great pity if such positive initiatives on children's autonomy were taken to indicate an implied and general criticism of parents and their role. Because a very great deal is asked of parents of disabled children and because they are often thrown into a closer and more protracted relationship with their sons and daughters, there is a danger that they may too easily become prime suspects when questions are raised about the quality of their sons' and daughters' childhood experiences. If the child's experience is rather restricted, then some may be tempted to draw too hasty conclusions about the ability and intentions of parents (Read 2000). While some disabled adults recall their families as confining and difficult, there are others who remember their parents as valued allies who supported them to make important gains that often flew in the face of more conventional and lower expectations. Some, unsurprisingly, describe a mixture of experiences (Reisser 1992; Thomas 1999). As with non-disabled children, the quality of family life varies. As we have seen, however, one important difference between the two groups is that much more is routinely asked of parents of disabled children and often in circumstances where they have fewer resources than other families. It would seem very harsh indeed to judge any parents as having offered too restrictive an upbringing to their child without asking questions about what they might have wished for and been able to achieve had they had the resources that allowed both adults and children greater freedom of choice and room for manoeuvre. It is important to acknowledge that the independence, however limited, that many children achieve comes as a direct result of their parents' hard work and perseverance. It is also crucial for us to appreciate that in the face of a lack of service provision, parents often feel that they have to become their child's sole advocate. Any practitioner or service provider needs to be sensitive to the dangers of appearing to set the child's need and right for autonomy in opposition to parents' often strong sense of responsibility. Drawing on the knowledge of all family members to learn lessons from the past and to plan for the future is an essential feature of good practice.

Getting a decent education

In the UK, the beginning of what was to become a major change in thinking about the education of disabled children occurred during the late 1970s and early 1980s. At that time, a small but growing number of academics, practitioners, policy-makers and parents began to challenge the established wisdom that it was both necessary and desirable for disabled children to be educated in separate or segregated institutions (Barton 1986; Booth and Potts 1983; Booth and Swann 1987; Family Focus 1984; Walker 1982). The movement arguing first for the integration and later for the inclusion of disabled children in mainstream settings gathered strength in the 1980s and 1990s, with the concept gaining increased official recognition and support across that period (DfEE 1998).

Among other things, it was argued that a segregated education system reproduced and maintained the disadvantaged position of disabled children and young people in a variety of ways. It was seen to play a major part in ensuring that disabled children started on a course of segregation and unequal opportunities that would continue for the rest of their lives. It was reported that the schooling they were offered was frequently of inferior quality and narrower dimensions than that of their non-disabled peers and that this ensured that the majority were unprepared for employment and autonomy in adult life. Early campaigners pointed out that there was no reason why support services most often associated with special education could not follow disabled children where necessary and allow them to be supported in a mainstream setting. As time went on, it was emphasised more frequently that the major challenge was how the education system as a whole and schools within it might change in fundamental ways in order to meet the needs of a more diverse range of children – and be the richer for it (Booth 1999; Priestley and Rabiee 2002; Reisser and Mason 1992). In the 1990s, as more children, parents and teachers had practical experience of working on these issues, a range of material became available that began to identify the factors that made for successful and positive inclusion in education. Sebba and Sachdev (1997) provide a clear and accessible review of research and practice in this area.

As one would expect, the reactions of disabled children and adults and their families to these shifts in thinking and to experiences of inclusive and separate education vary. Shaw (1998) reports a strong commitment on the part of both disabled and non-disabled pupils to the principle and practice of inclusion, together with concerns about whether the necessary changes that make it work for the pupils concerned are always in place in the education system. The views of parents in Dobson and Middleton's (1998) study are not untypical of those reported by others. Parents whose children had less complex and severe impairments were happier with the principle of mainstream provision but nevertheless described continual problems over ensuring that adequate and appropriate supports and facilities were provided. Within mainstream education, their children could find themselves excluded from taking part in some activities that were timetabled for everyone else. Necessary organisational arrangements and resources were not always in place, and some teachers did not have the required skills to meet the children's educational needs. Other parents whose children were in special schools were unhappy about the distances they were transported and the way in which these arrangements isolated their sons and daughters from others in the neighbourhood. They also found that they had repeated requests for contributions for school events, funds and trips.

Parents of disabled children have to make difficult choices about what they genuinely regard as being in their children's interests at any particular time. They have to consider the information they have, take all circumstances and human and material resources into account, and decide what seems to them the best option. The choices they make have to be pragmatic to some degree, but this does not mean that decisions are not driven by strong moral or ethical considerations. Parents' determination to minimise their disabled children's disadvantage, maximise their room for manoeuvre and strive for what they regard as the best achievable option has been reported repeatedly (e.g. Beresford 1994; Dobson and Middleton 1998; Read 2000). Some parents make a considered and positive choice in favour of mainstream school. Some parents genuinely believe that there are some forms of specialised provision that make a distinctive, high-quality and desirable contribution to their children's development and well-being (e.g. Read 1996). Others may have a commitment in principle to inclusive education but cannot see how it can be made to work for their child's benefit as things stand. It is not uncommon for parents to feel that they have to trade off some desirable things to get others. In Chapter 8, we deal with the issues and experiences related to placement in a residential school.

Information can make a very great difference to the basis on which parents make these difficult decisions and to the confidence they feel about them. As we have already seen, however, families often find themselves without adequate information. Parents should expect to be able to have informed discussions about a range of educational provision with those practitioners with whom they have contact. It is also reasonable for parents to expect to be able to visit different schools in order to ascertain how they think their child's needs could be met in a particular setting, whether in the mainstream or special education sector. Some families may feel that the information provided by their local education authority is very sound and that they are satisfied with the choices of schooling they have seen. However, some may feel they need additional or different information than that readily on offer. A comprehensive guide to the process of accessing special education is provided by Wright and Ruebain (2002). Some parents may also find it helpful to know that a number of voluntary organisations and groups provide information and advice about these crucial issues; some of these organisations have websites and telephone helplines. Two organisations specialising in advice on education are the Advisory Centre for Education (ACE, www.ace-ed.org.uk) and the Independent Panel for Special Education Advice (IPSEA, www.ipsea.org.uk). As increasing numbers of households gain access to the Internet, more parents are searching online for information about education and other matters and to make contact with organisations that represent the interests of disabled children and their families sharing similar experiences or concerns (Blackburn and Read 2005). Contact a Family (www.cafamily.org.uk) offers a telephone and online advisory service for families with disabled children on a range of matters, including education.

The specialist organisations that we have mentioned can also help children and their parents with a further problem that is identified consistently in research: the complexities of the statementing process by which a child's special educational needs are assessed and provision made accordingly. In other words, even when parents feel well-informed or clear about what they would regard as a good choice of education or a particular school for their child, they may find that the process of achieving it is not so easy. In the 1990s, a series of reports and studies highlighted the fact that parents found the procedures lengthy, complex and alienating (Association of Metropolitan Authorities 1994; Audit Commission 1992; Beresford 1995; Spastics Society 1992). It was also argued that there was a significant gap between the rhetoric of individualised needs-led assessment and a reality that was provision-focused (Swann 1987). Despite revisions of the code of practice governing assessment of special educational needs and the making of a statement (DfES 2001), the process undoubtedly remains perplexing and stressful for many children and their parents. Those who wish to challenge any aspect of the assessment or related decision-making may find it particularly taxing and frustrating. Parents may be aware one way or another that they are operating in territory that is more familiar to the professionals and that this places them at a disadvantage. Despite the fact that legislation and guidance emphasise the importance of practitioners working in partnership with parents, many service users do not experience it this way and find the whole business anxiety-provoking and intimidating. Many people are simply unused to the language that professionals employ in their reports and discussions and may find it difficult to frame their own ideas and to intervene effectively in a set of unfamiliar procedures. As has been observed, for those whose mother tongue is not English and who may have had less exposure to the services involved, the problems can be magnified, leaving them very disadvantaged indeed (Baxter *et al.* 1990).

As we discussed in Chapter 5, the local education authority should name an officer who is responsible for giving the parents information and assistance in relation to all aspects of their child's assessment of special educational needs. We have no wish to undermine the efforts of those in this position who take a proactive and positive role in relation to families, and we recognise that in some authorities such officers act as helpful consultants and valuable guides through the maze. In other authorities, however, their approach may at best be rather minimalist, making sources of alternative advice and support crucial. The local education authority is obliged to make arrangements for provision called parent partnership services (PPSs). These exist to provide independent advice and support to parents whose children have special educational needs. PPSs can put parents in touch with an independent parental supporter who can offer support and information, attend meetings with them, and so on. A comprehensive guide to the process of accessing special education is provided by Wright and Ruebain (2002). In addition, advice can be obtained from the Independent Panel for Special Education Advice (IPSEA), the Advisory Centre for Education (ACE), the National Autistic Society (NAS) and the National Deaf Children Society (NDCS). Contact a Family (www.cafamily.org.uk) has also produced a clear online guide to education for parents of disabled children. This includes a section on pre-school options and the procedures that families and professionals need to understand.

Leisure, play and social life

Within the general population, there are probably greater expectations than ever before about the provision of opportunities for leisure and play. There has been an expansion of leisure and holiday facilities for both adults and children, although the distribution varies from one geographical area to another and there is substantial variation of access between income groups (Williams 1993).

In addition to these changing expectations in relation to the standards of formally provided facilities, informal leisure and play activities, and the friendships and social life that are associated with them, form an important element of childhood and contribute significantly to the personal development of children (Association of Metropolitan Authorities 1994; Cavet 1998).

These enjoyable childhood experiences are as formative and important for disabled children as their non-disabled peers, and research indicates that they are viewed as a priority by both young people and their parents (Contact a Family 2003; Cuckle and Wilson 2002; Mitchell and Sloper 2003). Unfortunately, there is evidence that there are far fewer play, leisure and social opportunities available to disabled children (Beresford et al. 1996; ONS 2004). The ONS (2004) reports that in addition to factors related to disabled children's impairments, lower participation rates in sport outside school hours by disabled children compared with non-disabled children can be attributed to lack of money and unsuitability of local facilities to accommodate disability.

Beresford et al. (1996) and Cavet (1998) provide helpful reviews of the range of factors that contribute to disabled children's limited leisure opportunities. Children often form friendships that are based around contacts made at school. Disabled children who attend special schools some distance from home may not maintain contact so easily out of school hours unless they have assistance from adults to enable them to do so. For example, research has indicated that some disabled children have informal play contacts only once a week (Sloper et al. 1990). In addition, as Beresford et al. (1996) suggest, children mostly choose to play with peers who are at the same developmental level as themselves. The widening developmental gap between children with learning difficulties and their non-disabled peers may in part account for the diminishing social contact between them as they get older compared with frequency of informal contact at a younger age.

Beresford *et al.* (1996) also point out that the family plays a crucial mediating role in relation to the disabled child's social life. Arranging play and leisure for children who are not best placed to find them for themselves spontaneously often requires money, transport, time and energy. We have already seen that many families are hard pressed to meet everyone's needs, are frequently on very low incomes and do not always have transport.

In addition, there are other environmental factors within and outside the home that create barriers to leisure, play and social contact. The built environment and facilities within it are not always accessible or safe for the disabled child. There have been improvements, however, and further positive developments are likely to come about as a result of the implementation of Part 3 of the Disability Discrimination Act 1995. The Council for Disabled Children (2004) provides a helpful guide to good practice under the Act.

As we saw in Chapter 3, the homes in which families live are frequently unsuitable for disabled children and their carers, and this can act as a further impediment to ordinary shared childhood activities. Children and their families sometimes also encounter negative attitudes or a lack of positive awareness on the part of the general public and providers of leisure and play facilities, and this can make outings unpleasant or cause them to limit what they do (Association of Metropolitan Authorities 1994; Beresford 1995; Ryan 2005). Continually having to do battle, challenge or make out a case for arrangements to be adjusted can cause families to feel as if all the fun has been taken out of the outing and the purpose therefore defeated.

If this is the case, then it is small wonder that some parents and children opt to make use of the quite wide variety of specialist and separate leisure activities and facilities provided for disabled children. While there has been considerable debate about the importance of avoiding ghettoisation and ensuring that mainstream community facilities routinely include disabled children (Jigsaw Partnerships 1994), Cavet (1998) points to the arguments for disabled children and young people making the positive choice (as long as that is what it is) to associate with each other. She gives the example of the role that deaf clubs play in promoting and sustaining a positive deaf culture and identity. She highlights too the importance of ensuring that leisure activities are culturally appropriate for the child or young person concerned.

Research also draws attention to the part that short-term breaks and befriending schemes can play in extending the child's social world and creating enjoyable opportunities for contact with additional adults and children, both disabled and non-disabled (Beresford *et al.* 1996; Mitchell and Sloper 2003; Prewett 1999; Robinson 1996). Child support workers and children's personal assistants can also play a positive role. These services may be centred on the family home or elsewhere. Support workers or befrienders may do something enjoyable with children at home or take them out. They may accompany children to specialist provision or enable and assist access alongside other children to a mainstream community facility. Participation in a family link scheme provides another example of an opportunity for extending social contact outside the child's own family. Increasingly, whatever the arrangement, there is an assumption that, like any child, the disabled schoolchild should be consulted about preferences and experience of breaks and play provision (Beresford *et al.* 1996; Mitchell and Sloper 2003; Minkes *et al.* 1994).

Having acknowledged the importance of play, leisure and social contact in relation to the development and well-being of all children, it clearly has to be unacceptable for disabled children to have a more impoverished childhood than others in this respect. Good practice therefore demands that we use the measures we have at our disposal to create the chances they need that are so often not available. As we discuss later in this chapter, Section 2 of the Chronically Sick and Disabled Persons Act 1970 and Section 17 of the Children Act 1989 can potentially be used to improve these opportunities for children and their families. The Family Fund may also be a source of funding for these purposes.

Personal, material and practical support needs of individuals and families

By the time a disabled child is of school age, everyone involved may have become accustomed to the situation and developed their own ways of coping and keeping going. The fact that the situation is not new may mean that many children and families are left to soldier on without their needs for practical, personal and family support being reassessed in order to take account of the ways in which people and circumstances change.

When researchers explore the experiences of such disabled children and their families, they often pay tribute to the ways in which those involved manage a workload that is by anyone's standards complex and demanding. The question 'How do they do it?' is posed frequently. As we discussed in Chapter 3, substantial attention has been paid by researchers to both the positive and characteristic coping strategies that families establish (Beresford 1994) and the personal and practical costs of dealing with so many demands for a protracted period (Beresford 1995; Russell 1998; Sloper 1999).

We neither wish to minimise the importance of coping strategies that those involved develop nor detract in any way from families' achievements in this respect. We believe strongly, however, that the positive features of their lives and the rewards they describe should never be mistaken for an absence of need or used to justify a lack of services. We should undoubtedly be impressed with the way in which the majority cope, but we need to remind ourselves frequently of some of the ongoing costs that may put those concerned in jeopardy (Sloper 1999). Good practice should focus on and bolster their positive aspirations and achievements at the same time as providing integrated family services that help them to avoid some of the danger zones. The approach to such service provision and the needs that it can address are discussed in some detail in Chapter 3.

Beresford (1994) describes how 'keeping going' becomes a way of life in families with disabled children. Those coming in from the outside can see the stresses but frequently not the features that parents regard as positive. Beresford (p.67) argues: 'Until research can look at the child as the parents do, we will never fully understand how parents manage and what keeps them going.' When parents define the things that ensure they carry on providing high levels of care and assistance, they tend to talk about love for the child combined with their assumptions about what naturally comes with the territory of being a mother or father (Beresford 1994; Read 2000). Helping one's children to develop and taking pride and pleasure in their achievements, as well as deriving satisfaction from meeting a challenge and winning some ground, are often reported as very important. As Russell (1998) warns, however, many families are only just managing. The demands are often so great, their circumstances so fragile, and human and practical resources so limited that an unforeseen crisis or change of circumstances can upset the equilibrium.

We have also referred previously to research that reports that in many households these issues become even more pressing as time goes on (Beresford 1995). As we have seen, for example, the logistics of assisting and caring for older and larger children can become more complicated and demanding, particularly when suitably adapted accommodation and equipment are not available. Parents report that challenging behaviour creates more management problems and greater restrictions in family activities. Over time, the toll on the well-being and energy of main carers caused by physically strenuous work such as lifting growing children can be considerable. Limited income over a longer-term period leaves less margin for error and less room for manoeuvre. Other children do not stand still either: interests may diverge and additional demands may need to be met by already overstretched parents.

The long-term and taxing nature of some of the problems faced by the individuals and families concerned make it crucial for them to have their needs reviewed or reassessed at regular intervals, taking account of the range of issues that were identified in Chapter 3. In addition to the fact that the provision of some community-based services can undoubtedly raise the standard of living of all family members quite substantially, it is also important to consider whether they may play a part in enabling some children and their parents to continue living together. Further research is needed to establish the issues and circumstances that trigger the separation of substantial numbers of disabled children from their families of origin (see Chapter 8), but it would be surprising if the stress and workload that many manage long-term were not shown to be contributory factors in some cases at least.

LEGAL COMMENTARY

Introduction

Regrettably, many disabled children reach their school-age years having had little or nothing by way of specific assistance from the health, social services and education authorities. It is, however, during their school years that the provision of practical help and appropriate services can often have the most profound influence in ensuring that disabled children have the best opportunity of maximising not only their potential in terms of intellectual achievement but also social integration.

Typically it will often have been the health services that had most contact with the child during the early years, but unsurprisingly it will generally be the education department that is the lead organisation during the school-age years. Clearly, this will not always be the case, however: some children with severe and complex impairments or major health problems may also have significant contact with health and social services. As we have noted, however, it does not follow that children and their families with substantial and complex support needs receive services to meet those needs.

Education

In the 1980s, educational provision for disabled children (including those with physical impairments, learning difficulties, mental illnesses, sensory impairments and challenging behaviour) was transformed as a result of legislation introduced in 1981 (the Education Act 1981, which came into force in April 1983). Until then, education authorities determined provision for disabled children according to the label they were given; these labels referred to contemporary categories of physical, sensory and intellectual impairment or behavioural difficulty. Consequently, children who were deemed physically handicapped tended to be sent to schools designated for physically handicapped children, children who were blind were sent to schools for blind children, and so on. However, these labels bore little relation to a child's learning difficulties or educational needs. Other examples of labels include 'maladjusted', 'backward', 'delicate' and 'educationally subnormal', for which there were two subcategories: severe and moderate.

However, the 1981 Act, which followed from a report chaired by Baroness Mary Warnock, introduced two key principles in determining education provision for disabled children (DES 1978):

- Provision should, broadly, be child-centred, so that educational provision was tailored for the needs of each child.

- Wherever possible, disabled children should be educated alongside their non-disabled peers.

The Act established a statutory framework, which remains today, requiring consideration of the needs of disabled children, if necessary by way of what is known as a 'statutory assessment', which may lead to a legal document known as a 'statement of special educational needs'. Although the 1981 Act has long since been repealed and replaced, the current legislation – contained within Part 4 of the Education Act 1981 as amended by Part 1 of the Special Educational Needs and Disability Act 2001 – broadly maintains the assessment and statementing procedures for the more severely disabled child.

Assistance for parents and children through the assessment and statementing process

As we noted earlier in this chapter, many parents and their children find the procedures related to assessment and statementing confusing and stressful. Below, we note a number of organisations independent of LEAs that parents may approach if they wish to challenge any of the decisions that are made in relation to their child's education. In addition, all parents are entitled to guidance and information from their LEA to support them through the process of assessment and statementing. The Code of Practice (Para. 2.20) requires LEAs to 'provide a range of flexible services, including access to an Independent Parental Supporter for all parents who want one' – this person being someone who 'can support parents for example by attending meetings, encouraging parental participation, and helping the parent understand the SEN framework' (p.203).

Special educational needs

It is important to note, however, that not all disabled children will have a statement of special educational needs. Indeed, only those with high-level needs that require that the LEA arrange additional or different educational provision will have statements. In fact, the majority of children with special educational needs will not have a statement. Sections 312 and 321 of the 1996 Act define children as having special educational needs if they:

- have a significantly greater difficulty in learning than the majority of children of the same age; or
- have a disability that either prevents or hinders them from making use of educational facilities of a kind generally provided for children of the same age in schools within the area of the LEA; or
- are under the age of five years and are, or would be, likely to fall within these categories.

Accordingly, a child has special educational needs depending, in part, on the nature of their learning difficulties/disabilities but also depending on what is available in local schools. In fact, although many children may have learning difficulties either throughout or for a period of time during their educational career, only a minority will have needs of such a degree as to require that the LEA arranges provision, so only a minority will have a statement.

The majority of disabled children will, in fact, have their needs considered at what is known as School Action or School Action Plus (two stages that are explained further in the Statutory Guidance – the Special Educational Needs Code of Practice[1]). School Action and School Action Plus are similar to Early Years Action and Early Years Action Plus (see Chapter 5) and provide for graduated intervention and support from school staff of a nature that nevertheless does not require the LEA to directly intervene and therefore does not require a statutory assessment leading to a statement of special educational needs.

In any event, regardless of whether a child with special educational needs has a statement, the Code of Practice at Para. 1.5 establishes a series of fundamental principles that are meant to guide provision for all disabled children:

- A child with special educational needs should have their needs met.
- The special educational needs of children normally will be met in mainstream schools or settings.
- The views of the child should be sought and taken into account.
- Parents have a vital role to play in supporting their child's education.

- Children with special educational needs should be offered full access to a broad, balanced and relevant education, including an appropriate curriculum for the Foundation Stage and the National Curriculum.

The statementing process

As we have already outlined, a child will be considered for a statutory assessment only if he or she has educational needs that are likely to require the LEA to arrange additional or different provision beyond that which is available in local ordinary schools for children of their age. In these circumstances, an assessment can be triggered by:

- the LEA itself, upon receipt of advice from another agency that the child may require a statement
- the child's parents requesting an assessment
- the governing body of the school that the child attends requesting assessment.

If an assessment is undertaken, then the LEA must serve a notice on the child's parents advising them of this. After giving the parents 29 days to make representations about the decision to undertake an assessment, the LEA must then obtain written advices or opinions from at least the following:

- the appropriate children's social services unit
- the appropriate primary care trust/local health board
- the headteacher of any school or nursery that the child attends
- the child's parents
- an educational psychologist engaged by the local education authority
- possibly others where required, such as a speech and language therapist, a physician, etc.

Upon receipt of these advices, the LEA will then decide whether the evidence shows that the child does require a statement, in other words requires education provision that is additional to or different from that available in local ordinary schools for children of the child's age.

If the authority decides that a statement is necessary, then it must first of all serve a draft copy on the parents for consideration. The parents then have 15 days within which to make representations on the draft; those representations will include the parents' views as to the appropriate school for the child. Following this, the LEA will finalise the statement. Once the statement is finalised, a copy will be served on the parents and on the school concerned, and it will be at that point that it becomes a legally enforceable document. The process by which a statement can be challenged, generally by appeal to the Special Educational Needs and Disability Tribunal, is considered below.

The nature and content of a statement is proscribed in law. Broadly, the document is in six parts:

- *Part 1* contains basic details such as the name, date of birth, address, religion, home language and telephone number of the child concerned and the names and contact details of the child's parents. Part 1 will also list the advice and evidence considered in drafting the statement.

- *Part 2* should set out details of all of the child's special educational needs.

- *Part 3* is meant to contain all of the provision that the LEA considers necessary to meet the needs set out in Part 2. In addition, Part 3 will itself be subdivided into three subsections: the objectives, the educational provision itself and monitoring arrangements. Further, usually the provision set out in Part 3 should be quantified to an extent that makes it clear to everyone concerned with the child's education precisely what should be arranged for the child. For example, if the child requires a level of adult support, such as individual teaching support or learning support assistance, then that level of support should be particularised as, for instance, five hours per week or full-time support on a one-to-one basis, or whatever is required.[2] There are very limited circumstances where the obligation to particularise is not as great, and these are where the child's needs fluctuate to such a degree, and/or so frequently, that specifying provision in a statement would be inappropriate, or if a child attends a special school.

- *Part 4* names the school or type of school or other institution at which the provision will be made. In most cases, what will be set out here will be the particular school that the child should attend. Occasionally, a description of a type of school may be set out and, very occasionally, provision otherwise than at school, for example where parents want a home-based programme, may be set out.

- *Parts 5 and 6* mirror Parts 2 and 3 (dealing with special educational needs and special educational provision) and set out what is considered to be non-educational needs and non-educational provision. However, occasionally, what is set out in Parts 5 and 6 should, in fact, be set out in Parts 2 and 3. For example, the law provides that in the vast majority of cases, a child's needs for speech and language therapy constitutes an educational need, so it should be set out in Part 2 and the provision required to meet it should be in Part 3. This is important because provision that is set out in Part 3 *must* be arranged by an LEA,[3] whereas provision set out in Part 6 need not necessarily be arranged (although an LEA may do so if it wishes). In fact, what is and what is not educational provision is not always straightforward, but, broadly, teaching support and provision, including speech and language therapy (which is related broadly to teaching and learning and to the curriculum), is likely to be educational provision. However, not all occupational therapy or physiotherapy that a child may need is necessarily educational provision,[4] and nursing support or transport will not normally be educational provision.

- *Appendices* contain all of the advices obtained by the LEA in the course of the statutory assessment.

Choice of school

With regards to choice of school or other placement, the law sets out in detail the considerations that the LEA must have in determining whether to accede to parental preference. First, if a parent wants a maintained school (i.e. a state school), the LEA must generally accede to that preference unless one of the conditions set out in Schedule 27 to the Education Act 1996 apply. These conditions are:

- the school is unsuitable, with regard to the child's age, ability, aptitude or special educational needs
- the attendance of the child at the school would be incompatible with the provision of efficient education for the children with whom he or she would be educated
- the attendance of the child at the school would be incompatible with the efficient use of resources.

Separately, if a parent wants a mainstream (i.e. not special) school, in addition to the above criteria the LEA has a general duty pursuant to Sections 316 and 316A of the Education Act 1996 to ensure provision in an ordinary school unless the placement of the child at that school would be incompatible with the provision of efficient education for other children, and providing that there are no steps that either the school or the LEA can take to overcome any such difficulty.[5]

If an independent or non-maintained special school (i.e. not a state school) is sought, Section 9 of the Education Act 1996 requires the LEA generally to have regard to the wishes of the parents with respect to the education of their children, providing that this is not incompatible with the efficient use of the LEA's resources. In fact, it is usually the case that an independent school is materially more expensive than a maintained school in part because of the way that costs are considered for maintained schools. Consequently, if a parent wants their child to attend an independent school, it is usually necessary to show that there is no alternative maintained school that could meet the child's educational needs.

Finally, very occasionally, parents seek provision for their child other than at a school. For example, many parents of children with autism seek to secure funding for an intensive home-based programme such as LOVAAS[6] or Applied Behavioural Analysis . This is possible, pursuant to Section 319 of the Education Act 1996. However, the High Court has held that, in effect, an LEA may fund such provision only if placement at a school is 'inappropriate', which in practice means that a child's needs cannot be met at a school.[7]

Sometimes, parents seek provision for their child at a residential school; we deal with this issue mainly in Chapter 8. Para. 8.74 of the Code of Practice gives general guidance on this and provides that LEAs should agree a residential placement in only four circumstances:

- The child has severe or multiple special educational needs that cannot be met in local day provision.

- The child has severe or multiple special educational needs that require a consistent programme both during and after school hours and that cannot be provided by the parents with support from other agencies.

- The child is looked after by the local authority and has complex social and learning needs, and placement is joint funded with the social services department.

- The child has complex medical needs and learning needs that cannot be managed in local day provision, and the placement is joint funded with the health authority.

Timescales

The law provides for detailed time limits for the assessment and statementing procedure.[8] Broadly, they provide that the entire process should take no more than 26 weeks (six months), which consists of six weeks to decide whether to undertake an assessment, ten weeks to actually undertake the assessment, two weeks to serve a draft statement or to advise the parents that no statement will be produced (in which event, an alternative informal 'note in lieu' will be produced), and eight weeks to finalise the statement. These various time limits may be exceeded in certain limited circumstances. Meanwhile, pending a statement, it is sometimes possible to place a child temporarily at a special school for the purposes of assessment.

Challenging education decisions

Sometimes parents disagree with the LEA about decisions regarding this process. In particular, if against the wishes of the parents the LEA determines not to conduct a statutory assessment, not to make a statement following an assessment, not to amend a statement and name a different maintained school, not to undertake a reassessment, or to cease to maintain a statement, the parents then have a right of appeal to the Special Educational Needs and Disability Tribunal. First, it is important to note that any appeal against an LEA decision must be lodged with the Tribunal within two months of the date that the parents received the decision that will form the subject of the appeal. Information about how to appeal may be obtained from the Tribunal through a booklet entitled *How to Appeal*.[9] At the centre of the booklet is a form that contains all of the information that the Tribunal will require in order for an appeal to be lodged successfully.

Tribunals are relatively straightforward, but because special educational needs law is fairly complex many parents choose to obtain advice and assistance in progressing appeals to a tribunal. Such assistance is available from a number of voluntary organisations, including the Independent Panel for Special Education Advice (IPSEA), the Advisory Centre for Education (ACE), the National Autistic Society (NAS) and the National Deaf Children Society (NDCS), and also from specialist lawyers and advice centres. Tribunals take some three to four months to determine an appeal, and their decisions are binding on the parents and the LEA. Following a tribunal appeal, there is no further right of appeal, although in certain limited circumstances, parents can request a review of the tribunal decision within ten working days of receiving the decision if the tribunal has clearly made an error. Very occasionally, parents bring an appeal against a tribunal decision to the High Court on a point of law within 28 days of receiving the decision.

Legal aid is not available for any legal representation before the tribunal stage, but it is sometimes available to parents to assist in bringing appeals to tribunals. It needs to be borne in mind, however, that legal aid is limited in a number of ways, including by reference to the parents' (rather than the child's) financial means.

Sometimes, other disputes regarding special educational needs may arise that cannot be remedied by an appeal to a tribunal. For example, a school named on a child's statement may refuse to admit the child, or the LEA may not arrange the provision set out in a child's statement. In such an event, alternative remedies, such as complaint to the Secretary of State or, occasionally, proceedings in the High Court known as judicial review, may be appropriate.

Finally, statements once made must be reviewed at least once a year. In addition, reviews of statements of children in the tenth year of compulsory education have a particular importance and involve those who may be responsible for considering provision for a child once he or she leaves school (see Chapter 7).

If the parent moves home from the area of one LEA and into the area of another, the statement in effect transfers with them, so that the new LEA takes over responsibility for the child's statement.

Disability discrimination and education

Although the law that deals specifically with special educational needs and provision is clearly crucial, legislation designed to prevent discrimination against disabled people is also of great importance in the context of education.

The Disability Discrimination Act 1995 (DDA), when originally enacted, expressly excluded education services from its provisions, with the exception of a few very minor information-providing duties. However, since September 2002, as a result of amendments brought in by Part 2 of the Special Educational Needs and Disability Act 2001, the DDA has to a degree been extended to provide for anti-discrimination provisions within schools, colleges and universities.

The Disability Rights Commission (DRC) has produced helpful guidance on the operation of these provisions in two codes of practice, one for schools and one for post-16 providers.

Who is 'disabled' under the DDA?

First, it is very important to note that the definition of disability contained in Part 1 of the DDA is materially different from the definition of learning difficulty contained in Part 4 of the Education Act 1996, which governs provisions for children with special educational needs, and in Section 13 of the Learning and Skills Act 2000, in respect of students in further education. For the purposes of the DDA, a person is disabled if he or she has *a physical or mental impairment that has a substantial and long-term adverse effect on his or her ability to carry out normal day-to-day activities*. There are, currently, eight so-called 'day-to-day activities' defined in law:

- mobility
- manual dexterity
- physical coordination
- continence
- ability to lift, carry or otherwise move everyday objects
- speech, hearing or eyesight
- memory or ability to concentrate, learn or understand
- perception of the risk of physical danger.

In addition, the DDA also covers people with:

- severe disfigurements
- impairments that are controlled or corrected by the use of medication prostheses and aid or otherwise
- progressive symptomatic conditions
- a history of impairment
- most forms of cancer, human immunodeficiency virus (HIV) infection and multiple sclerosis at the point of diagnosis
- children under the age of six years who have impairments that in an older person would result in that person falling within the definition of disability described.

However, the Act expressly excludes:

- the fact of addiction to or dependency on nicotine, tobacco or other non-prescribed drugs or substances
- seasonal allergic rhinitis (hayfever)
- certain mental illnesses with antisocial consequences.

Accordingly, not all children with special educational needs will be defined as disabled for the purposes of the DDA and, conversely, not all disabled children, who are entitled to protection under the DDA, will have special educational needs. However, it is likely that there will be a considerable overlap.

The obligations for schools

Schools, including independent schools and special schools, now have the following obligations towards disabled pupils or disabled applicants for places at schools:

- They must not treat the disabled pupil or applicant less favourably for a reason relating to their disability, without justification.

- They must make reasonable adjustments to arrangements for determining admission to the school or in the provision of education and associated services, so as to prevent that student or applicant from being placed at a substantial disadvantage, unless they can legally justify not doing so.

Accordingly, there are effectively two obligations: one to not treat a disabled pupil or applicant less favourably and the other to remove barriers to participation. However, in relation to the obligation to make reasonable adjustments, in determining whether what may be required is reasonable and therefore legally required, the law proscribes a number of factors that may be taken into account, including:

- the need to maintain academic, music, sporting and other standards
- the money available
- the cost
- the availability of provision through special educational needs law
- the practicalities of making a particular adjustment
- the health and safety of the disabled pupil or applicant and others
- the interests of other pupils.

In addition, because the obligation to make an adjustment arises only if otherwise the disabled pupil or applicant would be placed at a substantial disadvantage, the law provides that the test for when this arises includes the following considerations:

- the time and effort that the disabled pupil or applicant might need to expend
- the inconvenience, indignity or discomfort that the child might suffer
- the loss of opportunity or lack of progress that a disabled child may make compared with other non-disabled children.

However, discrimination is permitted and is, therefore, not unlawful if it is in accordance with:

- a permitted form of selection; or
- where it is for reasons that are both material to the circumstances of the particular case and substantial, provided that there are no reasonable adjustments that could be made that would overcome this difficulty.

There are, then, confusing but important differences between special educational needs law and disability discrimination law. Most critically, the DDA is not meant to provide a basis for securing extra staffing or equipment for a child, since this is meant to be the sole preserve of the special educational needs framework, even though not all disabled children will have special educational needs. In addition, the law expressly provides that schools need not make physical adjustments to their premises. Accordingly, the adjustments that may be required are likely to be in the realm of policy, practices and procedures.

Accessibility strategies and plans and local education authorities' duties

LEAs and schools are required to prepare and maintain accessibility strategies (in the case of LEAs) and accessibility plans (in the case of schools). Further, LEAs have obligations under the DDA in respect of services that they may provide to disabled pupils in matters concerning:

- their policies for special educational needs
- practical building programmes
- sports, cultural activities, transport, early years provision, etc.
- schools' admissions and exclusions arrangements
- the deployment of a non-delegated budget
- services to pupils such as weekend or after-school leisure and sporting activities, school trips and cultural activities.

Complaints of discrimination

In most cases, complaints of discrimination must be brought before the Special Educational Needs and Disability Tribunal (SENDIST). Any such complaint must be brought within six months of the date of the incident that gives cause for complaint. However, in two specific cases, there are separate remedies instead of a complaint to SENDIST:

- If the complaint relates to the refusal to admit a disabled child without a statement of special educational needs to a maintained (state) school, the complaint must be brought before an independent appeal panel for admissions.[10]
- If the complaint relates to a permanent exclusion from a maintained school, the complaint must be brought before an independent appeal panel for exclusions.[11]

The procedures for bringing a complaint to a tribunal are similar to those for an appeal in respect of a special educational needs matter. The procedures are laid out in the Special Educational Needs and Disability Tribunal (General Provisions Disability Claim Procedure) Regulations 2002 and explained further in a booklet published by the Special Educational Needs and Disability Tribunal entitled *Disability Discrimination in Schools: How to Make a Claim.*

Successful claims to the tribunal may result in a number of orders, including an apology, provision of training or guidance for staff, provision of a replacement trip or tuition, or the implementation of new policies. In addition, a school could be ordered to admit a child. However, the law does not provide for monetary compensation. In addition, successful complaints to an independent appeal panel for admission or exclusion may result in the overturning of the decision not to admit or to permanently exclude.

Social services

In addition to its obligation to provide care services, children's social services is the key networking agency to which the family should be able to turn as and when they experience difficulties. If the problem relates to healthcare or an unmet educational need, then it is the duty of children's social services to intercede with the health body or colleagues in children's education services in order to ensure that the matter is resolved. If, however, the problem concerns matters such as the need for general advice (including welfare benefits advice), counselling, homecare services, transport, day-centre or other recreational needs, respite care, home adaptations or appliances, then the children's social services unit must decide whether it should make the necessary assistance available.

The first step in this process will almost invariably be an assessment. On pp.49 and 76 we consider the legal and good practice requirements for the assessment process, and on p.252 we describe the subsequent care-planning process, which culminates in the provision of care services.

As we have seen, research and Department of Health policy (DH 1998a, Para. 7.1) have identified a number of services frequently mentioned by disabled children and their families as being of particular importance. Some of these services have already been considered, including the importance of the family having a named social care manager, a key worker to coordinate the relevant professional support services, access to an advocacy service (see p.59) and the need for authorities to publish clear criteria for entitlement to their services (see p.44). Other services mentioned include access to interpreters and home adaptations (see p.259) as well as aids and equipment, laundry service, (see p.261) respite care/short-term break services, (see pp.63 and 262) transport, homecare and support workers.

As we have noted above, research has highlighted not only the importance of support for informal leisure and play activities but also that such activities do not necessarily occur spontaneously and often require money, transport, time and energy. Social services have substantial powers under both the Children Act 1989 and the Chronically Sick and Disabled Persons Act 1970 to provide and fund the necessary support (see p.258). Both of these Acts can be used to fund adaptations to the built environment in order to provide the child with safe access to leisure and play activities; in addition disabled facilities grants may, in certain situations, be used for such purposes (see p.271).

The needs of every disabled child and his or her family are, of course, unique and vary with time. In the early years, the need to access an upstairs bathroom may be met by being carried by a parent. As the child grows, this will cease to be both tenable and appropriate, and a stair lift, a through-floor lift or adaptations to construct ground-floor facilities may be required. As we have noted above, needs change, particularly during the school-age years, and on each occasion a reassessment will be necessary.

The social services department must consider not only the needs of the disabled child but also the needs of the wider family and, in particular, carers. In relation to carers, the obligations of social services are twofold: the duty under statute to assess and respond with appropriate assistance (see p.264) and a duty at common law to take steps to ensure, so far as is reasonable, that they do not come to harm as a result of their caring tasks.

Health risks for carers

The health risks to which carers are exposed are well documented.[12] Research undertaken by Carers UK (2003) found that over 55 per cent of carers reported they had significant health problems and that almost 43 per cent had sought medical treatment for depression, stress or anxiety since becoming a carer. Carers assessments should, therefore, address specifically the health and safety risks that could jeopardise the sustainability of the caring relationship. In this context, the practice guidance to the Carers and Disabled Children Act 2000[13] describes 'the development of major health problems' as a 'critical risk' for a carer, i.e. a risk that demands a response by the local authority. Such a situation would arise not only if a carer was diagnosed with a serious illness but also where a link had been established between an illness and the carer's caring responsibilities, e.g. a risk of a manual handling injury, or of chronic stress and anxiety in a carer who already had high blood pressure or a history of stress-related illness.

Health services

Department of Health (1998a, Para. 7.1) research has, as we have seen already (see p.00), identified a variety of health services that are frequently mentioned by disabled children and their families as being of particular importance. A number of these were considered in Chapter 5, including good access to primary care, with a named GP and support from a health visitor; contact with a community paediatrician and paediatric community nursing team; access to incontinence advice; the opportunity of respite care; and access to good-quality physiotherapy, speech therapy, occupational therapy and conductive education services. Other important services include the use of a range of laundry services (see p.261) and access to equipment on loan.

The Audit Commission (1995) has identified as one of the five key impediments to interagency working the problems involved in organising aids and appliances and has published highly critical reports[14] on the state of public provision of equipment for disabled people, characterised by 'long delays for equipment of dubious quality'. As a response, the government has required the establishment of 'community equipment services', where both NHS and social services equipment can be accessed at a single point.[15] The guidance accompanying this initiative[16] defines community equipment as follows:

Community equipment is equipment for home nursing usually provided by the NHS, such as pressure relief mattresses and commodes, and equipment for daily living such as shower chairs and raised toilet seats, usually provided by local authorities. It also includes, but is not limited to:

minor adaptations, such as grab rails, lever taps and improved domestic lighting

ancillary equipment for people with sensory impairments, such as liquid level indicators, hearing loops, assistive listening devices and flashing doorbells.

communication aids for people with speech impairments

wheelchairs for short term loan, but not those for permanent wheelchair users, as these are prescribed and funded by different NHS services [see Wheelchairs below]

telecare equipment such as fall alarms, gas escape alarms and health state monitoring for people who are vulnerable.

The above guidance makes plain that the provision of some forms of equipment may be construed as joint social services/NHS responsibility. Similarly, some forms of equipment can be viewed as a joint social services/housing authority responsibility. Circular LAC (90)7 seeks to clarify this question at Para. 19:

> equipment which can be installed and removed with little or no structural modification to the dwelling should usually be considered the responsibility of the [social services] authority. However, items such as stair lifts and through-floor lifts, which are designed to facilitate access into or around the dwelling, would, in the view of the Secretaries of State, be eligible for disabled facilities grant. With items such as electric hoists, it is suggested that any structural modification of the property – such as strengthened joists or modified lintels – could be grant aidable under the disabled facilities grant, but that the hoisting equipment itself should be the responsibility of the [social services] authority.

Wheelchairs

Wheelchairs may be obtained from NHS trusts for temporary use on discharge from hospital. In general, the disabled person will be referred to an occupational therapist, physiotherapist or consultant for assessment as to the most suitable wheelchair. Wheelchairs are provided in England by the local NHS wheelchair service and in Wales by the Artificial Limb and Appliance Service (ALAS) (which is also generally responsible for assessments, usually undertaken at one of its three centres in Cardiff, Swansea and Wrexham).

Despite new best practice guidance issued by the Department of Health (2004), considerable user dissatisfaction exists concerning access to specialist wheelchairs, including electrically powered indoor/outdoor chairs (EPIOCs).[17]

The Jennifer Trust for Spinal Muscular Atrophy argues that children who receive mobility aids at the age of about two years quickly adapt to wheelchairs and become accomplished wheelchair users.[18] It cites Department of Health advice that the eligibility criteria for EPIOCs do not and should not include restrictions on the grounds of a person's age and that the key entitlement factors are that the disabled person is:

- unable to propel a manual wheelchair outdoors
- able to benefit from the chair through increased mobility, leading to improved quality of life
- able to handle the chair safely.

The NHS in England operates a wheelchair voucher scheme that gives users the option of purchasing from an independent supplier or from the wheelchair service. In either case, the user can top up the voucher, which covers only the cost of a standard wheelchair to meet the user's needs, to enable them to buy a more expensive model if desired. However, if the chair is purchased from an independent supplier, it is owned by the user, who is responsible for its maintenance and repair, whereas if the wheelchair services option is chosen, the NHS trust retains ownership and is responsible for maintenance.[19]

Notes

1   Para. 5.43 and Para. 5.54. Department for Education and Skills (2001) and Welsh Assembly (2004).

2   There are numerous cases that establish this obligation, but the lead authority is that of *L* v. *Clarke and Somerset County Council* [1998] ELR 129 and also the Court of Appeal's decision in *Bromley* v. *Special Educational Needs Tribunal* [1999] ELR 260.

3   S. 324(5)(a)(i) Education Act 1996. See also *R* v. *London Borough of Harrow ex p. M* [1997] ELR 62.

4   *London Borough of Bromley* v. *Special Educational Needs Tribunal* [1999] ELR 260.

5   The interface between the Schedule 27 and the Sections 316 and 316A provisions was considered in detail by the Court of Appeal in *H* v. *Special Educational Needs and Disability Tribunal and Hounslow LBC* [2004] EWCA Civ 770: 2004 LGR 844.

6   A system of education for children with autism and related disabilities developed by Dr O. Ivar Lovaas.

7   *T* v. *Special Educational Needs Tribunal and Wiltshire County Council* [2002] ELR 704.

8   See in particular Regulations 12 and 18 of the Education (Special Educational Needs) (England) (Consolidation) Regulations 2001.

9   Available from SENDIST at SEN Appeals, Mowden Hall, Staindrop Road, Darlington DL3 9BG; tel. 01325 392555, email tribunalqueries@sendist.gis.giv.uk; please quote reference TR1 022.

10 An LEA organised panel.

11 An LEA organised panel.

12 See, for instance, Princess Royal Trust for Carers (2002) *Carers Speak Out Project: Report on Findings and Recommendations*. London: Princess Royal Trust for Carers.

13 Practice guidance to the 2000 Act (Para. 70).

14 *Fully Equipped: The Provision of Equipment to Older or Disabled People by the NHS and Social Services in England and Wales* (29 March 2000) and *Fully Equipped 2002: Assisting Independence* (27 June 2002); accessible at www.audit-commission.gov.uk.

15 For general information on this initiative, see www.doh.gov.uk/assetRoot/04/07/51/55/04075155.pdf.

16 Community Equipment Services HSC 2001/008: LAC (2001) 13 Para. 7.

17 See, for instance, Muscular Dystrophy Campaign (2004) *Hard Pushed: How the NHS Fails Powered Wheelchair Users*. www.muscular-dystrophy.org.

18 Information Sheet 002 at www.jtsma.org.uk/in002.html.

19 Health Service Guideline HSG (96)53.

CHAPTER 7

Becoming an Adult

Introduction

In previous chapters we have stressed the importance of gradually creating opportunities for disabled children in order to develop an appropriate degree of independence and autonomy. We have suggested that a range of supports and services may need to be available if disabled children and people close to them are to have experiences comparable in this respect to those enjoyed by non-disabled children and their families. The life that someone has as an adult will depend in part at least on the groundwork laid throughout childhood.

While our emphasis so far has been on the fact that becoming an adult begins the day you are born, we shall concentrate in this chapter on particular issues related to the transition from childhood to adulthood. In Chapter 3, we identified this period as one of the critical transitional points in the lives of young people and their families. It is a time when a range of legal and organisational arrangements change, new information needs to be accessed, and new plans have to be formulated and put into operation. All the evidence we have indicates that this may turn out to be a particularly hazardous time in the lives of those concerned (Beresford 2004; Ward *et al.* 2003). This is partly because of what has gone before, partly because of specific experiences associated with this point in the lifecourse and partly because of the way that services are organised and delivered. All the indications are that unless very positive and proactive steps are taken, certain things may happen by default or design that do not augur well for the young people concerned and their families. The need to tackle the problems associated with transition to adulthood has been emphasised increasingly in government policy and guidance (Audit Commission 2003; DfES and DH 2004; DH 2001b; PMSU 2005). In this chapter, we consider:

- what it means to become an adult
- key findings from research on disabled young people's experience of progressing towards adulthood

- representation, support and information
- service provision and planning for transition to adult life.

What it means to become an adult

In a paper on the dynamics of transition to adulthood for both disabled and non-disabled young people, Riddell (1998, p.193) argues:

> Development from childhood through adolescence to adulthood is at one level a process of biological change and as such is not merely a social construction. At the same time, it is evident that within different cultures and at different historical periods the social construction of childhood, adolescence and adulthood changes markedly (Aries 1973). This implies the existence of a state of interaction between biology and culture so that the physiological and emotional process of maturation is overlaid by a range of cultural expectations which will be subject to change over time and will be influenced by the wider economic context.

Riddell proceeds to describe the ways in which adulthood in modern industrialised societies is construed as a central social status. The achievement of this status entails the crossing of certain age-specific thresholds and this, in turn, carries with it both rights and obligations. Examples of the thresholds she describes include criminal responsibility, sexual consent, voting rights, conditional or unconditional marriage rights and the giving of medical consent. Obligations may include paying income tax when employed and attending for jury service.

Riddell's analysis raises a number of important issues that can inform our discussion on the process of transition to adulthood for disabled young people. First, she indicates the diversity of social and cultural experiences, expectations and practices that may be associated with progression to adult status. This would lead us to be circumspect about the yardsticks we use for measuring the degree to which any young person has moved towards adulthood. In other words, we should be hesitant about assuming that models that may in fact be relevant only to specific ethnic and social groupings are universally applicable. For example, the fact that a young person is living separately from his or her family of origin before marriage cannot be used without qualification as an indicator of progression to adult status. The authors of a study of the experiences of South Asian young disabled people and their families argue that notions of 'independence' were not shared with those of their white counterparts. Living separately or having control of resources did not always have the same significance for the two groups (Hussain, Atkin and Ahmad 2002). In addition, the extent to which such arrangements prove possible, even when regarded as desirable, may be influenced in the UK, for example, by matters such as youth unemployment and policies on eligibility to state benefits.

Second, Riddell draws to our attention the significance often attributed to normative biological maturation. When this is regarded as a key indicator, there are clearly implications for those whose development may not be defined as falling within the normal range or who are living with impairment. There may be a dominant and widespread assumption that access to the rights and obligations associated with adulthood is contingent upon having a particular physiological and intellectual status. Riddell's general discussion of the dynamics of transition reminds us that definitions of childhood, adulthood and transition are by no means straightforward. It also begins to signal some of the ways in which the legal markers of adulthood, however variously defined, may be withheld from disabled young people and just how difficult it may be for them to attain some of the orthodox benchmarks of adult status.

Our view is that even though the dominant templates used by the majority to define progression to adulthood do not always sit easily with the needs and circumstances of many disabled young people, there can be no assumption that disabled young people should be deprived of those experiences and aspirations frequently associated with an adult way of life. While these things may be difficult to achieve for some, we should nevertheless start from the premise that there are some basic rights that all adult citizens should enjoy unless a case can specifically be made to the contrary. Good policy and practice should, therefore, be directed towards supporting and enabling young disabled people and their families to work towards having choices that are within the range regarded as ordinary for the general population.

Disabled young people and transition to adulthood

Quality of life

There is now a substantial body of empirical research and other literature that indicates the extent of the limitations on their quality of life experienced by many disabled young people and those close to them as childhood is left behind (e.g. Baxter et al. 1990; Beresford 1995, 2004; Corbett and Barton 1992; Flynn and Hirst 1992; Hirst and Baldwin 1994; Morris 1999b; PMSU 2005; Social Services Inspectorate 1995a; Thompson, Ward and Wishard 1995; Ward et al. 2003). As Hirst and Baldwin (1994) point out, concern over disabled young people's quality of life and experience in adulthood is by no means new. Since the early 1960s, research and official reports have repeatedly raised serious questions about the quality of health, education and social support services available to them in the post-school period, as well as drawing attention to widespread inequalities in access to the labour market (DH 1976; Ferguson and Kerr 1960; Walker 1982; DES 1978; Younghusband *et al.* 1970). Hirst (1987, p.73) summarised the findings of his study of the careers of 274 disabled young people between the ages of 15 and 21 years as follows:

> First, the vast majority of young people in this sample can look forward to an occupational role which is both undervalued by and segregated from ordinary adult society. Secondly, they face long-term dependence on the social security system, incomes close to the official poverty line and low living standards. Thirdly, and as a consequence, they will have few opportunities to develop control over and responsibility for their own lives. The net result will be that these young people will suffer restricted activities and choice not only in their vocational activities but also in their living arrangements and social lives. Young people with disabilities are particularly dependent for the quality of their adult lives on the services provided for them. Those services need to extend the range of options available to young disabled people and enable them to exercise their own preferences.

More recent research confirms that substantial problems continue to exist for large numbers of the young people and adults concerned. Beresford's (1995) survey in the mid 1990s of 1100 households with a disabled child up to the age of 14 years explored the nature of a wide range of needs on the part of both parents and their sons and daughters. The study indicates some trends that are pertinent to the issue of transition to adulthood. Beresford found that as children grew older, there was a greater likelihood of their having unmet needs for services. Similarly, the extent to which parents' needs remained unmet also increased with the child's age. Parents of older children not only needed more financial support and assistance with day-to-day caring tasks but also wanted help with planning their child's future. Children with more severe impairments had more unmet needs than others, as did their parents. In summary, as many children grew older, they and their families often had increased needs, which were not being met by adequate interventions and supports.

Hirst and Baldwin's (1994) study of around 1000 young people in adolescence and young adulthood is generally regarded as one of the most comprehensive pieces of research on the topic and therefore merits detailed consideration. The study set out to investigate the extent to which disabled young people manage to attain an independent adult life more or less easily than young people in general. It did so by comparing the circumstances and lifestyles of disabled and non-disabled young people. The study also investigated differences in experience of adulthood among disabled young people according to type and severity of impairment.

Hirst and Baldwin report that while transition to adulthood remains a very difficult time for disabled young people, the experience was not uniformly bleak for everyone. Quite substantial numbers were progressing towards adulthood in ways that did not diverge significantly from their non-disabled peers. They had a measure of independence, age-appropriate social activities, a good image of themselves and some sense of personal control over their lives. Some were in paid employment.

Sadly, however, the study also reveals other experiences that give rise to considerable concern. It reports that between 30 and 40 per cent of the disabled young people were likely to have great difficulty in attaining a degree of independence in adult life compared with that of their non-disabled peers. Hirst and Baldwin (1994, pp.109–110) highlight a number of key findings:

- Disabled young people were less prepared for and less likely to be living independently of their parents than young people in general.

- Achieving independence through employment was difficult for most disabled young people, who were half as likely as their non-disabled peers to be in paid work.

- While financial independence increased with age for all the young people, many of those who were disabled faced long-term dependence on the social security system, incomes substantially below those of young people in general and restricted personal spending. Fewer disabled young people controlled money from their social security benefits. Where they did, it was often regarded as a contribution to their keep, thus restricting the income over which they had direct control.

- Although most disabled young people recorded positive views of themselves and the experience of a degree of autonomy, they were more likely than their non-disabled peers to report feelings reflecting a poor sense of their own worth and abilities and a limited sense of control over their lives. Disabled young people who had attended special school and had no post-school provision were at greatest risk of feeling worthless and helpless.

- Although most disabled young people had social and friendship networks, their social lives and use of leisure were more limited and more likely to be dependent on their parents than non-disabled young people. Non-disabled young people tended to have a wider circle of friends, closer friendships and more frequent contacts. Generally, lower participation by the disabled young people in ordinary social activities was offset to some degree by participation in clubs, including those exclusively for disabled people.

- The medical care for the disabled young people was provided more in hospital outpatient departments or clinics rather than through GPs. There was, however, a lack of adequate provision to keep their health needs under review following discharge from paediatric services. There was widespread uncertainty about the ways in which disabled young people could take responsibility for their own health.

- Despite their health needs, there was a lack of continuity in the provision for disabled young people of therapy or paramedical services in the post-school period.

- Few of the disabled young people had had recent contact with a social worker.

Hirst and Baldwin also point out that the circumstances, lifestyles and aspirations of the disabled and non-disabled populations diverged more as they got older, largely as a result of unequal access to employment and, therefore, independent income. As the young people went through their late teens and entered their twenties, the existing gap widened, to the extent that it was unlikely that the disabled young adults could ever catch up.

This study also draws our attention to the particularly disadvantaged position of young people living with severe and multiple impairments. Their access to experiences that others could regard as ordinary was severely limited and their lives were described as 'marginalised and isolated'. Hirst and Baldwin refute any suggestion, however, that there is an inevitable connection between severity of impairment and these quality-of-life outcomes. They point out that there were substantial differences in the experiences of those living with severe impairment and that these reflected inequalities in the support and opportunities made available to them rather than their functional abilities.

More recent work indicates that for many young people, the barriers graphically described by Hirst and Baldwin in 1994 still exist (Beresford 2004; PMSU 2005; Ward et al. 2003).

Barriers to opportunity

In considering the barriers that young people and their families face at this point in their lives, we are not suggesting that the nature of impairment is an insignificant factor but rather that the restrictions that many experience are not a necessary consequence of it. Such restrictions can be mitigated and, thus, the quality of life substantially enhanced by the introduction of appropriate supports and opportunities. What we are arguing is that the degree of autonomy to which a disabled young person may aspire has to be understood with reference to a complex relationship between impairment, social and economic disadvantage, and available opportunities.

The limited availability of supported living and personal assistance services for disabled young people is significant in that it may inhibit the extent to which disabled young people can take control of their own lives and broaden their horizons beyond their immediate family. It also has the effect of keeping the young person and other family members in a protracted and close relationship, which may prove demanding and restrictive in at least some respects for all concerned. We do not, of course, wish to undermine or be critical of close familial and other relationships that are important to those involved. Rather, we are suggesting that whatever disabled young people and their families might otherwise wish, force of circumstances and unmet needs combine to define the parameters of their relationships in particular ways. This is, however, only one element of a series of interlocking factors that restrict disabled young people and adults. In many cases, the disadvantage experienced in one area will have a knock-on effect on others.

The question of restricted employment opportunities is crucial in its own right, but it also provides a useful example of the way in which a number of inter-related factors together operate as barriers or disincentives. It is evident how the circle becomes tightly closed and employment placed beyond the reach of many young people. Having a job is one of the most significant single issues in any adult's life. Research has indicated consistently that economically active disabled people face greater barriers than their non-disabled peers in relation to employment opportunities (Anderson 1995; Barnes 1991; Lonsdale 1990; NACAB 1994; PMSU 2005; Simons 1998; Thornton *et al.* 1997). As a group, disabled people are more likely to face unemployment and to be among the long-term unemployed. When they have jobs, they are more likely than comparable workers in the general population to be in low-paid, low- status positions.

These disadvantages cannot be explained wholly in terms of their functional abilities. Disabled young people frequently have had a more restricted education than others and have often been afforded fewer training opportunities. In addition, there has been reluctance on the part of employers to comply with even the very limited legal obligations that were established in relation to the employment of disabled people in the period after the Second World War, let alone to contribute to the creation of equal opportunities (Gooding 1994). There have been many reported experiences of discrimination in recruitment and in the workplace (Morris 1999b). While the provisions of the Disability Discrimination Act place disabled people in a stronger legal position in the face of such discrimination in employment, there is clearly still much work to be done to change deep-seated negative attitudes and low expectations. A number of measures that have been introduced in an effort to improve disabled people's employment opportunities will be outlined later in this chapter.

In addition to the related issues of education, training and the workplace, young people may find that the vexed question of transport has a bearing on whether they are able to be economically active. Without appropriate transport, getting to the workplace, or doing so without undue difficulty and fatigue, may prove to be a significant barrier. Frequently, family and friends may be the only source of support in this respect.

Some people with learning difficulties who use supported housing schemes have also been found to face barriers to employment because of the fact that it is almost impossible for them to earn enough to meet the rent for such schemes. For many, being a service user of supported housing is contingent upon being in receipt of housing benefit (Morris 1999b; Simons 1998).

It is evident, then, that the barriers and disincentives to employment may prove insurmountable for many disabled young people. As we have already suggested, however, for those who are not in paid employment there are considerable personal and financial consequences. People are often accorded, and in turn accord themselves, value and esteem from being in paid work. The workplace provides a location for making and maintaining social contacts. The working day and the working week give a structure and routine that many people need and value. Finding purposeful activity, social contacts and self-esteem in other ways is extremely important but not always straightforward. In addition, disabled people who are without jobs face restrictions in income combined with high costs of disabled living and, therefore, limited access to goods and services (Bertoud, Lakey and McKay 1993). As we have seen in earlier chapters, the same is true of the household as a whole if the disabled young person is living with his or her family of origin. It is all too easy to see how financial pressures on the whole family may make it difficult for the young person to be allocated a distinct and separate income that they control themselves.

A further problem encountered by many disabled young people and those close to them is in part related to some of the barriers and difficulties that we have already described, but nevertheless it deserves consideration in its own right. As we have suggested earlier, throughout their lives many children and their families have substantial unmet needs for services that are essential to their well-being. As young disabled people approach adulthood, however, there is a tendency for services to fragment, become even more difficult to access or become completely unavailable (Beresford 2004; Ward et al. 2003). The transition from children's services to adult services is fraught with problems, and there is a danger that many young people and their families fall through the net. For some, the fact of being in the school system and having a statement of their special educational needs meant that at least some information and services came their way. These may not be replaced easily when the young person leaves school. For example, once paediatric services no longer have responsibility for the young person, appropriate medical and healthcare services may prove uncoordinated and difficult to access, and advice and guidance on these crucial matters may not be made available (DH 2001b; Ward *et al.* 2003). Young people who have complex healthcare needs may require services and treatment from a variety of practitioners within the health service; this provision is frequently uncoordinated. Within the health service, practitioners who take specialist or lead responsibility for ensuring that young disabled people's needs are met are still rare, as are organisational arrangements set up to deal with the problems of transition (Morris 1999b). Many young people find that physiotherapy and speech and language therapy cease to be available once they leave school. They and their families may also find themselves unsure about their rights in relation to provision of essential equipment as well as the procedures for obtaining it.

The provision of social care and support services may also present problems. As we have seen, despite their statutory duties in this respect, local authorities have not always kept registers of disabled children to aid service planning for populations and individuals. In any location, there are often inconsistencies in the ways that different services organise transition to adult provision, not only across agencies but also within organisations (Audit Commission 2003). For example, the progression from local authority children's social services to adult social services is frequently far from seamless (Audit Commission 2003). The type of interagency cooperation and planning that we consider later in this chapter is frequently not undertaken in ways that would safeguard the future interests of the service users concerned. Many of the relevant agencies undertake planning or review at a very late stage and with little involvement by the young people and their parents. Even when local education authorities comply with the statutory requirement (described later in this chapter) to initiate the formal process of 'transition planning', this by no means guarantees that the young people concerned will have an assessment of their needs for community care and support services or that there will be meaningful planning for other significant aspects of their future lives (Beresford 2004; Ward *et al.* 2003). This, combined with a shortage of post-school educational, vocational or employment opportunities, means that the service users and their families often make choices from a very restricted range of options (Audit Commission 2003). Research has shown that in the face of such enormous difficulties, positive outcomes for young people often are achieved only because of the proactive role played by their parents (Beresford 2004).

Adequate health and social care services are essential in their own right. In addition, we have also seen that for many disabled young people there is a clear and undeniable association between the nature of services with which they are provided and the degree of autonomy and quality of life that they are able to attain as they progress towards adulthood (Hirst and Baldwin 1994). This makes the gap between children's and adults' provision, the falling away of some services and the limited range of options available extremely significant and deserving of the attention of those involved in policy and practice. It also indicates the fragility of the position of young people and their families at this point and underlines the need for extremely positive and proactive steps to be taken to counter the potentially damaging effects of the organisational arrangements as they frequently operate.

Representation, support and information

Some organisations have recognised the need to develop focused or special projects in order to make a significant difference to young disabled people's experience of transition to adult life; some have developed guidance for good practice (e.g. Morris 1999a; Ward et al. 2003). These include voluntary-sector organisations as well as those with statutory responsibilities. Some young people and their families are fortunate enough to have access to practitioners, projects or agencies attempting to develop and adhere to good practice guidelines; many, however, do not. Currently, there are simply too few specialist and experienced practitioners and services to meet demand (Beresford 2004), and provision is far from uniform across the country. This makes it extremely important for as many young people and their families as possible to have access to advocates and key workers as well as sources of direct information. In other words, it is a time when people are likely to need all the human and information resources they can muster if they are to find their way through the maze and get a result they regard as successful. Currently, as we have seen, the outcomes for many young people are contingent on the persistence, knowledge and commitment of those closest to them – usually their parents.

There are a number of reports and guides that may prove useful to young people, their families and practitioners who want to be better informed about good practice, service users' rights and the duties of the various agencies at this time of transition. These include:

- Contact a Family fact sheets *Transition in England and Wales* and *Transition in Scotland*, accessible at www.cafamily.org.uk.

- *After 16 – What's New? Choices and Challenges for Young Disabled People*, accessible at www.after16.org.uk.

- *Move On Up: Supporting Young Disabled People in their Transition to Adulthood*, by Morris, J. (1999) Barkingside: Barnardo's.

We have recommended these particular sources of information because they are free or inexpensive and because they reflect a number of key trends in current work on transition. A great deal of this work stresses the duties and responsibilities of service providers as well as what service users want and should have a right to expect by way of good practice.

It is important to acknowledge that any practitioner involved in working with young people and their families will need to go beyond merely enabling them to find their way through the existing service maze, difficult though that may be in itself. What already exists in a given area may simply not meet the young person's needs and may provide them with only very restricted opportunities. If young people and their families are to have a decent quality of life, then they will require a thorough assessment of their needs in order to determine appropriate service provision. As part of this, they may benefit from the chance to develop their ideas about what would really be in their interests and, therefore, what their aspirations might be. They may need information about options they are unaware of and that do not yet exist in their area. As we have seen, many young people and their families will have led lives fraught with difficulty, and they may need time and a variety of appropriate supports if they are to become confident that better and realistic alternatives are possible in the future.

It also needs to be recognised that young people and their parents may need separate and different forms of information, support, advocacy and representation. When the lives of different family members have often been bound together inextricably, they may each require a distinctive service if they are to explore their different needs and rights. For example, young people who are lacking in self-esteem and have had only limited social networks may benefit from the opportunity to build their confidence within a peer group of other disabled young people and explore the nature of the personal, sexual and social relationships that they would like to develop. This approach has been developed through some peer-mentoring projects (e.g. Bethell and Harrison 2003; Bignall, Butt and Pagarani 2002). They may also welcome a variety of other interventions that enable them to extend their personal development, exercise choice and become aware of their rights. Some mothers who have never been able to go out to work because of their caring responsibilities may welcome the chance to look at how positive future provision for their sons or daughters might enable them, too, to have a wider range of choices.

Even when they are committed to building a life that is gradually more independent of one another, some young people and their parents may still have misgivings about the idea of living separately for a whole range of reasons. For example, when research indicates that alarming numbers of disabled young people have abusive experiences outside the home, ranging from routine unkindness through to bullying and serious assault, it is hardly surprising that concern about risk and safety may impact on aspirations and plans (Ward *et al.* 2003). Young people and those closest to them may value personal and practical support as they try to deal with these and other difficult issues (McConkey and Smyth 2003).

Service provision and planning for transition to adult life

A range of agencies have formal duties in respect of transition planning, and there is a clear expectation that they should work together to secure the best outcome. It is a requirement that a transitional plan should be produced for every young person who has a statement of special educational needs and that the process should be initiated by the local education authority at the first annual review after the person's fourteenth birthday. This would seem to indicate official recognition that successful transition to adulthood takes time and careful preparation. It is also recognised that it requires coordinated effort, planning and service delivery by key agencies with different responsibilities. The legal duties placed on the various parties involved and the procedures that they are required to follow will be specified in the legal commentary later in this chapter. Here, we will focus on what young people and those close to them ought to be able to expect in the way of basic good practice in transitional planning.

The first and perhaps most obvious issue is that disabled young people and their families should be able to expect that those involved do not simply go through the motions. The process of transitional planning should be undertaken in a manner that is meaningful to the young people and their parents and carried out in the spirit as well as to the letter of the law. The perspectives of both the young person and the parents should be central, and they should be regarded as partners with the professionals. The approach known as person-centred planning has been promoted strongly in policy and practice (DfES and DH 2004; DH 2001b). It is founded on a simple set of principles: that planning starts with the person and not the provision, and takes account of the young person's and their family's wishes; and that practice places the needs and preferences of service users at the centre of the planning process and finds ways of exploring the outcomes that are of most importance to them. As we discussed in Chapter 2, the deceptively simple questions that inform decisions about these outcomes might be:

- Where do you want to spend your time living, working, learning and socialising?
- What activities are important to you in those settings?
- Who are important people to interact with in these environments and activities?

Efforts are then directed at ways of achieving those outcomes. *The National Service Framework for Children, Young People and Maternity Services* (NSF) (DfES and DH 2004, Standard 8, p.38) describes the main focus of transition planning as 'the fulfilment of the hopes, dreams and potential of the disabled young person, in particular to maximize education, training and employment opportunities, to enjoy social relationships and to live independently'. Good practice involves a developmental process that takes time, skill and sensitivity and works to avoid common pitfalls. For example, formal procedures may prove important for all concerned and may safeguard rights, but some young people and their families may feel at a disadvantage in such a context and may, therefore, be hesitant about raising issues that are important to them. Some may feel that it is difficult to make headway if policy and practice appear to privilege cultural norms that are not their own (Jones *et al.* 2001). Some young people may require forms of communication other than speech (Rabiee *et al.* 2005) and may be marginalised if this is not acknowledged fully. In addition, in what is an essentially personal process, understandable concerns, tensions and differences of view may emerge between family members. All of this may necessitate using responsive, diverse and innovative ways of consulting with young people and those close to them.

Second, there needs to be a well-developed local policy to which all relevant agencies are committed with robust mechanisms for operationalising it. The NSF stipulates that local authorities, primary care trusts and NHS trusts should be responsible for putting in place multi-agency transition groups in their areas. These are to assume strategic and operational responsibility and are to agree interagency protocols. In addition to the standards set by the NSF, good practice would indicate the need for agreements about what young people and their families have the right to expect from different agencies and what will happen at every stage. It would be advantageous if, by interagency agreement, individual practitioners were designated to take lead responsibility for coordinating the work to be undertaken and for acting as the key worker or point of contact for the young person and the parents. This does not, of course, preclude the parents or young person having access to independent advocates or advisors. There is substantial research evidence to support the view that sound multi-agency working, including in the form of specialist multidisciplinary teams, improves outcomes for disabled young people at transition (Beresford 2004).

It is also important to recognise that the responsibilities of the agencies concerned are not limited only to their specific duties related to the transitional planning process. This process may bring to light current unmet needs for services that it is the duty of an agency to address. For example, if the local education authority notifies social services that a young person who is disabled has now reached their fourteenth birthday, it may trigger an immediate assessment of need for community care services as well as planning for the future.

In summary, good practice demands that everything about the process should be geared towards enabling young people to have choices that are comparable to those made by people in their age group in the general population as they progress towards adulthood. This requires a careful review of experience to date, the current and future needs of the young person and their family, and services that will have to be put in place to meet these needs.

We now consider in more detail five key areas that should be addressed in transition planning:

- future plans in education
- careers and employment
- healthcare
- community care services
- housing, accommodation and supported living schemes.

Future plans in education

As well as reviewing what the school curriculum aims specifically to offer the young person so that they may best be prepared personally and academically for adult life, consideration will also need to be given to whether it is in the young person's interests to continue at school beyond the age of 16 years.

Some young people will, for example, follow an academic curriculum that leads them to stay at school until they are 18 years old and take GCSEs and A-levels. Some may progress to higher education. Others who are also set to follow GCSE and A-level courses may prefer to leave school at 16 years and complete this part of their education either in a local standard college of further education or at a specialist college. These colleges may also be an option for people not following this type of academic curriculum. For some disabled young people who have been deemed to have special educational needs, there may also be the option of continuing in school until they are 19 years old.

It has been argued that extended school provision and places in the further education sector are sometimes offered almost as a default option rather than a planned choice with a clear purpose (PMSU 2005). Parents and young people should expect to be given a range of information about the available options. Discussion about the impact of choices on the young person's medium- and longer-term future should be integrated into the transitional planning process.

The responsibilities of a number of bodies for providing funding for different purposes for students who wish to take up places in further education colleges are outlined later in this chapter. Funding arrangements are often complex. This makes early planning essential so that they can be negotiated in good time.

Careers and employment

The Connexions Service is expected to make a comprehensive contribution to the transitional planning process. The service has responsibility for supporting and guiding all young people aged between 13 and 19 years as they progress towards adulthood, further and higher education, training and employment. Its personal advisors consequently have an advisory role in relation to disabled young people within this age group and to those aged between 20 and 25 years. As we have already suggested, despite a greater focus on the employment rights of disabled people and on schemes to assist them in the workplace, entry into paid work is by no means easy for many. It has been argued that the most effective provision to date has focused more on return to work and retention rather than targeting those entering the labour market for the first time (PMSU 2005). Consequently, it is stressed that in transitional planning, employment should be regarded as an important option, with clear goals being identified within a realistic timeframe. In addition, it is seen to be important to develop training packages for the individual along with flexible and supported work experience placements. Appropriate and ongoing support for both the disabled young person and the employer is argued to be crucial (PMSU 2005).

Day services provided or purchased by local authority adult social services departments may prove to be important for some young people. There has been substantial criticism of the segregated and limiting nature of some day services, particularly perhaps those for people with learning disabilities (Morris 1999b). Recent years have seen raised expectations and some innovation in this area of provision as a result, in part at least, of the work of the National Development Team. There has been an increased emphasis on the importance of putting together more individualised flexible programmes designed to enable young people to acquire skills, knowledge and contacts that can enhance their quality of life and prove useful for independent living. As part of this, they may be assisted to access mainstream leisure, educational and other facilities (Morris 1999b; Social Services Inspectorate 1995a, 1995b, 1997). While these trends are apparent, there is considerable variation in the type, quality and availability of day services from one authority to another.

Healthcare

As we have seen, disabled young people in transition may be in danger of having unmet healthcare needs when they are no longer eligible for children's services (DH 2001b). This makes the active involvement of the health service in transitional planning extremely important (DH 2001b). Young people and their parents need the opportunity to review with professionals the continuing healthcare needs and come to an agreement about how these should be met. They should be given information about how the necessary services will be delivered and what the key points of contact within the health service will be.

Community care services

Local authorities have a duty to assess disabled young people's needs for community care services provided under a variety of statutory provisions, including Section 2 of the Chronically Sick and Disabled Persons Act 1970. As we have already seen, a wide range of services may be provided that can enable the young person to live more independently and to approach a quality of life comparable to that of others in the general population. The day services of the types already described, practical and personal assistance and support in the home, assistance with travel, access to leisure, holidays and recreation, home adaptations and equipment and the provision of meals can all be made available to aid the young person's chances of living more autonomously. These can be provided within the young adult's own accommodation or at the family home if that is where the young person is living. We should not assume that no measure of independent living can be achieved by young people who do not live separately from their families of origin. For those living with their parents, a range of the interventions discussed in Chapters 3 and 6, including mutually beneficial short-term breaks, can be tailored so that they are age-appropriate and fit the lifestyle of a young adult (Flynn et al. 1998).

Earlier, we discussed the provision of support workers and personal assistants to enable children and young people to have access to a wider range of ordinary experiences without always having to rely on their parents or other family members. As young people progress towards adulthood, it becomes even more important to consider such options. Even though the young person's care needs may to date have been met by family members, consideration can be given to whether it is now more appropriate to introduce support and assistance provided by someone else. This may be organised or provided by the local authority, or by the young person and his or her family themselves but with local authority funding. Disabled young people are eligible to apply for funding from the Independent Living Fund from the age of 16 years, and local authorities can also make direct payments to them from the same age.

The option to have either direct personal care and assistance services or the money to buy and control them offers young people and their families scope for improving their lives and increasing the autonomy of everyone concerned. Those who have experience of receiving and providing personal assistance testify to the importance of clear and sensitive agreements, preparation and planning, as well as the piloting and readjustment of arrangements so that a service is reliable and appropriate. Now that there are greater numbers of disabled young people and adults using personal assistants, more source materials are available so that practitioners and service users new to this form of provision can learn from the experience of others (Hasler, Campbell and Zarb 1999). What is needed is likely to change over time, but the transitional planning process, if used positively, can provide the opportunity for young people and their families gradually to find out what services aid the progression to adulthood.

Housing, accommodation and supported living schemes

Research has pointed consistently to the limited housing and accommodation options available to disabled children and adults and those close to them (e.g. Harker and King 1999; Morris 1999b; Oldman and Beresford 1998; Ward et al. 2003). It is clear that the quantity and range of accommodation combined with appropriate and necessary support services do not match the potential need. The private rented market, the sector that many non-disabled young people rely on to provide their first independent home, often has little that is suitable for their disabled peers. Consequently, young disabled adults may find themselves having to stay with their families of origin for longer than they would otherwise choose or accepting options that they or their families do not regard as suitable. For example, while residential units may be regarded as a positive choice for some people, there are circumstances when this provision can almost be taken as a foregone conclusion without other forms of accommodation and support having been considered. Morris (1999b) suggests that for young people with high support needs leaving residential school, long-term nursing-home care is too often assumed to be the inevitable next stage. Similarly, having a flat of one's own may sometimes be ruled out for young people with learning disabilities, even though this could be viable given the provision of appropriate community care services.

In view of the fact that accommodation and housing difficulties are well known, it is crucial that as a young person approaches adulthood steps are taken to look at what their needs are and to work towards meeting them in a planned way. This may require cooperation between local authority adult social services, housing departments and independent providers. Some specialised housing and accommodation schemes have support services incorporated within them. In others, personal assistance and community care support packages are provided entirely separately by the local authority adult social services department, according to the needs of the tenant. For some young adults, there is no need for a specialist scheme, although they may need accommodation to be adapted and some community care services arranged that enable them to live more independently. A central government initiative, the Supporting People programme, which came into being in 2003, was designed to provide housing-related support to a range of adults defined as 'vulnerable' in order to enable them to live more independently. The eligible groups include people with learning difficulties and people with physical and sensory impairments. The programmes are jointly commissioned and implemented by local authority housing and social care agencies.

The idea that young disabled people can live independently of their parents may be unfamiliar to both the young person and his or her parents. Again, they may require a great deal of information and discussion about the way different approaches might meet their particular needs. They may need to build confidence that a suitable arrangement can be created, modified and made to work.

Because suitable provision is frequently hard to come by, there is often a strong feeling that choices have to be certain and that mistakes cannot be made. While this caution is understandable in the circumstances, we have to remind ourselves that we would not regard it as unusual for non-disabled young adults to try something and find that they want to change their minds. Many of us, both young and old, do not find our preferred living arrangements first time round and sort out what works only by at least a little trial and error.

LEGAL COMMENTARY
Introduction

As we have stressed throughout, disabled children have to negotiate a series of transitions. On each occasion, encounters take place with new procedures, new personnel and new administrative cultures.

Although the transition into adulthood is a major episode for all adolescents, for disabled young people it can represent a period characterised by acute anxiety and profound difficulties. At this stage, many of the key support agencies change, and young people and their families experience the gradual or abrupt withdrawal of education and children's services support, and the consequent need to engage in fresh dialogue with adult care services, learning and skills councils, and so on.

Statutory provisions exist that endeavour to ensure that there is a smooth handover of responsibility from those responsible for special education provision to the social services department responsible for the continuing community care needs of the disabled person.

It is essential, therefore, that new or revived contacts are forged with the new agencies – most obviously social services, although housing and the social security staff (i.e. those working for the Department of Work and Pensions) will also often have crucial roles. However, since the goal will be for the disabled young person to live as normal and as independent a life as is possible, crucial relationships may also involve the employment and careers services and learning and skills councils.

The statutory provisions that anticipate transition planning operate on the basis that if the social care services involvement is not already substantial, then the education section responsible for a special education statement (and possibly the Connexions Service; see p.185) will take the initiative to involve the other relevant agencies. If for any reason, however, this does not occur, or the initiative lacks the necessary vigour, early letters expressing concern and making direct contact with the other agencies should be sent.[1]

We consider the relevant legal issues under the following headings:

- education services' responsibilities
- social services
- NHS responsibilities
- the Independent Living Fund
- housing responsibilities
- mental capacity and parental wills/trusts.

For those children who have been looked after by the local authority (e.g. placed in foster care), the Children (Leaving Care) Act 2000 places additional transitional responsibilities on social services. These are considered in Chapter 8.

Education services' responsibilities

For children who have statements of special educational needs (see Chapter 6), the annual review in year 9 and subsequent years is extended to plan for the child's transition from school. In particular, the year 9 annual review must involve the Connexions Service and any other agency that may play a major role in the young person's life during the post-school years. Social services should attend so that any parallel assessments under the Disabled Person's (Services Consultation and Representations) Act 1986, the NHS and Community Care Act 1990 and the Chronically Sick and Disabled Persons Act 1970 can contribute to and draw information from the review process.

Following the meeting, a transition plan should be drawn up, and at subsequent reviews of the statement, the plan should be reviewed. This should draw together information from a range of individuals within and beyond school in order to plan coherently for the young person's transition to adult life. Transition plans are not simply about post-school arrangements; they are also there to plan for ongoing school provision if that is intended.

The Code of Practice on Special Educational Needs[2] requires that all those involved in the process of the production and review of a transition plan adhere to the principles that underpin the nature of transition and transition planning and the requirements of the young people and their families. In particular, Para. 9.52 of the Code requires that transition planning should be:

- participative
- holistic
- supportive
- evolving
- inclusive
- collaborative.

In addition, the Connexions Service is responsible for overseeing the delivery of the transition plan and the Connexions Personal Adviser should coordinate its delivery. Accordingly, there should not be a separate transition plan and Connexions Action Plan. In addition, the views of the young person should be sought and recorded wherever possible.

In the young person's final year of school, the Connexions Service has a separate responsibility under Section 140 of the Learning and Skills Act 2000 for ensuring that an assessment of the young person's needs on leaving school is undertaken and the provision identified.

Disability employment advisers

Where, because of a disability, a person faces complex employment problems, they may be referred to the Disability Employment Adviser by their Jobcentre. It is the responsibility of such advisers to provide assistance and access various schemes, in order to enable the disabled person to obtain employment. There are numerous schemes available, including the following.

Work Preparation Scheme

This scheme is directed at preparing disabled people for employment by concentrating on specific employment-related needs that result from the impairment and that would otherwise prevent the person from entering employment of vocational training. The scheme includes the possibility of paying to the disabled person an employment rehabilitation allowance.

Job Introductions Scheme

This scheme helps disabled people who are looking for work by providing a weekly grant to an employer for the first few weeks as a contribution to the wages or other employment costs, for example additional training. As at September 2005, it amounted to £75 per week for the first six weeks of employment. In exceptional circumstances, and after agreement with the Disability Employment Adviser, it may be extended to 13 weeks. The job can be full- or part-time but must be expected to last for at least six months.

Access to Work Scheme

This programme can, among other things, provide funding to cover the extra costs necessary because of disability, including the cost of:

- employing a communicator if the person is deaf or has a hearing impairment
- a part-time reader if the person has impaired vision
- support workers if the person needs practical help, either at work or getting to work
- special equipment or adaptations to equipment to suit individual needs
- alterations to premises or to the working environment so that an employee with disabilities can work there
- help with travel-to-work costs, such as adaptations to a car or taxi fares if public transport cannot be used.

The financial support available depends upon the length of time the disabled person has been employed, but for people about to start work the full cost of the support is available.

Workstep

This scheme provides job support to disabled people who face more complex barriers to getting and keeping a job but who can work effectively with the right support. It offers practical assistance to employers and is tailored to the disabled person's individual circumstances. It is available for almost any type of job.

The scheme provides for the disabled person to be paid the same wage as his or her non-disabled colleagues doing the same or similar work. It is based upon a development plan drawn up between the disabled person, the Workstep provider and the employer. The plan provides for, among other things, the necessary training and support.

Disability Discrimination Act 1995 and employment

The Disability Discrimination Act 1995 makes unlawful 'unjustified discrimination' against a disabled people in relation to many matters, including in the field of employment.

The Act's protection covers job applicants as well as existing employees and requires employers to take reasonable steps to change the working environment to reduce the discrimination experienced by disabled employees.

The provisions of the Act are relatively complex and beyond the scope of this text, but reference should be made to the specific Codes of Practice issued by the Disability Rights Commission.[3]

Further and higher education provision[4]

LEAs are responsible for the provision of a child's education until the age of 16 years, at which point statements of special educational needs also come to an end if the child is no longer on the roll of a school. After this age, responsibilities vary depending on the course chosen. The situation has many permutations, but the main options are as follows.

- Once a child has reached the age of 16 years, he or she may remain in school-based provision if there is provision available in the area. If the young person has a statement of special educational needs, they may continue to receive the protection afforded by the statement up to a maximum age of 19 years, providing that they remain on the roll of a school. LEAs are specifically obliged to have regard to the requirements of people with learning difficulties who are over the age of 16 years.[5]

- The young person may leave secondary school at the age of 16 years and commence further education or training at, for instance, a further education college.

- The young person may enter further education or training at the age of 19 years after the end of his or her secondary schooling.

- The young person may enter higher education by going to a university.

Further education

Since September 2000, the Learning and Skills Council (LSC) for England and the National Council for Education and Training for Wales have been the bodies primarily responsible for delivery of further education. The LSC has established 45 local skills councils in England with specific responsibilities and duties, pursuant to the Learning and Skills Act 2000. Broadly, these bodies are responsible for all post-16 education, except that which takes place in schools.

In relation to disabled students, the LSC in discharging its functions must have regard to the needs of such people and, as stated above, must obtain a specialist assessment of such a student pursuant to Section 140. If the LSC is satisfied that it cannot make arrangements for people aged between 16 and 19 years that are sufficient in quantity and adequate in quality without providing boarding accommodation, it must do so (Section 13(2)).

Likewise, it must provide boarding accommodation for those between the ages of 19 and 25 years if it cannot secure reasonable provision without this (Section 13(3)). The LSC has a power to make the same arrangements for anyone over the age of 25 years (Section 13(4)).

The LSC for England has outlined its procedures and criteria used in relation to specialist colleges for students with learning difficulties and disabilities in LSC Circular 02/14 (August 2002). The equivalent circular for Wales, issued by the National Council for Education and Training for Wales, is Circular NC/C/03/12LDF Securing Specialist Provision for Learners with Learning Difficulties and/or Disabilities. However, critically, statements of special educational needs effectively cease once a child is 16 if he or she is no longer on the roll of a school.

Disability discrimination and education

Further and higher education colleges and universities have similar obligations towards disabled students and applicants for places as those owed by schools to students in primary and secondary education (see p.157). However, in those cases, colleges may be required to make adjustments by way of additional staffing or equipment and also, from September 2005, may be required to make physical adjustments to premises.

Complaints about discrimination against colleges and universities must be brought through proceedings in the county court, which must be commenced within six months of the date that the incident that gives rise to the complaint arose. In this case, aside from seeking a specific remedy, such as an injunction requiring a college to admit a disabled applicant, the court can order monetary compensation.

Forthcoming changes

As a result of the European Community Directives and the Disability Discrimination Act 2005, new anti-discrimination provisions governing post-16 vocational training and obligations on general qualification bodies, such as those that prepare and deliver GCSEs, A-levels, etc., are likely to be introduced from September 2006.

Social services

While there may be good social work practice reasons for the departmental separation by the Children Act 2004 of children's services from adult social services, there is no significant justification for it in terms of the social care duties of local authorities to disabled people. Although in general services under the Children Act 1989 cease to be available when a disabled young person reaches the age of 18 years, entitlement to services under Section 2 of the Chronically Sick and Disabled Persons Act 1970 remains (see p.258). However, many young people and their families, and indeed practitioners, will be unaware that disabled children are entitled to services under Section 2 of the Chronically Sick and Disabled Persons Act 1970. As they approach transition to adulthood, therefore, they may have to go through the process of finding out about and accessing these entitlements.

There are, of course, dangers in separating adult and childcare services, and these often surface when the care responsibilities are being transferred from the child and families team to the adult social work team. As we note above, all too often at this stage, the quality of the services deteriorates significantly or the young person is effectively lost to the system and ceases to receive any continuing care. In this respect, the Children Act Guidance notes:[6]

> Although different agencies' statutory responsibilities for children vary by age, authorities may wish to plan around existing team structures to provide support to young people beyond the statutory age of responsibility and to provide support during the transitional period to adulthood. Unless the resources and experience of children's services can be used during the transition to adult life, it is unlikely that young people's special needs will be met. Additionally existing resources and professional expertise will not be used in the most consumer-sensitive and cost-effective way and the skills developed during the school years may be lost in adult life.

As detailed above, the LEA's obligations under the Disabled Persons (Services, Consultation and Representation) Act 1986 should ensure that social services are fully aware of the needs of the disabled child who has been statemented, well before his or her educational support comes to an end.

Some social services departments have care workers or occasionally even teams with specific responsibility for such transitional planning, but problems do occur at this stage, particularly in relation to the transitional arrangements for disabled children who do not have a statement of special educational needs.

As we have stressed repeatedly, social services have a crucial role in ensuring continuity of care and support throughout the disabled child's life, and this continues into adult life. If for any reason the social services provision or arrangements are considered to be inadequate, then the appropriate response will generally be for a comprehensive assessment (or reassessment), with a view to the production of a care plan aimed at the promotion of as independent and normal a life as is possible. We consider the assessment obligations of social services authorities on p.251 and the provision of community care services on p.252.

Upon the disabled person reaching the age of 18 years the statutory basis for a number of the services he or she may be receiving changes.[7] For instance, if the service received before the age of 18 years is residential accommodation (e.g. short periods of residential respite care), then after the age of 18 years the service will, in general, be made available under Section 21 of the National Assistance Act 1948 rather than under the Children Act 1989. This legislative changeover should not, however, in any way affect the services the young person receives.

Educational support services

Social services are required under Section 2(1)(c) of the Chronically Sick and Disabled Persons Act 1970 to provide certain non-educational support services for students who live away. The court has held that the provision enables social services to provide 'assistance to take advantage of education facilities which are available to [the student]', but it cannot be used to support 'purely education facilities'.[8] Department of Health guidance, LAC (93)12,[9] gives specific guidance on these responsibilities and, in particular, stresses that Section 2(1)(c) covers funding the personal care requirements of such students so as to enable them to pursue their studies, even if those studies are undertaken outside the local authority's area. The relevant part of the circular states:

> 9. SSDs have been reminded of their duty under s2(1)(c) of the Chronically Sick & Disabled Persons Act 1970 to make arrangements for assisting a disabled person who is ordinarily resident in their area in taking advantage of educational facilities available to him/her (even where provision is made outside that local authority's area), if they are satisfied that it is necessary in order to meet that person's needs. Such assistance might, in appropriate cases, include the funding by the local authority of the personal care required to enable the student in question to pursue his/her studies. It is, of course, for the authority to decide, in each case, what the individual's needs are, and how they are to be met.

> 10. Disabled students attending higher education courses may be eligible to receive up to three Disabled Students Allowances from the local education authority, as part of their mandatory award. These allowances are for a non-medical helper, major items of special equipment, or minor items such as tapes or braille paper. They are aimed at helping students with costs related to their course, and are not intended to meet other costs arising from their disability which would have to be met irrespective of whether or not they were in a course. For those attending further education courses, similar support may be provided at the discretion of the LEA.

> 11. There may be occasions where the social services department is asked to consider the provision of additional care support for an individual who will receive a Disabled Students Allowance or discretionary support from the LEA. It will, therefore, be appropriate in some circumstances for the support for an individual's personal care needs to be provided jointly by the SSD and the LEA.

NHS responsibilities

The NHS responsibilities for the healthcare needs of disabled young people do not change when such people attain adulthood, although inevitably the other changes in a young person's life may disrupt their contact with the health services. The guidance, therefore, stresses the 'crucial' role that GPs may play in this transitional period:

Their contribution to community care through knowledge of the whole family and the local community and their ability to monitor the individual young person's health and well-being – as well as the delivery of general medical services – are essential in terms of support to young people living in their local community.[10]

The main focus of recent health and social services guidance is to ensure that in so far as it is possible, young people are not accommodated in hospitals on a long-stay basis.

NHS-funded residential and respite care

The care needs of some disabled people are such that they require the provision of substantial or specialist nursing care in a residential setting. In relation to such young people, the guidance stresses that although they 'may spend substantial periods of time receiving care or treatment in an NHS facility, it is against government policy that [they] be placed for long-term residential care in a NHS hospital setting'.[11]

Thus, although the health authority may be responsible for the funding of a person's care package, the placement should be in 'small homely, locally-based units'.[12] In practice, these units will often be specialist independent or private nursing homes. Where a young person has been provided with accommodation by a health body for more than three months, the body is under a duty to notify the responsible social services department (i.e. the local authority for the area in which the child lives or was ordinarily resident immediately before being accommodated) of the arrangement.[13] We deal further with the issue of residential placements in health settings in Chapter 8.

The Independent Living Fund

A detailed consideration of welfare benefits law is outside the scope of this text, but excellent coverage of this field is given in the *Disability Rights Handbook* (Disability Allowance 2005), which is updated each year. We do, however, set out below the main rules for funding through the Independent Living (1993) Fund (ILF).

In order to qualify for a grant from the 1993 fund, an applicant must:

• be at least 16 and under 66 years of age

• live alone or with people who cannot fully meet his or her care needs

• be assessed by the local authority as being at risk of entering residential care, or capable of leaving it to live in the community

- receive at least £200 worth of services per week from the local authority (net of any charge) and be assessed as needing additional care

- receive the highest-rate care component of the Disability Living Allowance (DLA) and be able to live in the community for at least the next six months

- be on income support or income-based job seeker's allowance or have an income that is insufficient to cover the cost of the care needed (i.e. at or around income support levels after care costs are paid)

- have less than £18,500 capital (a tariff income of £1 per week is assumed for every £250 of capital between £11,500 and £18,500).

The maximum sum that the 1993 fund can pay is £420 per week. In addition, the combined contribution from the local authority and the ILF must be no greater than £715 per week, although the total cost of the care package may be more than this. As the guidance notes explain, any monies contributed by the applicant (by way of DLA, Severe Disability Premium (SDP), available income or money from savings), or by some other contributor (such as a friend or relative), do not count towards this maximum. Likewise, NHS funding is not included within the limit.

The ILF award is made on the basis that the care package will remain within the £715-per-week limit for the first six months. If the applicant's circumstances change within that period, the fund may be prepared to increase its funding, provided that it is satisfied that the change in circumstances was not foreseeable. However, if after the six-month period the local authority wishes to increase its contribution, taking the joint input to above £715 per week, then the award from the fund normally will not be withdrawn.

If the local authority contribution is variable, meaning that the combined weekly cost would occasionally exceed £715, the fund may still be prepared to contribute – for instance, where the variation in local authority contribution is part of a regular and established pattern and the overall cost averaged over 52 weeks is £715 a week or less.

Although applications can be made directly to the fund (see below), in general the social services department should first carry out a full community care assessment and agree to support the application to the fund. If an applicant appears to meet all the criteria, then the fund will arrange for an assessment visit to be made. The visit will be carried out jointly by one of the fund's visiting social workers together with a local authority social worker.

Applicants are required to contribute towards the overall cost of the care package, including all of their SDP and half of their DLA. Earnings are, however, disregarded, and if the applicant is not in receipt of income support, then specific charging rules apply – details are accessible from the ILF. The ILF entitlement terms are reviewed periodically. Guidance notes on the workings of the ILF schemes are accessible at www.ilf.org.uk/guidancenotes.htm.

Housing responsibilities

A detailed consideration of the entitlement of disabled people to access rented accommodation from the housing authority, either under the housing 'list' process or via the homelessness provisions of the Housing Act 1996, is outside the scope of this text, but we consider briefly three aspects of the duty to accommodate of particular relevance to disabled children.

Supporting People Programme

In an effort to streamline the housing benefit scheme, the costs attributable to various housing support services required by vulnerable people have been transferred to a separate budget – the Supporting People Programme. People who need these support services are no longer eligible for enhanced rates of housing benefit but instead seek assistance with the costs from the authority that administers these monies (generally the local social services authority).[14]

The services funded under the programme are not community care services and accordingly are subject to a distinct assessment and charging regime. Although the programme does not affect the responsibility of social services authorities to meet the assessed needs of service users, the funds it makes available do enable local authorities to provide a greater breadth of housing-related solutions in any particular case. Thus, instead of providing a person with a care home or home-help services, the local authority could utilise the supporting people's monies to fund a warden service[15] in a sheltered housing scheme or provide support for a person with learning disabilities or mental health problems in moving into more independent living, for instance by providing help in making rent payments and ensuring windows are locked at night and that other housing-related obligations are discharged.

Homelessness

The duty to house homeless people is contained in Part VIII of the Housing Act 1996 (Sections 175–218). Of particular relevance for disabled children, young people and their families are two aspects of the statutory definition of homelessness. A person is homeless if there is no accommodation that it would be reasonable for him or her to occupy (Section 175). In addition, the Act specifies that accommodation can be regarded as available for a person's occupation only if it is available for occupation by him or her together with:

- any other person who normally resides with him or her as a member of his or her family; or
- any other person who might be reasonably expected to reside with him or her.

Thus, accommodation that is manifestly unsuitable for a disabled child or young person may create a situation of homelessness, requiring action by the housing authority either to rehouse or to render the property habitable for the child.

Children Act housing duties

Housing may, in limited circumstances, be provided by social services authorities in pursuance of their community care or Children Act responsibilities. Thus, in *R v. Tower Hamlets LG ex p. Bradford* [1997],[16] the court ruled that the social services department had fundamentally misunderstood its powers under Section 17 of the Children Act 1989 when confronted with the needs of a disabled parent and her 11-year-old child in need. It had failed to appreciate, until immediately before the hearing, that it had power under Section 17 to provide virtually any service it deemed necessary, including the provision of accommodation for the whole family.

Subsequent to the *ex p. Bradford* decision, considerable controversy arose concerning the extent of the housing obligation under Section 17 of the Children Act 1989, culminating in the House of Lords' judgment in *R (G) v. Barnet LBC and others* [2003],[17] where the majority concluded that there was only a 'weak' duty under Section 17 to provide this service. The position has now been put beyond doubt by the amending of Section 17(6)[18] to expressly include the provision of 'accommodation' as one of the general services that may be provided and 22 amended so as to exclude children provided with accommodation under Section 17. Guidance on these amendments has been provided in England in LAC (2003)13, which includes the following:

> The amendment to section 17 did not affect the duties and powers of local authorities to provide accommodation for lone children under section 20 of the Children Act 1989, or under a care order. Accordingly, the power to provide accommodation under section 17 will almost always concern children needing to be accommodated with their families. However, there may be cases where a lone child who needs help with accommodation, but does not need to be looked after, might appropriately be assisted under section 17.

Disabled facilities grants

In addition to their housing provision responsibilities, housing authorities are responsible for administering grants to pay for the provision of disabled facilities in homes. These grants are primarily available to owner-occupiers/tenants for the purpose of:

- facilitating a disabled person's access to:
  - the dwelling
  - a room usable as the principal family room or for sleeping in
  - a WC, bath, shower, etc., or the provision of a room for these facilities
- facilitating the preparation of food by the disabled person
- improving/providing a heating system to meet the disabled person's needs
- facilitating the disabled person's use of a source of power
- facilitating access and movement around the home to enable the disabled person to care for someone dependent upon them
- making the dwelling safe for the disabled person and others residing with him or her.

The means test for these grants depends upon the financial resources of the disabled person and his or her partner. In England and Wales if the disabled person is under 18 years, there is no longer any means test in such cases. We set out the main rules for such grants in greater detail on p.271.

Not infrequently, social services assess a need for an adaptation but for one reason or another the costs of this are not covered by a disabled facilities grant. This may occur because the works in question do not come under the mandatory scheme, or because the housing authority does not consider the proposed works to be reasonable or practicable, or because the applicant fails the means test.[19] In addition, it may be that the proposed works cost significantly more than the maximum grant (currently £25,000 in England and £30,000 in Wales). In such situations, the failure of the grant application does not absolve the social services authority of its duty under Section 2 of the Chronically Sick and Disabled Persons Act 1970 to meet an assessed need. The social services obligation to provide adaptations under the 1970 Act is considered on p.259.

Mental capacity and parental wills/trusts

When young people attain the age of 18 years, the law treats them as adults and assumes that they have the ability to make any decision that they choose. If, however, they lack this capacity, then number of problems arise. For instance, they may lack the capacity to make a will or decide where they live or how they invest their money. As a child, some of these problems, for instance disputes about access or contact arrangements with parents or about their residence, are capable of resolution by way of an application under the Children Act 1989, but upon attaining the age of 18 years, these relatively simple procedures are no longer available; unfortunately, there is no simple equivalent procedures for adults. The Mental Capacity Act 2005 may resolve some of these difficulties when it comes into force, although this is not expected to occur until 2007 at the earliest. We accordingly outline some of the relevant legal provisions and principles below.

Mental capacity

Whether an adult has sufficient mental capacity to make a particular decision depends in large measure upon whether he or she has sufficient understanding of the consequence of making, or not making, that decision. The degree of mental capacity required by law varies, therefore, depending on the nature of the act that is to be undertaken. Thus, for example, a person may have sufficient mental capacity at law to conduct a simple transaction, for instance to handle his or her social security monies, but not sufficient capacity for a complex matter, such as buying a house.

If a person lacks capacity to make a particular decision, then any decision made on his or her behalf in relation to that matter must be made in the person's 'best interests'. Where the decision relates to the person's property or affairs, then legal mechanisms such as Enduring Powers of Attorney or the Court of Protection are available. Where the person has always lacked the necessary mental capacity, the use of an Enduring Powers of Attorney is not possible, and the authority of the Court of Protection generally will be required. This is of particular relevance to the transition to adulthood of disabled young people who are deemed to lack capacity.

The Court of Protection

The Court of Protection has wide powers to 'do or secure the doing of all such things as appear necessary or expedient' concerning people who lack mental capacity. It is presently regulated by the Mental Health Act 1983.[20] The court can only take action in relation to a person's property and affairs, and only after it has been satisfied (after considering medical evidence) of the necessary mental incapacity.

Generally, the court will act by appointing a 'receiver', although in certain situations this is not necessary, for instance when the patient's assets consist of only:

- social security benefits
- a pension or similar payment from a government department or local authority
- entitlement under a discretionary trust
- property that does not exceed £16,000 in value – in such cases, a 'short order' can be made, avoiding the necessity of a receiver.

Where a receivership order has been made, the incapacitated person generally is referred to as a 'patient' of the Court of Protection.

Parental wills/trusts

Many parents face considerable difficulties in deciding how to make financial provision for their disabled sons and daughters. This is especially so where the extent of a disabled child's impairments are such that he or she will almost certainly have to rely upon means-tested social security benefits during his or her adult life. The concern here is that if the son or daughter inherits or otherwise receives any substantial sum of money, this will lead to the loss of means-tested benefits until such time as the bulk of the capital has been spent.

In some cases, parents decide to make no financial provision for their disabled son or daughter, deciding instead, for example, to leave the money to another child. Such a will is, however, vulnerable to be challenged under the Inheritance (Provisions for Family and Dependants) Act 1975 on the grounds that provision should have been made for the dependent child.

A detailed consideration of this issue is beyond the scope of this book,[21] but in many cases the solution to the problem involves the making of a will that leaves the disabled child's share on a 'discretionary trust'. The money is then administered by trustees nominated by the parent in his or her will, and the capital value of the trust is ignored for means-tested benefit purposes. Although such discretionary trust arrangements appear relatively complex and can have certain unfavourable tax implications, most solicitors who specialise in probate law should be able to draft a suitable scheme without too much difficulty.

Notes

1 If the child has a special educational needs statement, then the initial letter should be sent to the LEA seeking clarification as to why there has been no planning and, in particular, why there has been no 14-plus review (see p.185). If there is no special educational needs statement, then the initial letter should be sent to social services, seeking their involvement to prepare care plans that will facilitate a smooth transfer into adulthood. Precedent letters (on p.275) can be adapted for these purposes.

2 Department for Education and Skills (2001) and Welsh Assembly (2004).

3 Accessible at www.drc-gb.org.

4 For legal analysis of the relevant law, see Further Education Funding Council (FEFC) (1996) *Duties and Powers: The Law Governing the Provision of Further Education to Students with Learning Difficulties and/or Disabilities*. London: The Stationery Office.

5 S.15(5)(b) Education Act 1996.

6 The Children Act 1989: Guidance and Regulations, Vol. 6, *Children with Disabilities*. London: HMSO, Para. 16.10.

7 Entitlement to adult services under the Community Care legislation is outside the scope of this book; reference should be made to Clements, L. (2004) *Community Care and the Law,* 3rd edn. London: Legal Action Group.

8 *R v. Further Education Funding Council and Bradford MBC ex p. Parkinson* [1997] 2 FCR 67.

9 See Paras 9–11.

10 The Children Act 1989: Guidance and Regulations, Vol. 6, *Children with Disabilities*. London: HMSO, Para. 16.11.

11 The Children Act 1989: Guidance and Regulations, Vol. 6, *Children with Disabilities*. London: HMSO, Para. 13.7.

12 The Children Act 1989: Guidance and Regulations, Vol. 6, *Children with Disabilities*. London: HMSO, Para. 13.8.

13 S.85 Children Act 1989. In addition, the body must also inform the social services department of the area in which a young person proposes to live if he or she has reached the age of 16 years and leaves accommodation that has been provided for at least three months.

14 Technically, the local authority only administers the scheme, which it does on behalf of its partners in the programme, e.g. health trusts, probation services and the housing authority (if this is a different authority to the social services authority).

15 This might be a 'floating' warden service, in which wardens visit a number of different homes, or an on-site warden service.

16 1 CCLR 294.

17 [2003] UKHL 57, [2003] 3 WLR 1194.

18 Via Adoption and Children Act 2002 s.116.

19 Research suggests that one in three families that, as a result of the means test, were assessed as needing to make a contribution towards an adaptation to their home for their children's needs could not afford to do so. It is estimated that the removal of the means test for disabled facilities grants for disabled children would cost the government in England between £10 million and £20 million a year: House of Lords Hansard Parliamentary Questions – Baroness Wilkins 5 January 2004: Column 2.

20 The court will be reformed when the Mental Capacity Act 2005 comes into force (expected to be in 2007) and then be regulated by ss.15–21 of that Act.

21 For a fuller account of such schemes, see Ashton, G. (1995) *Elderly People and the Law*. London: Butterworths; and Mind 'Making Provision', a guidance booklet obtainable from Mind, 15–19 Broadway, London E15 4BQ.

CHAPTER 8

Children Who Live Away from Home

Introduction

In earlier chapters, we have been concerned mainly with disabled children who are brought up by their families of origin and who live at home for the majority of the time. We turn now to those who spend a significant proportion of their childhood elsewhere. We shall focus primarily on children who have substantial experience of living in communal or residential settings of some sort, although we also refer briefly to substitute family care.

It is only in relatively recent times that disabled children who live away from home have begun to have any significant presence on the major policy and research agendas. For a very long time, the experiences of the general population of children living away from their families have come under scrutiny. A large body of research and official reports have investigated a range of key issues relevant to their circumstances and to policy and practice seen to affect their life chances and well-being. These have included:

- factors that trigger family breakdown and make it likely for children to need to be 'looked after'* by the local authority (e.g. Bebbington and Miles 1989; DH 1991)

- practice that enables or inhibits the maintenance of appropriate contact between separated children and their families (e.g. Marsh and Treseliotis 1993; Masson, Harrison and Pavlovic 1999; Milham *et al.* 1986; Neil and Howe 2004; Quinton *et al.* 1997)

---

*   The definitions of 'looked after' and 'accommodated' children are given in the legal commentary section of this chapter.

- the patterns of the 'care careers' of separated children (e.g. Barn 1993; Bebbington and Miles 1989; Bullock, Little and Milham 1993; Milham *et al.* 1986; Rowe and Lambert 1973)

- the abuse, protection and well-being of children in residential settings (e.g. Stuart and Baines 2004; Utting 1997; Warner 1992)

- placements and other arrangements that offer the most positive and stable upbringing for those who cannot be with their birth families (Berridge 1996; Berridge and Brodie 1998; Jackson and Thomas 1999; Parker *et al.* 1991; Sellick and Thoburn 1996; Thoburn 1990, 1994)

- the ways in which children's experience may be differentiated with reference to, for example, their social status and ethnic origin (e.g. Barn 1993; Bebbington and Miles 1989; Jackson and Thomas 1999)

- young people leaving the care system (e.g. Biehal *et al.* 1995; Broad 1998; Stein 1997)

- the perspectives of children and young people on their own experience of public care (e.g. Coventry Who Cares 1984; Page and Clark 1977; Voice for the Child in Care 1998; Who Cares? Trust 1993).

Later in this chapter we will consider whether the key issues identified in relation to the general population of separated children may be used as a framework to guide the development of appropriate policy, practice and research in relation to disabled children. The level of research activity in relation to other children living away from their families should not, of course, be taken to mean that their situations are problem-free. There has long been professional, academic and public recognition that the care system and residential schooling have not invariably served children's interests too well. The 1990s saw a particularly heightened sense of concern as a result of continuing revelations of unsatisfactory standards and sexual, physical and emotional abuse of children in some children's homes and residential schools in the post-war period (Utting 1991, 1997). A number of reports and policy initiatives have given attention to ways of improving the care offered to looked-after children and monitoring whether progress has been made (DH 1998b; Stuart and Baines 2004; Utting 1997; Warner 1992). There have also been other more general trends in service development and delivery that have relevance to the situations of children in public care. Partly as a result of professional and public concern about abuse and, therefore, standards of care and partly as a response to a more consumerist approach to the provision of public services, the 1990s saw increasing attempts to systematically define and improve quality in social care, including residential provision for a range of service user groups (Kelly and Warr 1992; Residential Forum 1996).

Sadly, however, until the mid 1990s, disabled children were frequently notable by their absence from many of the major policy, practice and research debates about the experience of children living away from their families. In the early 1990s, however, significant findings became available on the patterns of care of disabled children living in communal establishments (Loughran, Parker and Gordon 1992). Loughran *et al.*'s reanalysis of the data from the OPCS disability surveys of the 1980s (see Chapter 3) highlighted important trends in the care of disabled children living away from home as well as the limitations of the information available about such children. At about the same time, important work began to emerge on the abuse experienced by some disabled children, including some in residential settings (Marchant and Cross 1993; Marchant and Page 1992; Westcott 1991, 1993). By the mid 1990s, it was becoming clear that a more comprehensive reassessment was needed in relation to the experiences, quality of life and standards of care for disabled children who spend substantial periods of time living away from their families (Ball 1998; Morris 1995, 1998a, 1998b; Russell 1995).

In this chapter, we review and evaluate the available information about disabled children who live away from home. We consider what is known, what is not known and what can reasonably be regarded as issues that warrant the attention of policy-makers, service providers and service users. We begin by looking at the work of those researchers in the 1990s who raised awareness of the experience of these children. They evaluated the information then available and began the process of generating new research and other forms of enquiry. It is important to be familiar with this work, because we are still to some degree reliant on both the data generated during the 1990s and the insights that were derived from them. We also consider efforts to build better sources of information on disabled children away from home and what they have to tell us. Finally, we explore how policy and practice might be improved for the benefit of these children and those close to them.

The deficit of information and data

There is now unequivocal official recognition that, for a long time, the information collected about disabled children who live away from home has been inadequate (DfES 2003c; DH 2001b). It is acknowledged that this basic lack of reliable data has made it very difficult to describe and make sense of the experience of these children as well as to develop models of good practice.

Scoping the problem: work in the 1990s

In the mid 1990s in her preface to the report *Positive Choices: Services for Disabled Children Living Away from Home* (Russell 1995), the late Barbara Kahan drew attention to just how little was known about the use of residential provision for disabled children: 'We do not even have reliable statistics of how many children and young people are cared for in local authority provision, voluntary organisations and private sector establishments' (Russell 1995, p.vi). Others too expressed deep concern about the implications of the fragmented and unsatisfactory nature of the available information about disabled children's care careers and experience away from home:

> One of the major barriers to meeting the needs of disabled children who are living away from their families is the hidden nature of their experiences: we don't know enough about who they are, where they are, what their life feels like to them. (Morris 1995, p.89)

In summary, then as now, disabled children who live away from home may be found in a range of different settings. Some are placed in non-educational residential establishments in the local authority, voluntary and private sectors. In addition, there are those who spend the majority of their year, and in some cases their childhoods, away at residential school. There is also a group of children who spend long periods of time in hospitals or other health service establishments. Some children are placed with foster parents for significant periods. Some appear to use family-based and residential short-term break provision not as one part of a community-based child and family support service but rather as an element of a substantial package of provision primarily based away from home.

The researchers of the 1990s identified three main issues as contributing to the difficulty of building up a reliable picture of the experiences and lifecourses of these children. First, the total pool of reliable data held on disabled children generally at local and national levels was very limited. As we discussed in Chapter 3, there remains a serious lack of up-to-date national demographic data on disabled children and their households: to a large degree, they have been rendered invisible in government statistics (Gordon *et al.* 2000b). Second, the data specifically on disabled children living away from their families were found to be limited and in some respects confusing. Third, as we have already suggested, the population of disabled children has frequently been excluded from the frame when important research questions have been posed about children separated from their families. As a result, the pool of research on disabled children living away from home is smaller and less developed than that on other separated children.

This information deficit has meant that we have been heavily reliant on the OPCS surveys of the disabled population in Britain, published at the end of the 1980s, as the major data source on disabled children and their circumstances (Bone and Meltzer 1989; Meltzer *et al.* 1989; Smyth and Robus 1989). As we have already acknowledged, these surveys were undeniably of great importance, but the work of Gordon and colleagues during the 1990s drew attention to their limitations in relation to disabled children living away from home. They also reanalysed the data to highlight significant trends that previously were unclear (Gordon *et al.* 2000b; Loughran *et al.* 1992; Morris 1995).

Before turning to the issues raised by the reanalysis in the 1990s of the OPCS material on the experience of disabled children away from home, we must acknowledge that the definitions of disability used generally within these surveys have not been without their detractors. They have been challenged for, among other things, adopting what was argued to be an over-medicalised and individualised set of definitions that drew on the International Classification of Impairments, Disabilities and Handicaps (Abberley 1992, 1996). In addition, there are more specific difficulties associated with definitions of disability and impairment used in the surveys on disabled children in the public care system. Gordon, *et al.* (2000b), Loughran *et al.* (1992) and Morris (1995) point out that because of the definitions of disability used, the findings encompassed large numbers (almost 50 per cent of the total) who had behavioural problems alone and no physical, sensory or intellectual impairment. Gordon *et al.* (2000b) also argue that the threshold for inclusion of behavioural and emotional difficulties was set at a fairly low level. While no one would wish to detract from the needs of children and young people with behavioural and emotional difficulties however defined, the work of Gordon *et al.* would indicate that it is important to be circumspect about the nature and size of the population revealed by the survey. They argue that the decision to include children with a wide range of behavioural and emotional difficulties enlarged the conventional definition of disability and increased the proportion of disabled children found to be in local authority care. Making a related but different point, Morris (1995) suggests that the undifferentiated nature of the definition may have had the effect of obscuring the particular experience of some of those living with impairment who would usually be regarded as disabled.

In a different respect, it has been argued that the data collection for the OPCS survey of children in communal establishments may also have served to obscure very significant or even dominant experiences of care away from home for some particular groups of disabled children. Morris (1995), drawing on the reanalysis by Loughran *et al.* (1992), argues that the data generated by the survey had three major limitations, which may lead us to underestimate the extent of institutional living experienced by disabled children. First, the survey did not include young people between the ages of 16 and 19 years. Second, the survey excluded large numbers of children who spent considerable proportions of their time in residential provision, the most significant of group being those at boarding schools. Despite the fact that many of the latter spend the majority of the year and a significant amount of their childhood away from home, they were included in the private households survey as if they lived with their families. Third, within the 5–15 years age group, children who lived in communal establishments but who went home to their families at least once a fortnight were not included. On the basis of this evidence, Gordon *et al.* (2000b) argue that it is likely that the OPCS surveys substantially underestimated the numbers of disabled children living in residential care.

The work of the 1990s also revealed that potential sources of information other than the OPCS surveys were disappointing. The way that local authorities collected data on children who were subject to the provisions of the Children Act 1989 did not allow a clear and detailed picture of the position of disabled children to emerge (Morris 1995). Neither was the legal status of disabled children always clear when they were living away from home. While some may have been in a residential or foster care placement on a long-term basis, their status as accommodated or looked-after children was not always clarified and recorded (Morris 1998b). Concern was also expressed about the fact that some disabled children were spending substantial periods away from home in short-term break or respite care provision without appropriate legal safeguards (Robinson 1996) and without their appearing in Department of Health returns on looked-after children. In addition, there appeared to be confusion among practitioners about the legal status of some children in residential schools and about the duties that local authorities had towards them (Abbott, Morris and Ward 2000). The way that formal data are collected also tended not to allow a clear view of children's likely 'care careers' through the placements and systems where they found themselves. Snapshots of populations in particular establishments do not necessarily give indications of either the well-worn paths that children go down or the triggers that set them off and maintain them on a particular course. Finally, it was noted that local authority registers of disabled children remained under-developed (Ball 1998) and did not collect data that would fill identified information gaps (Russell 1995).

Piecing together the fragments

As the findings of early investigations and research began to emerge, it was possible to begin to piece together what was known about at least some disabled children living away from home, the scale of the information deficit and the issues that merited attention (Read and Clements 2001). Emerging findings caused considerable concern. Perhaps most notably, Morris (1995) argued that many disabled children experienced patterns of care that simply would not be tolerated for their non-disabled peers:

> We all need to feel outraged that so many children have 'gone missing' from our society, that they are denied the things that we all take for granted and that, as they reach adulthood, so many of them 'disappear' into long-term residential provision. (Morris 1995, p.89)

While it needs to be stressed again that the majority of disabled children live at home with their families of origin, a major issue that came to the fore in the 1990s was that disabled children appeared to have a substantially greater chance of being separated from their families than non-disabled children. Gordon et al. (2000b) highlighted the fact that 4 per cent of the population of disabled children (as defined in the OPCS disability surveys) were in the care of local authorities. This rate was some ten times greater than that which prevailed in the child population as a whole. The very least to be said about this trend was that it warranted more attention and investigation than it had been given hitherto. Parker (1998) summarised the findings from the reanalysis of the OPCS data on disabled children in the care of local authorities: 'Our best estimate from the data available is that at the time of the surveys some 18,700 of the 327,000 children under 16 estimated to be disabled were in local authority care: that is 5.7 per cent' (p.11).

As we have already indicated, in addition to those disabled children in local authority residential and foster care, there was concern about those who were often assumed to be living with their families but who appeared to be spending large amounts of time away at school. Research indicates that at least some of these are quite young children (Abbott et al. 2000). Gordon et al. (2000b) point out that the OPCS private households survey revealed 14,400 children at boarding school, making this the most common form of residential provision and out-of-home care for disabled children at the time. The great majority (75%) were attending residential special schools. Children with severe behavioural and emotional problems were the largest group placed in boarding schools; children with the most severe and multiple disabilities represented the second highest percentage (Gordon et al. 2000b). Subsequent research indicates that the likelihood of such a placement being made varies substantially from one authority to another (Abbott et al. 2000). Despite the fact that many of these children spend considerable periods away from home, there is often a lack of clarity among practitioners and their employing authorities about the children's legal status and, therefore, the duties of the authorities towards them. This may mean that, even when appropriate, local authorities do not always fulfil their statutory duties to review their circumstances and plan for their future as looked-after children (Abbott *et al.* 2000; Morris 1998b).

In addition to children in schools, residential care and substitute family placement, Gordon *et al.* (2000b) draw attention to the role of health authorities in making residential provision for disabled children. At the time of the OPCS surveys, one in ten children in residential care was placed in such a setting, and the health sector was looking after a disproportionate number of the most severely disabled children, sometimes for very long periods. Gordon *et al.* also point out that this flies in the face of Children Act 1989 guidance, which emphasises that such health placements should never be regarded as permanent.

Updating and improving national data

In 2001, the White Paper *Valuing People* (DH 2001b) made a commitment that more information would be collected on the numbers and characteristics of disabled children living away from home in residential placements provided by social services, health authorities and education authorities. There was also recognition of the need to know more about outcomes for such children. There was a further commitment to developing arrangements that created better linkages between those children and their families and that ensured that they were properly supported and protected by key agencies. The report *Disabled Children in Residential Placements* (DfES 2003c) was published in response both to enduring concerns about the welfare of this group of children and to the specific commitments given in *Valuing People*. It contains an up-to-date digest of the numbers of disabled children away from home together with guidance on how to interpret the information. It is important to note that the administrative data in the report relates only to children in England, but some of the research to which it refers is not limited to the English experience.

The report refers to the familiar problem of differing definitions across placements in health, education and social services settings. It points out that each sector may describe the same child in different ways: health services are more likely to record a specific medical diagnosis, education services to use the framework of special educational needs and social services to refer to the child as disabled. Some children may, therefore, be recorded more than once and in a number of guises. In addition, practice varies as to whether children with moderate learning disabilities or emotional and behavioural difficulties are included within the category of disabled children. The report also indicates how administrative data-collection methods may serve to obscure information on some disabled children. For example, children who are looked after by local authorities will be recorded as disabled only if the authority identifies that as the principal reason why they are looked after. Thus, those disabled children whose primary reason for being looked after is that they have been abused will not appear as disabled in the annual returns.

The DfES (2003c) report indicates that there are 1320 looked-after disabled children in residential settings, 610 of whom are in children's homes and 595 in residential schools. A further 965 are in foster care, 80 in other care homes and 15 in healthcare establishments. It is important to take a number of provisos into account in relation to this total of 2380. This number represents a snapshot of those looked after on a single day (31 March 2002) and, therefore, does not show what are likely to be the larger total numbers placed across the course of a year. It is also subject to the data-collection anomaly identified earlier, namely that children are excluded if the primary reason for their being looked after is identified as something other than their being disabled. In addition, it excludes children who have a series of short-term placements, many of whom would be disabled children. The report indicates that the majority of looked-after disabled children in residential settings are white and between the ages 10 and 15 years. It confirms, however, that we still have relatively little information on why children are looked after in residential homes or on the specific nature of the placements used. The report also raises concerns about the 39 per cent of the looked-after disabled children who are placed outside their home authority and the likely problems that this may create for maintaining family contact in at least some cases. Concern is also expressed about the fact that disabled children are less likely to be placed in foster care and more likely to be placed in residential care than the general population of looked-after children.

While some disabled children in residential schools are counted in the returns on looked-after children, separate data are also collected on pupils in maintained, non-maintained and independent residential special schools on a single day each year (see p.154–5 for the meaning of these terms). Most of the 10,500 children in these schools have statements of special educational need (see Chapter 6). There is considerable overlap between this population of children and those who would be defined as disabled, but the two groups are not coterminous. The DfES (2003c) reports that, as yet, data are not collected on the needs or impairments of individual children and young people in residential special schools but rather on numbers within schools approved to take specific categories of pupils. Some schools are approved to take more than one category of pupil. The largest single group by far is comprised of teenage boys attending schools approved to educate children with emotional and behavioural difficulties. The majority of boarders in residential special schools are aged between 11 and 15 years, three-quarters are male and the majority are white. Most children return home at least one night each week. The DfES has undertaken to refine the data collected on disabled children attending residential special schools.

The DfES (2003c) report also analyses the available data on disabled children in healthcare settings. Currently, data on NHS admissions do not identify disabled children as a group about whom information is collected. Some of the ways in which children are classified by the NHS, however, make it not unreasonable to define them as disabled. These might include at least some of those who are categorised as having 'mental and behavioural disorders'. The report also points out that much of what is known about the experience of disabled children in health settings is mainly reliant on small-scale studies. Drawing on Department of Health Hospital Episode Statistics, the report indicates that between 1998 and 2001, 2200 children spent more than six months in hospital. Of these, 245 had spent more than five years there. The largest proportion of young people spending more than six months in hospital were aged between 15 and 19 years. The most common reason for the admission of those who spent long periods in healthcare settings was 'mental and behavioural disorders'. These data are consistent with recent research on disabled children in hospital settings in England and Scotland. The work of Stalker *et al.* (2003) also identified significant numbers of children and young people with complex needs staying in healthcare settings for long periods and drew attention to the fact that the children's legal status was a source of confusion in many instances.

Implications for policy and practice

It is apparent from the previous sections that although efforts are being made to provide more up-to-date data, there is still a huge information deficit about disabled children who are placed away from home. Despite these limitations, some issues are apparent that may alert both professionals and service users to some hazards in the system and to action that could be taken in order to improve the life chances of the children concerned. One way of highlighting these hazards and moving towards improved practice is to keep asking the research and practice questions in relation to disabled children that have already been asked in relation to other children in the public care system. Some of these are summarised in the introduction to this chapter.

The first of a series of inter-related and overlapping questions that we feel are important to ask has to be about why a significant minority of disabled children spend so much time away from their families and what determines where they are placed. It is important to stress once more how fragmented and insufficient is the available information on these important matters. The lack of evidence about what determines whether children leave home and whether they are placed in school, residential care, family placement or a health setting should make us cautious about drawing too firm conclusions. In their discussion of why some children are placed in residential care, Gordon *et al.* (2000b) argue that a combination of factors related to the children's disabilities, the social circumstances of their families and their 'care careers' propels children towards this sector. They highlight the fact that two-thirds of the children in the OPCS surveys were subject to compulsory orders of some sort. They also point out that the extent to which children in residential care had multiple disabilities was pronounced, but that there is very limited reliable information on what distinguishes those disabled children from others placed in substitute families. No conclusions can be drawn about the extent to which severity of disability acts as a determinant in relation to the type of placement.

There are some indications, however, that age may be a determinant, with older children more likely to find themselves in communal establishments rather than foster care. Administrative data on the ages of looked-after disabled children and those in residential special schools also indicate that the majority are beyond primary school age (DfES 2003c). Added to this, some research on residential schooling, together with anecdotal accounts and conventional wisdom (Abbott *et al.* 2000; Morris 1995; Russell 1995), suggests that as children get older, particularly if they have high support needs, some families may simply not be able to continue to provide the type and level of care and assistance that they require. This may be particularly the case if the families have other stresses, crises or significant calls on their time and personal resources and if they have been offered little in the way of community care services. In Chapter 3, we referred to research that indicated that for many families, social and practical problems increased as the disabled child grew older (Beresford 1995). It is important to note that according to the OPCS data, children from lone-parent households have a disproportionate chance of being at boarding school. While 19 per cent of disabled children in the 5–15 years age group were living with a lone parent, such children comprised 27 per cent of those at boarding school (Gordon *et al.* 2000b).

It is often suggested that even when the reasons for going away from home are primarily social and familial, some families may find residential schooling a more acceptable option than other provision (Abbott *et al.* 2000; Russell 1995). It has also been argued that in some cases, placement in residential school may come about as a result of the fact that suitable educational provision to meet the children's needs may not always be available in their own locality (Abbott *et al.* 2000). As rates of placement in boarding school vary substantially from one local authority to another (Abbott *et al.* 2000), it is not unreasonable to conclude that decisions have at least as much to do with local policy and resources as with children's social and educational needs. A similar point can be made in relation to away-from-home services for looked-after disabled children. McConkey *et al.* (2004) argue that it is very difficult to reconcile the aspiration for developing locally based services with the need for specialist facilities that can be cost-effective only if they serve a sufficiently wide area.

Earlier in this book, we drew attention to the frequently limited nature of the child and family support services that are made available to disabled children and those close to them. We have also pointed to the way in which short-term break provision or respite care is often the primary (and sometimes the only) service on offer. It seems important, therefore, that practitioners as well as researchers investigate further the relationship between stress on families, the lack of availability of flexible community care support, and the substantial and sometimes multiple use of provision of various sorts away from home. Research by Stalker *et al.* (2003) on children with complex needs who spend long periods in healthcare settings indicates that a lack of adequate community-based services for them and their families contributes to their remaining for long stays in hospital. Without such supports, families are left with the prospect of managing the anxiety and stress of sometimes complex care.

Relatedly, it is important to consider the educational provision, including flexible packages of learning support, that would enable children to stay in their home authorities rather than go elsewhere. This is not to assume that a place in boarding school, for example, is always a negative choice, but rather to be aware of the factors that may make such a placement almost inevitable by default rather than a positive choice for a child and the family.

In Chapter 3, we discussed the fact that having a disabled child increased the likelihood of families living on low incomes. We also commented earlier on the differential experience that children and their families have in accessing services. Socioeconomic status and ethnic origin are key factors associated with differential access to community-based services that meet needs effectively. We need to know more about the ways in which such factors may affect children's and families' chances of living away from each other. The over-representation of children from lone-parent households in residential education would suggest a possible association between socioeconomic status and predisposition to separation that is worthy of investigation by practitioners and others.

A second major question has to be concerned with the ways in which some disabled children become cut off from their families and isolated in provision away from home (Abbott *et al.* 2000; Ball 1998; Knight 1998). Gordon *et al.* (2000b) point out that a quarter of those in residential establishments in the 1980s neither received visits from parents nor went home. When these children are taken together with those who had only infrequent visits, around one-third of disabled children in residential care were living in isolation from their parents and other family members. We know that there is still concern about the numbers of looked-after disabled children placed outside their home authorities and the implications that this may have for contact with their families (DfES 2003c). As we have already indicated, information about the needs and circumstances of disabled children within the care system remains too limited to allow conclusions to be drawn about what the precise nature and purpose of the contact with their families should be. It needs to be emphasised, however, that local authorities have clear duties in relation to those children who are subject to the provisions of the Children Act 1989, so that appropriate contact with families and significant others may be agreed, planned for, put into practice and adjusted.

It is encouraging to see that the majority of children in residential special schools go home regularly (DfES 2003c). It is important to recognise, however, that maintaining contact is not easy for all children and their families. School and home may be some considerable distance apart, and arrangements for keeping in close touch may prove expensive. Even when this is not the case, there may be a variety of personal, familial and organisational circumstances that create barriers and make it difficult for everyone involved to maintain a close and sustaining relationship between the disabled child and the rest of the family. Some disabled adults have offered illuminating retrospective accounts of their experiences of becoming dislocated from their families and communities (French 1996; Humphries and Gordon 1992; Smith 1994).

When children are out of contact with their parents, there is growing recognition of the importance of their having consistent contact with or access to a key person from outside the residential setting, whether at school or home. This person may be, for example, a children's advocate or an independent visitor (Wynne Oakley and Masson 2000). While the Children Act 1989 requires local authorities to appoint independent visitors for those children who are looked after and have had no contact with their parents for more than 12 months, there can be no assumption that such provision will be made available to the majority of disabled children away from home who fall within this category (Knight 1998). Apart from any other considerations, it is not unlikely that the confusion among practitioners about the legal status of many such children that we have already highlighted may lead to their being overlooked in this respect. There are indications from research, however, that when disabled children are provided with independent visitors they find the experience positive. The benefits associated with having a visitor include the chance to do ordinary activities, access to the experience of family life, support at reviews, and having someone to monitor the child's welfare and assist with planning for the future (Knight 1998).

A third area of concern is related to the 'care careers' that some children may have when they are away from home. The lack of information on why children do or do not stay where they are placed and the outcomes for them of particular types of away-from-home provision (DfES 2003c) also leave us with limited evidence on which to base policy and practice.

A combination of factors that we have already acknowledged (lack of clarity over their legal status and the duties that authorities have towards them, a lack of comprehensive and long-term planning, substantial amounts of time away from their families in one or more placements, isolation, lack of community connections and support) may predispose some children, particularly perhaps those with high support needs, to live in a state of drift. In other words, some children may live for long periods in situations that have significant implications for their present and future well-being without anyone taking an appropriate degree of responsibility for looking at all aspects of their current circumstances as well as the directions of their future lives (Morris 1995). Attention needs to be given to how the most positive alternative choices can be systematically reviewed for those disabled children who cannot be with their families of origin and steps taken to ensure that the most effective and active planning is undertaken with their immediate and longer-term future in mind. This should include, for example, considerations related to their transition to adulthood. We have seen in earlier chapters how difficult the satisfactory transition from childhood to adulthood and from children's services to adult services can be for those at home with their families. Concern has been raised about the particularly hazardous position of those young people who face such issues away from their families (Morris 1995). At this point, there is no doubt that we are seriously under-informed about outcomes for disabled children who live away from their families (DfES 2003c).

The fourth matter to warrant serious attention has to do with the abuse, protection and well-being of disabled children separated from their families. First, there has been a growing debate about the fact that in some institutional settings for disabled children, the standards of care, routine practices and quality of life offered at particular points or over time may be so poor that they should be regarded as abusive or an infringement of human rights (Morris 1998c). Second, it has been argued that individual disabled children may be particularly vulnerable to physical, sexual and emotional abuse, whether in residential settings or elsewhere (e.g. Cross 1992; Kennedy 1992, 1996; Marchant and Page 1992; Westcott 1993, 1998). While there are relatively few UK studies on this issue, the view that disabled children are very vulnerable to abuse is held widely (DfES 2003c; Stuart and Baines 2004). There are a number of reasons why this is argued to be the case. Disabled children are often reliant upon a number of other people for intimate care and other assistance, and this may mask abusive or exploitative practices. They may have difficulty in making themselves understood, and thus it may prove harder for them to let others know of distressing or abusive experiences without mediation. Their relative isolation from other children and adults and the reduced opportunities they have for unhindered social contact may make it easier for abuse and neglect to be hidden.

It is not difficult to speculate how any general vulnerability can be magnified by some of the factors that have already been discussed in this chapter. There may be potentially very serious hazards for children who are out of touch with their families and for whom there is no key person who knows them intimately, reviews their situation, monitors their well-being and plans for their future. The welfare of the children who have 'gone missing' in the system (Morris 1995), who are in a state of 'drift' and who may have a number of unplanned placement experiences has to be a cause for concern. Again, these matters highlight the importance of ongoing contact with outside individuals who know the child well, individual planning, monitoring and review for children, and the adoption of a comprehensive range of strategies to raise general care standards at the same time as protecting individual children (DH 1999; DfES 2003c; Stuart and Baines 2004; Utting 1997).

The fifth set of issues that need to claim our attention is related to the complexities of deciding which placements and other circumstances offer the most positive and stable upbringing for disabled children who cannot be with their birth families for the majority of the time. Again, because of the fragmented and limited nature of the available information on outcomes, we, like others, can only pose what seem to be key policy and practice questions.

A number of reports have acknowledged and expressed concern about the way that the residential or group care sector has been under-valued and relegated to an option of last resort (Berridge and Brodie 1998; Russell 1995; Utting 1997). The revelations of abuse to which we referred earlier have undoubtedly had a negative effect, but it has also been suggested that financial retrenchment and ideological prejudice have contributed substantially to the destabilisation of a sector that can have a valuable role within a range of care services (Utting 1997). It has been argued that for some children, some of the time, group living should be seen as a positive option. It is also recognised that if disabled children with complex care and support needs are to be offered a safe and enhancing experience in residential settings, then there is a need to raise standards, address lowered morale and increase staff training (Argent and Kerrane 1997; Gordon *et al.* 2000b; Marchant and Cross 1993; Utting 1997). The case for a more positive role for group care is reported in summary by Russell:

> Part of a range of positive options for disabled children, regarded as a valued and well-managed service that is part of – not distant from – mainstream thinking about children's needs but that can also respond to some of the most challenging children and facilitate their return to family and community in due course.

> Assuming that all children live in families all the time is optimistic but unrealistic. A good residential service should facilitate home life, but it has a distinct contribution of its own to make in caring for disabled children in the community (Russell 1995, p.66).

It is possible to argue a similar perspective in relation to residential education. Earlier, we called into question the way that residential education can sometimes be used as a default option and we challenged some of the arrangements made for children who are placed in this sector. Nevertheless, it is important to acknowledge that some parents and children may regard residential school as a very positive option and may successfully integrate such a placement within a strong network of family and community links. Just as some parents of non-disabled children may believe strongly that some boarding schools offer their children the opportunities to enhance their life chances by receiving what they regard as the best education on offer, some who have disabled sons and daughters may feel that the specialist provision offered by a good residential school of their choice cannot be matched elsewhere. As we have already argued, the necessity to provide a high quality of provision and adequate safeguards for children in such settings is increasingly recognised and of paramount importance (DfES 2003c; DH 1999; Stuart and Baines 2004; Utting 1997). In addition, it is important to draw attention to work that has also already been undertaken to provide parents and their children with practical guidance about choosing the right residential school (Morris 2003).

Another significant provision for disabled children is family placement or foster care. This may be temporary, permanent or on a 'shared-care' basis. Since the 1980s, there has been a growth in local authority family placement schemes of various sorts for disabled children (Argent and Kerrane 1997; Stalker 1996). We have already referred in this chapter to Parker's (1998) observations on disabled children in the care of local authorities. He also draws attention to the substantial role played by foster care in providing for disabled children living away from their families and raises the question of what kind of support these substitute families are being given as they undertake this extremely complex work.

While there exists a substantial body of work on shared-care short-term break provision for disabled children (Robinson 1996; Robinson and Jackson 1999; Russell 1996; Stalker 1991, 1996), there is more limited research evidence about outcomes in permanent family placement (Phillips 1998; Sellick and Thoburn 1996). In addition, although social workers and others may have been developing schemes and placing disabled children, it has sometimes been argued that there has been only a limited range of practice guides and manuals that might help them with these complex tasks (Argent and Kerrane 1997).

Many foster carers undoubtedly offer a valued service, and it is important that they receive sufficient support and resources to enable them to do so. Disabled children together with their foster families need access to the range of community-based services that we have already suggested are essential to the well-being of the children's families of origin. Argent and Kerrane's (1997) helpful guide, *Taking Extra Care*, addresses a range of essential practice issues related to the family placement of disabled children. These include assessment and planning in relation to disabled children who may need alternative family care; recruitment of substitute families; training preparation and support for substitute families; working directly with disabled children before, during and after placement; and working with parents.

The final issue which we wish to address here is the way in which the voices of disabled children living away from their families have frequently not been heard. Earlier in this book, we emphasised that it is essential to consult with disabled children, to take account of their wishes, preferences and aspirations, and to do so in an imaginative way that is likely to enable them to participate in planning their lives in the short and longer term. This is no less true for children away from home than for those living with their families. In the 1970s and 1980s, the Who Cares? movement, the National Association of Young People in Care and the Voice for the Child in Care were formed in response to a recognition that children in public care needed a voice (Coventry Who Cares 1984; Page and Clark 1977). Again, however, it was the voices of non-disabled children that were primarily heard. There can be few more momentous issues in the life of a child than those on which we have touched in this chapter. This makes it of paramount importance for practitioners and significant others in the children's lives to make it a routine and central matter to involve them in day-to-day and longer-term decision-making. Again, it is important to stress that if the ability of children to influence their own lives is not to be restricted, then they need to be provided with or enabled to develop the means to communicate (Beecher 1998; Marchant and Martyn 1999; Marchant, Jones and Julyan 1999).

More recently, there have been concerted efforts to offer more disabled children away from home the chance to be consulted and to express their opinions about issues generally and about their own specific situations (Chailey Young People's Group 1998; Minkes *et al.* 1994; Morris 1995, 1998a). This not only offers the children positive opportunities to give commentary on and to shape their own lives but also offers practitioners and policy-makers unique insights into an essential set of perceptions of the world that they have long since denied themselves or been denied.

Concluding remarks

We have acknowledged that the majority of disabled children live at home for most of their childhoods, but it is clear that a significant minority spend substantial periods away their families. It is likely that this will continue to be the case and, this being so, we need to consider how to increase the responsiveness and quality of the services made available to them. It is our view that it is largely unhelpful to see the different living situations and placements away from home as discrete entities that bear no relation to each other or to community-based services. We believe that it is useful to consider the importance of developing and sustaining a network of varied service provision that children and their families may access appropriately at different points in their lives. We need to consider the way in which good-quality residential care or schooling might be seen as less of an all-or-nothing option of last resort and become one choice in a pattern of services that vary over time and in response to different circumstances. If a child's experience is dominated by one particular placement or one form of service provision, then it may be that significant needs will be neglected.

The DfES (2003c) has made a number of recommendations designed to improve future policy and practice in relation to disabled children who may be placed away from home. These include multi-agency assessment and planning and review of such children before and after placement, a recommendation that may prove administratively more feasible with the implementation of the Children Act 2004 (see Chapter 4). They also propose that data on disabled children separated from their families should be collected and collated in a form that can be utilised by local authorities and primary care trusts. These data should be linked to outcomes for children. It is also proposed that there should be a regional audit of provision and a record of disabled children in residential placements in each authority. The data from the individual assessments of disabled children should also be used to inform local and regional planning. It is recommended that the range of inspection agencies should focus on residential provision for disabled children and work towards a common inspection framework.

LEGAL COMMENTARY

Introduction

Disabled children may live apart from their parents and siblings for a variety of reasons. The period of separation may be short or prolonged and may be a one-off event or at planned and frequent intervals. The separation may occur in order to facilitate the provision of the child's special educational needs or in order to enable their carers to have a short break (sometimes referred to as respite care). Sometimes, however, the separation results from the parents being unable, for one reason or another, to provide the necessary care.

The law relating to these arrangements has been framed with the aim of ensuring that children are protected and their development is promoted. Although abuse (physical, sexual and financial) is a reality, of concern too is the potential for administrative neglect, of the child becoming isolated or left to 'drift' in the system. Accordingly, in the Children Act 1989 and the Care Standards Act 2000, in Regulations, Minimum Standards and in binding guidance, procedures exist that spell out what should be provided and who is responsible. These have, unfortunately, generated various legal terms that need to be understood.

Terminology

Care orders and secure accommodation orders

Most disabled children who live apart from their families do so with their parents' agreement and without any court order having been obtained. For a few, however, there is an element of compulsion, either because there is a care order in force (under Section 31 of the Children Act 1989) or because they are subject to a secure accommodation order (under Section 25 of the Children Act 1989). We do not consider the procedures for the making of such orders in this text, since invariably a lawyer will be instructed on behalf of the parents and child and separate and substantial texts exist on this subject.

Accommodated children

Colloquially, many parents refer to their children being 'in care' when they are not in fact the subject of a care order. In such cases, the parent has agreed to the arrangement with the local authority and no formal court order has been made. Under this voluntary arrangement, the child is 'accommodated'. This is a service provided by the local authority, and the parent may at any time bring the arrangement to an end. A child cannot be accommodated if anyone with parental responsibility objects and is able to offer them a home. This right includes the right to object to the kind of accommodation offered because the arrangements are a matter of cooperation and cannot be dictated by one party.[1]

Looked-after children

A child is 'looked after by a local authority' if he or she is in their care by reason of a court order or is being accommodated (i.e. under Section 20 of the Children Act 1989) for more than 24 hours by agreement with the parents (or with the child if aged over 16 years).

In general, however, a child provided with respite care accommodation, even if for more than 24 hours, is not legally 'looked after',[2] because this accommodation is provided under Section 17 rather than under Section 20 of the 1989 Act.

The legal differences between being provided with accommodation under Section 17 and Section 20 were considered in the case of *R (P)* v. *Essex County Council* [2004].[3] One of the main differences is that if the child is accommodated under Section 20 for more than 24 hours, then the child becomes looked after and the relevant regulations and guidance apply – this is not the case if the accommodation is provided under Section 17. Additionally, as the court noted at Para. 8 of its judgment:

> housing and other welfare benefits are not available to 'looked after' children, but are in principle available to children being accommodated under section 17. It follows that the financial and other burdens on a local authority are likely to be significantly greater if it accommodates a child under section 20 than if it does so under section 17.

The court went on to stress, however, at Para. 9, that:

> it is not open to a local authority to choose between providing accommodation under section 17 and section 20. Nor can a local authority decide to provide accommodation under section 17, rather than under section 20, merely because it believes that a section 17 package would be better or would offer more flexibility. If the conditions in either section 20(1) or section 20(3) are satisfied then, subject only to sections 20(6)[4] and 20(7), it is the duty of the local authority to provide accommodation under section 20, with all the consequences that flow from that.

Parental responsibility

Parental responsibility is defined by Section 3 of the Children Act 1989 as including all the rights, powers, authority and duties of parents in relation to a child and his or her property. The child's parents share parental responsibility if they were married at or after the time of conception[5] or if the father's name is on the birth certificate of a child whose birth was registered after 1 December 2003.[6] Otherwise, only the child's mother has parental responsibility, although the father can also acquire it by agreement or a court order.

A local authority does not acquire parental responsibility for children it is voluntarily accommodating. Although a care order does give the local authority parental responsibility, this does not extinguish the parental responsibilities of the parent, except to the extent that their actions are incompatible with the care order.

Local authority duties to looked-after children

As we have noted above, the Children Act 1989 places a general obligation on local authorities to provide an appropriate range and level of services in order to safeguard and promote the welfare of children in need and so far as is consistent with that duty to promote their family life (Section 17). This duty is reinforced by Section 23(6), which requires local authorities to make arrangements to enable accommodated children to live with a parent or relative and under Para. 6 of Schedule 2 to the Act, which requires that the services be designed to:

- minimise the effect on disabled children of their disabilities
- give such children the opportunity to lead lives that are as normal as possible.

The guidance emphasises this point by stressing (among other things):[7]

- The family home is the natural and most appropriate place for the majority of children.
- The family has a unique and special knowledge of a child and can therefore contribute significantly to that child's health and development – albeit often in partnership with a range of service providers.

In order to ensure that disabled children are provided for properly, local authorities must not only provide services themselves but also actively consider assisting voluntary organisations (and others, such as extended family members and friends) to provide help to the child and his or her family. The help may consist of day and domiciliary services (see p.258), guidance and counselling (see p.257), respite and other care services.

Duties before placement

All children looked after should have a comprehensive care plan based on their needs according to the Framework for Assessment of Children in Need (DH *et al.* 2000). If, during the assessment process, a local authority anticipates that the child may need to live apart from his or her family, then the authority is subject to specific care-planning obligations.[8] In each case, compliance with these obligations must be on the basis of fully involving the child and the family, clearly formulating objectives and considering all the available options to meet these. The care plan that emerges from this process must detail who is responsible for which service and the timescale in which tasks must be achieved or reassessed.[9] We consider the law and good practice in relation to assessment and care planning on p.252.

Local authorities must have particular regard to certain specified matters, namely healthcare, education, and race, culture, religion and linguistic background.

Healthcare

A health assessment is to be undertaken as soon as practicable after a child starts to be 'looked after' and includes physical and mental health and how this can be promoted.[10] A written report of the assessment and a health plan is then prepared and reviewed annually (or every six months if aged between two and five years). Following criticisms by children who were consulted about the previous system of 'medicals', the Department of Health issued new guidance jointly to local authorities and NHS agencies aimed at a more holistic and continuing assessment of health needs.[11]

Placements outside the local authority boundary should not be made without first making arrangements to secure appropriate health services for the child. Councils need to have a system in place to monitor whether children's health needs are being met. The review process is the normal mechanism for doing this on an individual basis, but the system needs to track children placed outside the area. A senior manager within social services should have specific responsibility for the health of looked-after children. The individual child's social worker is responsible for ensuring each stage of the health assessment, plan, implementation and review is initiated and, where any problems are encountered, for reporting these to the designated manager. The guidance also sets out principles regarding confidentiality and sharing of information.

Specific provisions relating to disabled children who are 'looked after' states:[12]

> Parents will retain the prime responsibility for ensuring the health of their children if using short-term breaks. These children do not need a full health assessment, but carers will need to have appropriate understanding of the child's disabilities and any medical, behavioural and social consequences; what to do in an emergency and who to contact. Disabled children in longer-term care should have a very detailed health history and health plan. Many disabled children are well known to consultant paediatricians and other specialists including dentists, whose advice is essential to health care planning, and in most circumstances they

will be the most appropriate person to undertake the health assessment and contribute to the health plan. The provision for the health assessment should take account of any communication barriers and ensure that the child's wishes and feelings are represented and respected.

A health assessment of a disabled child should recognise the importance of identifying any disabling barriers in the child's environment that exacerbate the effects of the child's impairments. Steps should be taken to ensure that the child's environment promotes the development of the child's potential. Disabled children have the same developmental needs for appropriate social, leisure and recreational activities as other children; if they are living away from home in the short or long term, attention must be given to ensuring the safe installation and use of any equipment and adaptations that may be necessary.[13]

Specific regulations and detailed minimum standards to promote the health and development of children apply to placements in children's homes,[14] by fostering services[15] and in residential special schools.[16]

Education

The Children Act 1989 guidance stresses that looked-after children have the same rights as all children to education, including further and higher education, and to other opportunities for development. Authorities therefore must bear in mind the need to provide extra help to compensate for early educational deprivation, the value of peer group relationships made in educational settings, and the importance of continuity of education and of taking a long-term view. The aim should be to help all children to achieve their full potential and equip themselves as well as possible for adult life.

Significant concerns about the low educational achievements of looked-after children have resulted in an amendment to Section 22(3)(a) of the Children Act 1989 by Section 52 of the Children Act 2004 to ensure that local authorities, in carrying out their duty to safeguard and promote the welfare of children looked after by them, give particular attention to the educational implications of any decision about the welfare of those children. Schools are expected to take a proactive approach to cooperating with and supporting local authorities in discharging this duty, which applies to all children looked after by an authority, including those it has placed out of authority.[17]

Children social services must notify the LEA of a placement 'in good time' so that arrangements for liaison and coordination can be put in place without delay.[18] Specifically, however, Section 28 of the Children Act 1989 provides that where a local authority proposes to place a child in an establishment at which education is provided for children accommodated there, it must consult the relevant LEA[19] before doing so. We consider the general provisions relating to special educational needs assessments on p.150.

Race, culture, religion and linguistic background

Guidance[20] advises that as a guiding principle of good practice (and other things being equal), 'in the great majority of cases, placement with a family of similar ethnic origin and religion is most likely to meet a child's needs as fully as possible'. It cautions, however, against generalisations in this area, stating that there will be cases where such a placement is not possible or desirable.

The care plan

The guidance[21] outlines the requirements for placement planning. These are set out in detail in practice materials issued under the Integrated Children's System,[22] now used by local authorities and scheduled to be implemented in electronic format by the end of 2005. The prescribed Care Plan form should be completed before a child is looked after or as soon as possible thereafter. This records:

- the overall aim and timescale of the plan
- placement details, showing the evidence for the preferred placement, contingency plans and likely duration; if the child is not in the preferred placement, then an explanation and outline of actions to secure this are needed
- the health plan
- the personal education plan
- identified needs and how these will be met, as follows:
  - emotional and behavioural development
  - identity
  - family and social relationships
  - contact with family members
  - social presentation
  - self-care skills
  - parental capacity
  - family and environmental factors, e.g. housing
- the views and wishes of the child and their family and whether these have been acted on
- dates for review.

The plan must be discussed with the child, those with parental responsibility and other carers (e.g. foster carers), and the written plan must be endorsed with their signatures as to their agreement or not. If any people in this list have not been consulted, then reasons must be given.

Placements outside England and Wales

The Children Act (Para. 19, Schedule 2) empowers local authorities to make placements for looked-after children outside England and Wales, subject to:

- suitable arrangements being made for the reception and welfare of the child in the new country
- the arrangements ebbing in the child's best interests
- the necessary consents being obtained (i.e. generally that of the parents).[23]

Duties during placement

Record-keeping

Local authorities must ensure that 'accurate, comprehensive and well organised' records are kept in relation to looked-after children, since such records are essential for continuity of care as social workers and carers change.[24] The Integrated Children's System forms mentioned above are grouped into four types:

1. *Information:*

- contact record (initial contact between the department and the family)
- referral and information record
- placement information record
- chronology
- closure.

2. *Assessment:*

- initial assessment
- records of any child-protection investigations
- core assessment
- assessment and progress record.

3. *Planning:*

- initial plan
- child's plan (if placed at home)
- care plan (if placed away from home)
- adoption plan (where appropriate)
- pathway plan (for care-leavers).

4. *Review records.*

In addition, the following material should be kept with the record:[25]

1. Copies of any written reports in the responsible authority's possession concerning the welfare of the child; this will include family history and home study reports, reports made at the request of a court, reports made of visits to the child, his family or his carer, health reports etc.

2. Copies of all the documents used to seek information, provide information or record views given to the authority in the course of planning and reviewing the child's case and review reports (see also Regulation 10 of the Review of Children's Cases Regulations).

3. Details of arrangements for contact and contact orders and any other court orders relating to the child.

4. Details of any arrangements made for another authority, agency or person to act on behalf of a local authority or organisation which placed a child.

5. Any contribution the child may wish to make such as written material, photographs, school certificates etc..

Access to such records and other local authority material is considered on p.92.

Reviews

The care-planning process for looked-after children is continuous. In order to ensure that the child's welfare is safeguarded and promoted in the most effective way, it is essential that progress is reviewed regularly. The Children Act Regulations put such reviews on a statutory basis.[26] Local authorities must hold review meetings at specified intervals, namely:

First review: within four weeks of the date on which the child begins to be looked after.

Second review: within three months of the first review.

Subsequent reviews: at six-monthly intervals thereafter, i.e. within six months of the date of the previous review.

The guidance deals with the good practice that local authorities must adopt in order to ensure that an efficient, fair and effective system of reviews occurs.[27] In particular, it must provide for:

- the full participation of both children and parents in the decision-making process

- a structured, coordinated approach to the planning of childcare work in individual cases

- a monitoring system for checking the operation of the review process.

Review meetings should be chaired by an independent reviewing officer (IRO), a role introduced by the Adoption and Children Act 2002, which also entitles children to independent advocacy services if they are pursuing a complaint against the local authority. The IRO's functions include monitoring the implementation of the plan and ensuring that the child's views are being taken into account.[28]

The meetings should have a proper agenda and should take place in a setting conducive to the relaxed participation of all those attending, with particular regard being paid to the needs of the child. As a minimum, reviews should consider:[29]

- the child's and the parents' views as to the local authority's care plan

- the extent to which the plan fulfils the authority's duty under the Children Act[30] to safeguard and promote the child's welfare examination or treatment.

The Looked After Review form addresses each of the aspects set out in the care plan described above and is completed by the social worker and the IRO, with the agreement or disagreement of the child and family duly recorded. Progress towards planned outcomes and continuing or newly identified needs is assessed in the context of the placement and developments since the last review. Any changes in plans are explained. The IRO must record the extent to which the child participated in the review, a copy of which is distributed to the family and all relevant agencies.

Contact

Whereas the procedures for determining 'reasonable' contact for children in the subject of a care order are governed by statute,[31] contact arrangements for accommodated children are merely 'a matter for negotiation and agreement' between the local authority, the older child, the parents and others seeking contact.[32] The guidance follows the research evidence by stressing the general importance of contact, particularly in the early days of a placement.

Contact visits can, of course, cause financial hardship to the visitor; accordingly, the Children Act (Para. 16, Schedule 2) provides local authorities with the power to help with such costs, and the guidance reminds authorities that 'the power is not limited to assistance with travelling expenses, but can be used to meet all reasonable costs associated with visiting'.[33]

Independent visitors

As we have noted above, a recurrent theme emerging from the research is the importance of the child's voice being heard. While our domestic law assumes that parents will fulfil this responsibility, and where necessary act as the child's advocate, they are not always able to discharge this role when the child is living away. Accordingly, the Children Act 1989[34] makes provision for the appointment of an 'independent visitor' in certain situations, namely where the local authority believes it is in the child's best interests and either it appears that communication between the child and parent has been infrequent or the child has not been visited by a parent during the preceding 12 months.

The guidance[35] states, however, that in certain circumstances the local authority may decide that an appointment is not in the child's best interests (even though no visits have occurred), if, for example, the child is well settled in a foster placement and has sufficient contacts, friends and, if necessary, opportunities to seek advice.

Independent visitors must be independent; regulations[36] specifically exclude local authority officers and people connected with the care home (and their spouses) from being considered. Independent visitors are unpaid, although they can be reimbursed their travel and other out-of-pocket expenses. Their role is to visit, advise and befriend the child[37] and to (among other things) encourage the child to exercise his or her rights and to participate in decisions that affect him or her. The guidance explores in some depth the range of roles and skills required, the process for recruitment and training[38] and the process for matching the visitor to the particular needs and personality of the child. It anticipates that the independent visitor will, on occasions, speak on behalf of the child ('as a friend') in order to resolve difficulties or deal with particular issues that have arisen. However, it is not the visitor's role to become involved where more serious complaints arise (for instance, a significant dispute between the child and the local authority or in relation to an allegation of abuse). In such cases, the concerns should be raised at an appropriate level within the local authority; it may be that additionally the child needs to be provided with a specialist advocacy service (see p.244, where advocacy as a service is considered).

Duties to young people leaving care

Section 24 of the Children Act 1989 obliges local authorities to prepare young people that they have been looking after for the time when they cease to be looked after and to provide a range of after-care advice and assistance services. In relation to young people between the ages of 16 and 21 years who cease to be looked after, the local authority has the additional power to make a leaving-care grant, the purpose of which is to provide help in the following ways:[39]

- by contributing to expenses incurred by the young person in living near the place where he or she is or will be employed or seeking employment or in receipt of education or training

- by making a grant to enable the young person to meet expenses connected with his or her education or training.

In Chapter 7, we considered the general legal duties on the statutory agencies to assist the disabled child in his or her transition into adulthood.

The Children (Leaving Care) Act 2000

The Children (Leaving Care) Act 2000 implemented proposals first detailed in the consultation document *Me, Survive, Out There? – New Arrangements for Young People Living in and Leaving Care* published in July 1999. The consultation document set out detailed proposals for improving the life chances of young people living in and leaving local authority care. Essentially, the new arrangements give practical effect to the Quality Protects policy (see p.48) and endeavour to ensure that local authorities provide the same level of support as children who have not been in care might in general expect from their parents. Guidance under the Act has been issued in both England[40] and Wales.[41]

The main purpose of the Act is to help young people who have been looked after by a local authority to move from care into living independently in as stable a fashion as possible; it achieves this aim by amending key provisions of the Children Act 1989 by placing a duty on local authorities[42] in respect of 'eligible' and 'relevant' children as described below.

'Eligible' children are those shortly to stop being looked after as they approach the age of 18 years.[43] The local authority has a duty to assess and meet the care and support needs of children in care aged between 16 and 17 years and who have been looked after for 13 weeks, either continuously or in aggregate (but excluding certain respite care periods). Local authorities are required to do the following:

- Undertake an assessment of young people's needs with a view to determining what advice, assistance and support it would be appropriate to provide:
  - while the local authority is still looking after them
  - after the local authority has ceased to look after them

and then to prepare a pathway plan for them.[44] The assessment must be completed not more than three months after the child reaches the age of 16 years.[45]

- Prepare a written statement describing the manner in which their needs would be assessed. The content of these statements is specified in the regulations[46] and must include, for instance, the complaints process, the name of the person responsible for conducting the assessment and so on.

- Appoint a personal adviser who is responsible for (among other things) the coordination of services, including ensuring that the person leaving care makes use of such services.[47] In R (J) v. Caerphilly CBC [2005],[48] the High Court held that it was essential that the personal adviser was independent of the authority and was not the person responsible for the preparation of the assessment or the pathway plan.

'Relevant' children are those aged between 16 and 17 years and who would have been 'eligible' before they ceased being looked after.[49] The local authority duties include:

- to keep in touch with such care-leavers, until aged 21 years, and beyond in some cases

- to prepare 'pathway plans'. These plans take over from the child's existing care plan and run at least until the age of 21 years, covering education, training, career plans and support needs. Such plans will be subject to review every six months. The guidance[50] identifies these plans as 'pivotal to the process whereby children and young people map out their future'.[51]

In R (P) v. Newham LBC,[52] it was held that a local authority had acted unlawfully by failing to provide a personal pathway plan before the severely disabled child in care turned 19 years of age.[53] It was irrelevant that the local authority had started an alternative process that it believed to be more appropriate, namely a transitional plan. As the judge (Ouseley J) observed: 'Whatever the merits of that process may be and however well it may be done, it is not one which meets the requirements of the statute. The requirements of the statute are clear':

- To provide each child with a personal adviser who will help to draw up the Pathway Plan and ensure that it develops with the young person's changing needs and that it is implemented. The personal adviser will be responsible for keeping in touch with the care-leaver (until the age of 21 years) and for ensuring that the care-leaver receives the advice and support to which he or she is entitled.

- To provide the advice and support assessed as required under the Pathway Plan, which may include accommodation and support in kind or in cash. Where appropriate, the cash may be given regularly; the circumstances need not be exceptional.

- The provision of 'vacation support' for care-leavers in higher education, e.g. vacation accommodation where needed.

- To provide assistance with employment, such as the costs associated with employment.

- To provide help with the costs of education and training support, extending beyond the age of 21 years if need be.

- To provide 'general assistance' to young people aged 18 years or over, which may include assistance in kind or, exceptionally, in cash.

The Act provides a unified structure for financial support by transferring to local authorities the funds that previously were paid to such care-leavers under the income support, housing benefit or income-based jobseeker's allowance schemes. Local authorities must use this money to support care-leavers (aged between 16 and 17 years) who, in turn, cease to be entitled entitlement to these means-tested benefits from 'eligible' and 'relevant' children.

Generally, 16- and 17-year-olds cannot claim benefits, but there is an exception for care-leavers who are unable to work because of disability.

Specific accommodation arrangements

Whether a child is provided with accommodation as a short-term break or as a long-term option – in a foster home placement or in residential care – the local authority should ensure not only that it is suitable for the child's needs[54] but also that it minimises the effects of the child's disability.[55] Every effort should be taken to place children as close to their family home as is practicable, so as to maintain family links.

The Care Standards Act 2000 covers residential establishments and care services used by people of all ages; the provisions relating to children are outlined below. Inspection and regulation is currently undertaken by the Commission for Social Care Inspection (CSCI) in accordance with separate sets of national minimum standards (NMS) and regulations relating to the type of service. In March 2005 it was announced that the CSCI is to merge with the Health Care Commission. NHS hospitals are excluded from the Act's definition of a 'children's home', and the relevant guidance is, therefore, dealt with separately.

Short-term breaks (respite care)

Short-term breaks should be provided as part of an overall care plan. They should be flexible, and local authorities should avoid seeing respite care merely as a crisis service but instead strive to make it:[56]

- a local service, where the child can continue to attend school as if still living at home
- good-quality childcare, in which parents have confidence and that ensures that the child is treated first as a child and then for any disability that may require special provision
- planned availability: research into different models of respite care has indicated clearly the importance of parents and older children choosing patterns of use and being able to use a service flexibly
- a service that meets the needs of all children. Concern has been expressed about the lack of respite care for children with complex needs. The service should be available to children living with long-term foster carers or adoptive parents
- care that is compatible with the child's family background and culture, racial origin, religious persuasion and language
- age-appropriate care, so that young children and adolescents are given relevant care and occupation
- an integrated programme of family support that sees planned respite care as part of a wider range of professional support services to meet family needs. Escalating use of respite care may indicate a need for other family support services.

Although the guidance reminds authorities of the NHS's continuing obligation to provide respite care for children who have substantial medical, paramedical and nursing needs, it stresses that such care should not be provided in long-stay mental handicap hospitals but in 'small homely, locally-based units'.[57]

Section 3 of the Carers and Disabled Children Act 2000 provided for regulations to enable a local authority to issue vouchers to the parents of disabled children, the vouchers being redeemable at various agreed providers of respite care. These regulations allow local authorities to set up schemes for vouchers either to a monetary value, or for the delivery of a service for a period of time, to be redeemed in exchange for services delivered by approved providers. The vouchers may be used for accommodation up to 28 days at one time, to a maximum of 120 days in a year.[58]

Fostering

Foster placements arranged by local authorities, including those made with independent agencies, are governed by the Fostering Regulations 2002,[59] supported by two sets of Standards: the UK National Standards for Foster Care 1999 (UKMS) and the National Minimum Standards for Fostering Services 2002 (NMS).[60] The guidance encourages local authorities to actively consider involving people with disabilities as foster carers or as contributors to training programmes. The assessment process for recruiting carers must address specific issues relevant to particular groups, including those with disabilities, and will consider their qualities in relation to a number of factors, such as their own experiences in relation to disability and attitudes to disability.[61] Continuity in education should be a high priority in making any placement, as should the need for foster carers to become involved, as appropriate, in such programmes as paired reading, speech therapy and physiotherapy and independence training exercises.[62]

One of the benefits of a foster placement is that it can enable the child to live in his or her local community. However, as the guidance notes, ordinary homes may be neither automatically accessible or suitable for children with disabilities. Accordingly, local authorities are required to make every effort to ensure that the accommodation is suitable, by (if necessary) providing appropriate equipment and adaptations to make sure that the child's living environment is as barrier-free as possible.[63] The guidance continues:

> 12.10. It is essential that children with disabilities (who may have incontinence or special personal care needs) should have privacy in bathroom and bedroom and that they should not be excluded from the main areas of the home such as living rooms and kitchen (and the social activities which take place in these areas) because of access difficulties. In many instances access problems can be resolved through the use of relatively simple and cheap modifications such as the use of moveable ramps and other aids. It is quite unacceptable for a child to be placed in a setting where he or she is more restricted than would have been the case in the natural home or in a residential setting. Similarly accommodation may be suitable in itself, but the child will be severely limited in his or her use of it if the carers lack confidence in the management of a child with, for example, a severe visual handicap or if the child concerned is hyperactive. SSDs should additionally ensure that the accommodation is safe for the child in question and that access (and egress) can be easily accomplished in the case of fire. If a child is hyperactive or for some other reason is liable to be at risk if playing outside the house, the safety of any garden gates and fences should also be assessed. It would be inappropriate for a child with a disability to have to be confined unnecessarily

to particular rooms because of problems of safety relating to the physical environment of the placement.

A Foster Placement Agreement will be drawn up that contains all the information necessary for full care of the child, including their identified health, safety and educational needs, and any other needs arising from a disability.[64] Carers are expected to promote the child's welfare and family ties, and help them build confidence in themselves and their self-worth.[65] Children should be provided with services and support to help make them as independent, and lead as full a life, as possible.[66]

Residential care

Section 53 of the Children Act 1989 provides that every local authority is under a duty to make arrangements to ensure that community homes are available for the care and accommodation of (among others) disabled children looked after by them. The statutory framework for the registration and inspection of children's homes has been simplified by the Care Standards Act to broadly define a children's home as an establishment to 'provide care and accommodation wholly or mainly for children'.[67] The definition includes what were previously known as community and voluntary homes, as well as any school accommodating a child for over 295 days a year. It excludes NHS hospitals, private hospitals and clinics, and residential family centres.

Homes that accommodate disabled children must provide the necessary equipment facilities and adaptations.[68] Although this is of great importance, the guidance advises that the aim should be to integrate the disabled child in every aspect of life in the home, not merely the physical aspects.[69]

Children accommodated by the NHS or an education authority

Because of the nature or degree of their disabilities, some children inevitably will spend prolonged periods of time in an NHS facility. The guidance, however, emphasises that 'it is against government policy that such children should be placed for long-term residential care in a NHS hospital setting'[70] and that the 'use of NHS facilities should reflect a child's need for assessment, treatment or other services which cannot' be provided by social services. Remaining in such a facility cannot, however, 'constitute a permanent placement'. Furthermore, in 'rare circumstances in which it is necessary for children and young people to receive specialist medical care and treatment which can only be provided in a hospital setting (for example children with terminal or life-threatening conditions)', the NHS should aim to provide this care in 'small homely, locally-based units'.

Notification duties

If a child is provided with accommodation by the NHS or LEA for more than three months on a consecutive basis or the intention is that this will happen, then the health authority, NHS trust or LEA must notify the 'responsible social services department'.[71] On being notified, the authority must 'take all reasonably practicable steps to enable them to decide whether the child's welfare is adequately safeguarded and promoted while he stays in the accommodation and to decide whether it is necessary to exercise any of their functions under the Act'.[72]

Educational and social services placements

In relation to such placements, the guidance[73] notes that:

> some children with disabilities and special needs attend independent or non-maintained residential special schools – some on a 52 weeks a year basis. The use of a residential school, after careful joint assessment by the LEA, the SSD and the relevant DHA, may represent an important resource for the development of a particular child. Residential school placements should be made with a clear understanding of the nature and objective of the placement. Close links with the SSD in question will ensure that there is clear and coherent planning for the school holidays, the maintenance of family and community links and future arrangements for the child when leaving school. Placements in a residential school should never be made by SSDs without consultation with their LEA.

Residential schools are inspected against national minimum standards to ensure that they are promoting and safeguarding the welfare of pupils. These include:

- children's rights – how children are encouraged to take part in decision-making
- child protection
- care and control
- quality of care
- planning and recording
- premises
- staff and management.[74]

Notes

1   *R* v. *Tameside MBC ex p. J* [2000] 1 FLR 942.

2   S.116 of the Adoption and Children Act 2002 amended s.22(1) CA 1989 to state specifically that a child is not a looked-after child if he or she is provided with accommodation under s.17. See also s.7

Carers and Disabled Children Act 2000, which inserted s.17B into Children Act 1989 explicitly dealing with s.17 respite care and allowing vouchers in lieu of direct service provision.

3   [2004] EWHC 2027 (Admin).

4   In relation to s.20(6), the court went on to comment that it 'requires the local authority to ascertain and give due consideration to the child's wishes regarding the provision of accommodation. Plainly when dealing with 16-year-old children, who are likely to have minds of their own and may well be Gillick competent – see *Gillick* v. *West Norfolk and Wisbech Area Health Authority* [1986] AC 112 – a local authority has to have regard to the realities. In particular, a local authority has to have regard to the reality that young people faced with proffered support packages which are perceived as being unacceptable may well reject the support being offered and simply vote with their feet. A young person may, for example, prefer the financial independence of managing their own benefits rather than living on local authority pocket-money, and for that reason prefer to be accommodated under s17.'

5   S.2(1) Children Act 1989.

6   S.4 (1A) Children Act 1989.

7   The Children Act 1989: Guidance and Regulations, Vol. 6, *Children with Disabilities.* London: HMSO, Para. 6.1.

8   The Arrangements for Placement of Children (General) Regulations 1991, Regulations 3, 4 and 5; and The Children Act 1989: Guidance and Regulations, Vol. 4, *Residential Care.* London: HMSO, Chapter 2.

9   The Children Act 1989: Guidance and Regulations, Vol. 4, *Residential Care.* London: HMSO, Para. 2.20.

10 Regulation 6 The Review of Children's Cases Regulations 1991 amended by Regulation 4 Children Act (Miscellaneous Amendments) (England) Regulations 2002 SI 546.

11 Department of Health (2002) *Promoting the Health of Looked After Children;* accessible at www.dh.gov.uk/assetRoot/04/06/04/24/04060424.pdf.

12 The Children Act 1989: Guidance and Regulations, Vol. 4, *Residential Care.* London: HMSO, Paras 10.2 and 10.3.

13 Ibid. Paras 10.2–10.5.

14 Department of Health (2002) National Minimum Standards and Regulations for Children's Homes. NMS 12, Regulation 20.

15 Department of Health (2002) National Minimum Standards and Regulations for Fostering Services. NMS 12, Regulation 15.

16 Department of Health (2002) National Minimum Standards for Residential Special Schools. NMS 14.

17 Statutory guidance on the new duty to promote the educational achievement of looked-after children has been issued by the DfES and is accessible at www.everychildmatters.gov.uk

18 The Children Act 1989: Guidance and Regulations, Vol. 4, *Residential Care.* London: HMSO, Para. 2.34.

19 That is, the LEA within whose area the local authority's area falls or, if there is a special educational needs statement, the LEA that maintains that statement. The Children Act 1989: Guidance and Regulations, Vol. 4, *Residential Care.* London: HMSO, Para. 2.39.

20 The Children Act 1989: Guidance and Regulations, Vol. 4, *Residential Care.* London: HMSO, Para. 2.40.

21 Accessible at www.dfes.gov.uk/integratedchildrenssystem/resources/.

22 Accessible at www.dfes.gov.uk/integratedchildrenssystem/.

23 The Children Act 1989: Guidance and Regulations, Vol. 4, *Residential Care.* London: HMSO, Para. 2.77.

24 Ibid. Para. 2.78.

25 Ibid. Para. 2.81.

26 Review of Children's Care Regulations 1991, SI 895, as amended by Children Short Term Placement (Miscellaneous Provisions) Regulations 1995. The reviews do not apply to series of

short-term break (respite) placements, provided that they all occur with the same carer at the same establishment and are individually shorter than four weeks and the total period in any one year does not exceed 120 days; Regulation 11.

27 The Children Act 1989: Guidance and Regulations. Vol. 4, *Residential Care*. London: HMSO, Paras 3.8–3.25.

28 The Review of Children's Cases (Amendment) (England) Regulations 2004 SI 2004/1419.

29 The Children Act 1989: Guidance and Regulations, Vol. 4, *Residential Care*. London: HMSO, Paras 3.10–3.120; and The Review of Children's Care Regulations 1991, Schedule 2.

30 Ss.22(3), 61(1) or 64(1).

31 S.34 Children Act 1989 and The Contact with Children Regulations 1991, No. 891.

32 The Children Act 1989: Guidance and Regulations, Vol. 4, *Residential Care*. London: HMSO, Para. 4.7.

33 Ibid. Para. 4.23.

34 Para. 17 Schedule 2.

35 The Children Act 1989: Guidance and Regulations, Vol. 4, *Residential Care*. London: HMSO, Para. 6.11.

36 Definition of Independent Visitors (Children) Regulations 1991, No. 892.

37 Para. 17(2) Schedule 2 Children Act 1989.

38 The Children Act 1989: Guidance and Regulations, Vol. 4, *Residential Care*. London: HMSO, Paras 6.12–6.46.

39 S.24(2) Children Act; and The Children Act 1989: Guidance and Regulations, Vol. 4, *Residential Care*. London: HMSO, Para. 7.10.

40 Department for Education and Skills. *Children (Leaving Care) Act 2000 Regulations and Guidance*, accessible at www.dfes.gov.uk/qualityprotects/pdfs/regs2000.pdf.

41 National Assembly for Wales. *Children Leaving Care Act Guidance*, accessible at www.wales.gov.uk/subichildren/toc-e.htm#b.

42 The responsible local authority is the one that last looked after the child, even if the child has since moved into the area of another authority.

43 Para. 19B(2) Schedule 2 Children Act 1989.

44 Para. 19B(4) Schedule 2 Children Act 1989.

45 Regulation 7 Children (Leaving Care) (England) Regulations 2001, SI 2001/2874; in Wales, the Children (Leaving Care) (Wales) Regulations 2001, SI 2001/2189 (W151).

46 Ibid. Regulation 5.

47 Ibid. Regulation 12.

48 [2005] EWHC 586 (Admin) at Para. 30.

49 S.23A Children Act 1989.

50 Department for Education and Skills. *Children (Leaving Care) Act 2000 Regulations and Guidance*, Para. 20, p.40; accessible at www.dfes.gov.uk/qualityprotects/pdfs/regs2000.pdf; and the National Assembly for Wales. *Children Leaving Care Act Guidance*, Para. 7.2; accessible at www.wales.gov.uk/subichildren/toc-e.htm#b.

51 See also *R (J) v. Caerphilly CBC* [2005] EWHC 586 (Admin), *The Times*, 21 April 2005.

52 [2004] 7 CCL Rep 553.

53 In breach of s.19B(4) of Schedule 2 of the Children Act 1989 and the Children (Leaving Care) (England) Regulations 2001. The equivalent regulations in Wales are the Children (Leaving Care) (Wales) Regulations 2001, SI 2001/2189 (W151).

54 S.23(8) Children Act 1989.

55 Ibid. Para. 6, Schedule 2.

56 The Children Act 1989: Guidance and Regulations, Vol. 6, *Children with Disabilities*. London: HMSO, Para. 11.11. See also The Children Act 1989: Guidance and Regulations, Vol. 4, *Residential Care*. London: HMSO, Para. 2.37, which advises that even during short-term placements, opportunities to develop and pursue leisure activities should be encouraged.

57 The Children Act 1989: Guidance and Regulations. Vol. 6, Children with Disabilities. London: HMSO, Para. 11.12.

58 Carers and Disabled Children (Vouchers) (England) Regulations 2003.

59 SI 2002/57.

60 SI no. 910 and general guidance for all children (whether or not disabled) contained in the Children Act 1989: Guidance and Regulations, Vol. 4, *Residential Care*. London: HMSO, Chapter 4.

61 NMS 17.7.

62 The Children Act 1989: Guidance and Regulations, Vol. 6, *Children with Disabilities*. London: HMSO, Para. 12.4.

63 The Children Act 1989: Guidance and Regulations, Vol. 6, *Children with Disabilities*. London: HMSO, Para. 12.9.

64 Fostering Regulations 2002 Schedule 6 Para. 34(3).

65 NMS 7.3.

66 NMS 7.7.

67 S.1(2) Care Standards Act 2000.

68 The Children Act 1989: Guidance and Regulations, Vol. 4, *Residential Care*. London: HMSO, Para. 1.78.

69 Ibid. Para. 1.81.

70 The Children Act 1989: Guidance and Regulations, Vol. 6, *Children with Disabilities*. London: HMSO, Para. 13.7.

71 S.85 Children Act 1989. Defined as the social services authority for the area in which the child lives or was ordinarily resident immediately before being accommodated or (if there is no such authority) the authority in whose area the accommodation for the child is being provided.

72 The Children Act 1989: Guidance and Regulations, Vol. 6, *Children with Disabilities*. London: HMSO, Para. 13.9.

73 Ibid. Para. 13.13.

74 Residential Special Schools: National Minimum Standards; Inspection Regulations DH 2002.

PART II

Resource Materials

Complaints Materials

Local authority complaints procedures

Local authorities must have fair and efficient complaints procedures. Although the law clearly defines the shape and content of the complaints system that social services must operate, this is not the case in relation to complaints about other local authority functions, such as housing and children's education services. We accordingly outline the social services procedures first and then consider briefly the requirements for other local authority sections.

At the time of writing, both adults' and children's social services complaints procedures are about to be the subject of major reform, and the final details of the new procedures (which are expected to come into effect in early 2006) have not been published. The new guidance for children's social services complaints will be published by the Department for Education and Skills (DfES) and will be accessible on its website at www.dfes.gov.uk. That for adults' social services complaints will be published by the Department of Health and will be accessible on its website at www.dh.gov.uk. The following account seeks to describe the new procedures based on current practices. In so doing, we make reference to the existing guidance. Although this will be replaced in due course, its advice as to best practice is unlikely to change, as best practice does not change merely because a procedure has been amended.

The reforms

The Health and Social Care (Community Health and Standards) Act 2003 provides the Secretary of State (in Wales, the National Assembly) with the power to make regulations providing for a two-stage process for representations and complaints dealing with local authority social services. In relation to complaints concerning adults this is achieved by Section 114, and in relation to children by Section 116 (which inserts a new section, 26ZA, into the Children Act 1989).

It is envisaged that the first stage will comprise informal and formal/registered procedures along the lines of the pre-existing process and that these will remain the responsibility of the local social services authority. The major reform concerns what happens if the local authority fails to resolve the complaint during the informal or formal procedure. If this occurs, then the resolution of the complaint becomes the responsibility of the Commission for Social Care Inspection (CSCI) in

England or an independent panel in Wales. (For the CSCI proposals concerning the new procedures, see www.csci.org.uk/publications/independant_voice.pdf.) The timescale for the implementation of the reforms has slipped and is now scheduled for early 2006.

Social services complaints

Although complaints concerning adults' and children's social services functions are governed by different regulations, the two systems are very similar and accordingly are considered as one below. Good practice guidance concerning the pre-2006 general complaints procedures was issued by the Department of Health as *The Right to Complain* (1991) and in relation to complaints under the Children Act 1989 as *Children Act 1989 Guidance Volume 3, Family Placements,* Paras 10.33 *et seq.*

Who can complain?

Complaints may be made by anyone for whom the authority has a power or duty to provide a service as well as by the parents of the disabled child.

The structure of the complaints system

Social services departments must appoint an officer who is responsible for coordinating all aspects of the complaints procedures. In practice, all social services complaints procedures have three distinct stages, namely:

- the informal or problem-solving stage
- the formal or registration stage
- the review stage.

The Children Act guidance[1] stresses that 'every effort should be made to work with local disability groups to ensure that the procedures are accessible, useable and effective when dealing with issues relating to disabilities'.

The informal or problem-solving stage

The initial stage is where the local authority must attempt to resolve the matter informally. At this stage, there is no requirement that the complaint be in writing. *The Right to Complain*[2] explains that:

> normal good practice should sort out, to the user's satisfaction, the queries and grumbles which are part of a social work department's daily workload. Stage 1 then alerts the relevant worker, supervisor or manager to the fact that there is a more fundamental problem, as perceived by the user or her or his representative. It gives users the right to decide whether or not to pursue the issue and ensures that it is taken seriously and not dismissed by busy staff. The fact, however, that this stage is not 'formal' does not mean that it is 'casual'.[3]

The first stage of the complaints process is simply an opportunity for the local authority to attempt problem-solving, conciliation and negotiation. It is not subject to any statutory timescale, although in practice many authorities specify in their local procedures maximum periods for this phase (often in the region of one to four weeks).

Local authorities should provide complainants with a simple explanation as to how the complaints process works and the relevant timescales. The provision of a leaflet with this information does not obviate the need to advise complainants in correspondence at the appropriate times of their rights at subsequent stages, i.e. of the right to seek a panel hearing if dissatisfied with the outcome of the formal stage.

Local authorities will need to ensure that advocacy assistance (see below) is available to disabled children and their parents in appropriate cases. In addition, the guidance[4] notes that 'many children and young people with sensory or learning disabilities will have more complex communication needs that can be met by the provision of an interpreter'.

The formal stage

If the local-level informal process fails to resolve the complaint speedily, then it moves to the formal stage (a complainant is entitled to go straight to this stage, omitting the informal stage, if he or she so wishes). At the formal stage, complaints should be put in writing. A precedent complaints letter can be found on p.278.

The Right to Complain at Para. 4.10 explains that:

> many people will need support and advice from someone they trust either from within or outside the department. Some people will need help in writing and sometimes formulating a complaint. Those who give help in writing down the complaint must ensure that it fully reflects what the complainant wishes to say and ask the complainant to sign it.

The fact that a complaint has progressed to the formal stage does not absolve the authority from its duty to try to resolve the problem.[5]

Social services must consider the complaint and then formulate a response within 28 days of its receipt. If for any reason it is not possible to comply with the 28-day period, the authority must within that period explain to the complainant why this is so and explain when the response will be given. In any event, the response must be forthcoming within three months.

Authorities may, if the need arises, appoint an independent person[6] at this stage to oversee the investigation. If the complaint concerns services under the Children Act 1989, authorities *must* appoint such an independent person.[7] When such an independent person is appointed, his or her role is, as stated, to 'oversee the investigation'. This means that he or she may accompany the local authority complaints investigator and also interview complainants separately. Generally, independent people file separate reports to those filed by the local authority investigator.

On some occasions, the investigation may need to call upon specialist outsiders, for instance:

> In some instances complaints may relate to inappropriate services for children with disabilities, for example where there are poor access facilities, unsuitable furnishings or equipment or where children are unnecessarily excluded from the full range of activities appropriate to their ages, interests and general ability. In these instances expert advice on the particular disability should be identified eg from within the SSD, from a [health authority] or from a voluntary organisation and the SSD's existing arrangements for placement reassessed to avoid similar difficulties in the future.[8]

At the conclusion of its investigation, the local authority must notify the complainant in writing of the result of its investigation. If the complaint has been made by a parent or carer on behalf of a disabled child, then notification must also be sent to the child, unless the authority considers that he or she is not able to understand. Complainants should generally be given the opportunity of commenting on a draft of the investigator's report,[9] particularly in relation to any contra-allegations that may have been made,[10] before the final report is produced.

The review stage

The disabled child or his or her parents or carers may, if dissatisfied with the outcome of the formal stage, request that the complaint be referred to a panel for review. This stage will be the subject of new procedures (not available at the time of writing). In England, the request for a review panel will be made to the CSCI; in Wales, the request will be made to an independent panel. In every case, however, it will be the responsibility of the local authority to explain the process and the relevant timescales to the complainant.

Panel hearings are in private and are conducted as informally as possible. The panel hearing must follow the rules of natural justice, although the chairperson is entitled to set reasonable time limits on the oral submissions to be made by the parties, provided these are used as 'guidelines rather than guillotines'.[11]

Advocacy in children's complaints

Since April 2004, all children involved in the complaints process have a statutory right to an advocate. The Adoption and Children Act 2002 (Section 119) imposes a duty on local authorities to provide advocacy services for certain categories of complainant under the Children Act 1989 representations procedure. It inserts into the 1989 Act a new section (Section 26A) that requires local authorities to make arrangements for the provision of assistance, including assistance by way of representation, to care-leavers and children who make or intend to make representations using the procedures under Sections 24D and 26(3) of the Act. Regulations have been issued fleshing out this function,[12] and guidance has been issued by the DES[13] and the Welsh Assembly.[14]

Local authority complaints not covered by the specific social services rules

Education complaints

With the exception of complaints concerning the national curriculum[15] of provision of information, there is no statutory complaints process for parental/student disputes with the LEA or school governors.

In 1989, the Department of Education issued guidance on the need for complaints procedures (Circular 1/89). As a consequence, most local authorities have adopted a model complaints code formulated jointly by the Associations of Metropolitan and County Councils. This involves a phased response, commencing at the first stage with local resolution via teacher and parent, followed by formal complaint to the governors and thence to the LEA. The LEA stage provides for a designated officer to investigate and for the results of the investigation to be considered by a panel of three LEA members.

Although LEAs are obliged to provide parents/students with information concerning their complaints process, the model procedure is far from perfect. It contains no time limits for the completion of each stage, and the final LEA stage has no independent element. Accordingly, where disputes arise, it is generally prudent to stress the following in the initial letter of complaint:

- The investigation (at each stage) must occur with expedition.
- The investigation must be impartial.
- The parent/student before must have the opportunity of responding to any contra-allegations made by the school/LEA.
- Throughout, the parent/student must be kept fully informed, particularly if any delay occurs, in which case an explanation for this must be provided.
- Given the absence of clear statutory guidance on the process, it is expected that the investigation will comply with the good practice guidance issued by the ombudsman (see below).

Other local authority complaints

Although, as noted, local authority complaints that concern non-social services matters are not governed by strict statutory procedures, the ombudsman has nevertheless emphasised that equally clear local procedures must also be in place to deal with such complaints. Thus, in a complaint against Nottingham County Council, the ombudsman noted that although the complainant was not a qualifying individual, it was nevertheless important that her 'complaints were still given full and proper consideration in a way which equated to the standard of service a complaint would have received under the council's formal complaints procedure'.[16]

The local ombudsman in pursuance of this policy has issued guidance to local authorities on how such complaints procedures should be operated,[17] in essence adopting many of the principles present in the social services statutory procedures.

NHS complaints materials

Complaints against NHS bodies such as health authorities, trusts and GPs are governed by statute, and there are many parallels between the NHS and social services procedures. In 2004, the NHS complaints process was the subject of fundamental reform[18] and is now governed by regulations that place responsibility on individual NHS bodies for the first local resolution stage of the complaints procedure and on the Health Care Commission (correctly entitled the Commission for Healthcare Audit and Inspection, CHAI) for the second independent review stage.[19]

The Department of Health has issued preliminary guidance on the new scheme, *Guidance to Support Implementation of the National Health Service (Complaints) Regulations 2004*, available at www.dh.gov.uk/assetRoot/04/08/81/57/04088157.pdf.

NHS complainants should have access to assistance from a variety of bodies, including the Patient Advice and Liaison Service (PALS), a complaints advocacy service and a complaints manager.

Patient Advice and Liaison Service

Every NHS trust must have a PALS. Essentially, this is an advice/signposting unit that should assist in resolving simple communication problems and very minor grumbles. It is not an advocacy services, although one of its functions is to explain to patients and their carers how complaints about the NHS can be made.

Complaints advocacy service

An Independent Complaints Advocacy Service (ICAS) exists in England to help individuals with each aspect of their NHS complaint. ICAS replaced the service previously provided by Community Health Councils in England; however, in Wales, the Community Health Council service remains.

In England, the ICAS has been provided largely by offices attached to Citizens Advice Bureaux and its development has encountered significant problems. Patients who want to complain about NHS services can approach ICAS directly or may be directed there by the PALS. Complaints managers at trust level are also expected to advise patients of the availability of this service and assist them in making contact. For further information on the service, and for a review of the progress made by ICAS in the year to August 2004, see www.dh.gov.uk/assetRoot/04/09/88/64/04098864.pdf.

Complaints manager

Every NHS body must appoint a complaints manager with responsibility for ensuring that complaints are investigated properly. In addition, every NHS body must appoint a member of its board of directors to take overall responsibility for the scheme. The system must be:

> accessible and such as to ensure that complaints are dealt with speedily and efficiently, and that complainants are treated courteously and sympathetically and as far as possible involved in decisions about how their complaints are handled and considered. (Regulation 3)

Who may complain?

Complaints may be made by a patient or anyone 'who is affected by or likely to be affected by the action, omission or decision of the NHS body which is the subject of the complaint' (Regulation 8). Where a complaint is made by a representative on behalf of a patient who has died or lacks the physical or mental capacity to make the complaint in person, then he or she must 'in the opinion of the complaints manager' (Regulation 8) have a sufficient interest in the patient's welfare and be 'a suitable person to act as representative' (Regulation 8).

Complaints on behalf of a child must be made by:

> a parent, guardian or other adult person who has care of the child and where the child is in the care of a local authority or a voluntary organisation, the representative must be a person authorised by the local authority or the voluntary organisation. (Regulation 8)

Time limits

Complaints must be made within six months of the date of the incident in question or within six months of the date on which the issue came to the notice of the complainant. Complaints can be made outside these time limits where good cause exists. Para. 3.37 of the Department of Health guidance advises:

> The discretion to vary the time limit should be used flexibly and with sensitivity. An example of where discretion might be exercised would be where the complainant has suffered such distress or trauma as to prevent him/her from making their complaint at an earlier stage.

Stage 1

Complaints may be made orally or in writing (including electronically) and must be recorded by the complaints manager. When a complaint is made orally, 'the complaints manager must make a written record of the complaint' (Regulations 11–13).

The regulations require the complaints manager to acknowledge the complaint in writing within two days of its receipt. If made orally, the acknowledgement must include a written record of the complaint. The complaints manager must send a copy of the complaint and his or her acknowledgement to any person who is the subject of the complaint. The letter of acknowledgement must also include information about the right to advocacy assistance from ICAS.

The complaints manager must investigate the complaint 'to the extent necessary and in the manner which appears to him most appropriate to resolve it speedily and efficiently' (Regulation 12). The regulations provide for conciliation and mediation and require the complaints manager to keep the complainant informed about the progress of the investigation. A written response is provided (generally signed by the chief executive of the NHS body) summarising the nature and substance of the complaint, describing the investigation and summarising its conclusions; this is to be provided within 20 working days of the date on which the complaint was made, unless this is impractical, in which case it is to be done 'as soon as reasonably practicable' (Regulation 13). The complaint should be copied to any person identified in the complaint as the subject of the complaint.

The response must advise of the right to have the complaint referred to the CHAI.

Stage 2

The CHAI issued guidance on the operation of the second-stage process in July 2004 as *Reforming the NHS Complaints Procedure*, accessible at www.chai.org.uk/ assetRoot/ 04/00/81/95/04008195.pdf. If the complainant is dissatisfied with the outcome of the first stage process, or the complaints manager has declined to investigate it, then the complainant can ask the CHAI to investigate (special rules relate to NHS foundation trusts). The request must be made 'within 2 months of, or as soon as reasonably practicable after', the response' (Regulation 14). It may be made orally or in writing (including electronically). The CHAI must acknowledge the request and then decide whether to:

- take no further action; in which case, the complainant must be advised of his or her right to complain to the NHS ombudsman
- refer the complaint back to the NHS body with recommendations as to what action might be taken to resolve it
- investigate the complaint further itself, either by convening a panel or otherwise
- consider the subject matter of the complaint as part of or in conjunction with any other investigation that it is conducting or proposes to conduct;
- refer the complaint to a health regulatory body
- refer the complaint to the NHS ombudsman.

CHAI investigation

If the CHAI decides to investigate the complaint itself, it must within ten working days advise the complainant of its proposed terms of reference for the investigation. The CHAI's report must be completed as soon as is reasonably practicable and must contain a reasoned response provided to the complainant together with advice of the right to take the matter to the NHS ombudsman if dissatisfied.

Panels

The CHAI maintains a list of people who are suitable to be members of an independent lay panel (employees and members of NHS bodies are excluded from membership). Individual panels consist of three such people, one of whom is designated by the CHAI as the chairperson.

Once a complaint has been referred to a panel, the CHAI must make arrangements for the panel to be convened.

Notes

1   The Children Act 1989: Guidance and Regulations, Vol. 6, *Children with Disabilities*. London: HMSO, Para. 14.4.

2   Para. 4.3.

3   Ibid. Para. 4.2-3.

4   The Children Act 1989: Guidance and Regulations, Vol. 6, *Children with Disabilities*. London: HMSO, Para. 14.7.

5   Local Government Ombudsman complaint against Liverpool (1999) 98/C/3591.

6   *The Right to Complain*, Para. 4.12.

7   See Representations Procedure (Children) Regulations 1991 SI no. 894 Regulations 5 and 6; and The Children Act 1989: Guidance and Regulations, Vol. 3, Paras 10.33 et seq.

8   The Children Act 1989: Guidance and Regulations, Vol. 6, *Children with Disabilities*. London: HMSO, Para. 14.8.

9   Local Government Ombudsman complaint against Cheshire (1999) 97/C/4618.

10   Local Government Ombudsman report against Calderdale MBC 98/C/1294.

11   Ibid.

12   In England as the Advocacy Services and Representations Procedure (Children) (Amendment) Regulations 2004 SI no. 719; in Wales as the Advocacy Services and Representations Procedure (Children) (Wales) Regulations 2004 SI no. 1448 (W.148).

13   LAC (2004)11; and Get it Sorted: Providing Effective Advocacy Services for Children and Young People making a Complaint under the Children Act 1989.

14   Providing Effective Advocacy Services for Children and Young People Making a Representation or Complaint under the Children Act 1989 (May 2004).

15   Curriculum/information disputes are subject to the provisions of s.409 Education Act 1996 and, if the local resolution of such a complaint fails, provision exists for them to be made directly to the Secretary of State under s.496-7 of the 1996 Act.

16   Report no. 94/C/2959 against Nottingham City Council, 28 November 1994. See also Local Government Ombudsman complaint against Bury MBC (1999) 97/C/1614, in which the ombudsman accepted that part of the complaint lay outside the statutory complaints process but nevertheless warranted investigation and commented 'It is hard to identify any aspect of the Council's handling of Mr Redfern's complaints which was in the proper manner or in full accordance with the statutory complaints procedure and/or the Council's own written complaints procedure.'

17   Local Government Ombudsman (February 1992). Good Practice 1: Devising a Complaints System.
18   S.113 Social Care (Community Health and Standards) Act 2003.
19   The National Health Service (Complaints) Regulations 2004 SI no. 1768.
19   Sedley J put it thus: 'The practice guidance ... counsels against trimming the assessment of need to fit the available provision.'

Social Services Materials

The social services assessment and care-planning obligations

Assessments under the Children Act 1989

Although there is no specific duty to assess under the Children Act 1989 equivalent to that found in NHS and Community Care Act 1990 (considered below), there is a power to assess. In *R (G)* v. *Barnet LBC and others* [2003][1] the House of Lords held that in practice local authorities were obliged to undertake and assess – that it was in effect implicit in the 1989 Act that such an obligation existed. Guidance issued by the Department of Health and the Welsh Assembly strongly reinforces the requirement that such assessments take place.

In many situations, disabled children will be entitled to a community care assessment under the NHS and Community Care Act 1990,[2] or the Chronically Sick and Disabled Persons Act 1970 and also to other assessments, such as for their special education needs. In order to avoid duplications, the Children Act 1989 provides that these various assessments can be combined,[3] stating that local authorities may, at the same time as assessing under the 1989 Act, also carry out an assessment under:

- the Chronically Sick and Disabled Persons Act 1970
- Part IV of the Education Act 1996
- the Disabled Persons (Services, Consultation and Representation) Act 1986
- any other enactment.

In discharging these various functions, social services departments must be sensitive to the needs and requirements of ethnic minority families and, in particular, ensure that assessments take into account individual circumstances and are not based on a stereotypical view of what may be required.[4]

The Children Act 1989 guidance (Vol. 2: *Family Support*) amplifies what is required in such assessments:

> 2.7 Good practice requires that the assessment of need should be undertaken in an open way and should involve those caring for the child, the child and other significant persons. Families with a child in need, whether the need results from family difficulties or the child's circumstances, have the right to receive sympathetic support and sensitive intervention in their family's life...

2.8 In making an assessment, the local authority should take account of the particular needs of the child – that is in relation to health, development, disability, education, religious persuasion, racial origin, cultural and linguistic background, the degree (if any) to which these needs are being met by existing services to the family or the child and which agencies' services are best suited to the child's needs.

The Children Act guidance concerned specifically with disabled children (Vol. 6) provides further detail, as follows:

5.1 SSDs will need to develop clear assessment procedures for children in need within agreed criteria which take account of the child's and family's needs and preferences, racial and ethnic origins, their culture, religion and any special needs relating to the circumstances of individual families…

5.2 In many cases children with disabilities will need continuing services throughout their lives. It will therefore be particularly important that for these children the assessment process takes a longer perspective than is usual or necessary for children without disabilities, who will usually cease to have a need for services after reaching adulthood.

5.3 The requirements of children with disabilities may need to be met from a number of sources. In conducting assessments and managing the care provided, SSDs will need to ensure that all necessary expertise is marshalled and that all those providing services are involved from both within and beyond the SSD. The outcome of assessment should be a holistic and realistic picture of the individual and family being assessed, which takes into account their strengths and capacities as well as any difficulties and which acknowledges the need to make provision appropriate to the family's cultural background and their expressed views and preferences.

Care planning

Government guidance[5] has characterised the community care assessment process as comprising three distinct processes, namely gathering relevant information, making a service-provision decision, and preparing and implementing a care plan.

Gathering relevant information

At this stage, the person undertaking the assessment must gather as much information as is necessary in order to establish the reasonable needs of the disabled child or his or her carers. This will usually involve contacting all relevant sources of information, such as family, carers, GPs, teachers and other specialists involved in the child's care.

Making a service-provision decision

Having accumulated information about the disabled person, the assessor (generally a social worker) decides which of the various needs are sufficiently substantial to warrant the provision of assistance or services. Generally, this decision is only made having regard to the likely consequences of not providing support. In essence, the assessor asks a 'What if?' question: 'What will happen if the specific need is not met by the provision of social support services?' There are many potential answers to this question, but three common scenarios are as follows:

- *Answer (a)*: If the answer is that the child would likely suffer harm or have impaired development, then the assistance must be provided. In social services jargon, this equates to the child 'meeting the eligibility criteria' for services (see below). This might be, for example, the need for an accessible bathroom or the need for help with feeding.

- *Answer (b)*: The answer may be that although the child would be at risk of harm if social services support was not provided, it is not necessary for the local authority to arrange such services because the child's carer can provide the necessary assistance. In such situations, the local authority is obliged to undertake a carers assessment before deciding that it is reasonable that it is not nevertheless necessary for it to provide the support. Carers assessments are considered separately below. However, an example of this situation might concern a child with exceptionally demanding day and night needs. The child's mother might be able to provide support, but this would require her to give up her job and even then would not be sustainable, since she would be unable to cope without respite from being 'on call' 24 hours a day. The carers assessment considers the sustainability of the caring role and also addresses specifically the carer's needs and aspirations in relation to work, education, training and leisure.

- *Answer (c)*: The answer may be that there is no risk of harm if social support services are not provided. In such a situation, the local authority is not responsible for providing support, although if circumstances change it will have then to undertake a reassessment and in all cases it must give a clear explanation as to the reasons for this, so that the disabled person or carer can invoke the complaints process if necessary (see p.241 for an outline of the complaints procedures).

Eligibility criteria

Although local authorities must have some rational process for deciding on where to apply their limited resources, the decision as to whether a disabled child receives support is, of course, a complex one that cannot be done merely by reference to an arbitrary two-dimensional scale of eligibility. The consequences of not providing support can be multidimensional, with impacts varying over time. Commenting upon the inappropriate use of eligibility criteria, Lord Laming said:[6]

1.53 The use of eligibility criteria to restrict access to services is not found either in legislation or in guidance, and its ill-founded application is not something I support. Only after a child and his or her home circumstances have been assessed can such criteria be justified in determining the suitability of a referral, the degree of risk, and the urgency of the response.

1.54 Local government in this country should be at the forefront of organisations serving the public. Sadly, little I heard persuades me that this is so. Many of the procedures that I heard about seemed to me to be self-serving – supporting the needs of the organisation, rather than the public they are set up to serve.

Preparing and implementing a care plan

The third and final stage is referred to as the care-planning stage. The local authority is required to construct a care plan that (among other things) describes the services that will be provided in order to meet the child's identified needs. For example, an assessment may identify that the child needs adaptations to the house in order that he or she can access the bathroom, that the child needs regular home-help support at feeding times, and that the child's parents need to have regular respite periods in order to be able to sustain their caring roles. The care plan should specify how these identified needs are going to be met. In relation to some needs, it may not be possible to state immediately how they will be met (for instance, the adaptations), and in this case the care plan should specify the steps that the local authority will take to ensure that the needs are met within a reasonable time. In general, care plans of this type should specify (among other things):[7]

- A description of the level and frequency of the help that is to be provided, stating which agency is responsible for what service.[8]

- The objectives of providing help and anticipated outcomes for the disabled child and carers.

- Details of what the carers are willing to do, and related needs and support.

- The name of the person coordinating the care plan and their contact number.

- A contact number or office in case of emergencies, and a contingency plan if things go wrong.

- Monitoring arrangements and a date for review.

The policy guidance, the *Framework for the Assessment of Children in Need and their Families*,[9] makes the following comment concerning care plans at Para. 4.37:

It is essential that the plan is constructed on the basis of the findings from the assessment and that this plan is reviewed and refined over time to ensure the agreed case objectives are achieved. Specific outcomes for the child, expressed in terms of their health and development, can be measured. These provide objective evidence against which to evaluate whether the child and family have been provided with appropriate services and ultimately whether the child's well-being is optimal.

Although the Children Act 1989 guidance concerning care plans is concerned primarily with children who are looked after (see p.224) or at risk of being taken into care, it provides useful general advice concerning 'areas in which clarity is required in child care planning' at Para. 4.36. In relation to disabled children in general (i.e. those who are not in contact with the local authority due to child-protection concerns), there is no definitive list of issues and questions that must be addressed in a care plan. Comments made by Sedley J (as he then was) in R v. *Islington LBC ex p. Rixon* [1996][10] are, however, useful in this context, even though the case involved an adult disabled person. The judge accepted the local authority's submission that 'nowhere in the legislation is a care plan, by that or any other name required', and that 'a care plan is nothing more than a clerical record of what has been decided and what is planned'. In his view, however, this state of affairs:

> far from marginalising the care plan, places it at the centre of any scrutiny of the local authority's due discharge of its functions… A care plan is the means by which the local authority assembles the relevant information and applies it to the statutory ends, and hence affords good evidence to any inquirer of the due discharge of its statutory duties.

Assessments are about outcomes – about producing a service designed to meet the disabled person's needs rather than trying to force him or her into an existing service. This aim is expressed in the following terms by guidance concerning community care assessments:[11]

> It is easy to slip out of thinking 'what does this person need?' into 'what have we got that he/she could have?' The focus on need is most clearly achieved where practitioners responsible for assessment do not also carry responsibility for the delivery or management of services arising from that assessment (at para 22 of the guide's summary).[12]

As noted, once a local authority has decided that a particular social care need has to be met, then it is obliged to provide services to this end and to specify these services in the disabled child's care plan. Frequently, a local authority will have various options as to how it meets a particular need. For instance, a need for constant supervision may be addressed by 24-hour support in the home or placement in a residential care home. A need to keep clean could be addressed by the provision of an accessible shower or bath or a regular visit by a nurse to provide a flannel wash. A need to have an accessible toilet could be addressed by the construction of a downstairs toilet or the provision of a commode. All things being equal, the local authority can take into account the cost of the various options in deciding which it will choose. However, this general principle is subject to three overriding constraints, as we explain below.

Assessed needs must be met

The chosen service must meet the disabled person's needs. This principle is illustrated by the facts of the case *R* v. *Sutton LBC ex p. Tucker* [1996][13] which concerned a rubella-impaired applicant. The applicant was blind and deaf, had learning difficulties and had been in short-term NHS accommodation for over two years awaiting a decision from the authority as to her long-term placement. All agreed that this would need to be in a small residential unit shared with one or two other residents with similar impairments. The local authority favoured a home in Birmingham run by the specialist charity SENSE, but the applicant's family, clinicians and indeed the SENSE staff considered that this would not be viable, since she needed to be close to her family in London. No such facility existed in Richmond, and the local authority baulked at the cost of commissioning a purpose-created unit solely for the applicant. The net result was that nothing concrete happened and the applicant remained inappropriately placed in short-term NHS accommodation.

In the judicial review proceedings, the local authority sought to explain its inaction by reference to the family's unreasonable refusal of a care option – namely, the placement in Birmingham. The court disagreed. This was not a situation where there was a choice of care plans; indeed, this was a case where there was no care plan at all. The court considered that the local authority's preference for the Birmingham placement was untenable. The only option was a local placement. Since there was no choice of care plan, the issue of resources was not relevant and Richmond London Borough Council had to prepare a plan to this effect.

The duty to avoid institutionalisation

A primary purpose underlying the assessment process is to promote independent living. Thus, where two alternative care packages involve a choice between institutionalisation and independent living, the decision should always come down in favour of independent living, unless the local authority concludes for sound professional reasons (i.e. not merely financial) that independent living is not a viable option.[14]

The issue of dignity

Certain services, although functional from a basic perspective, are objectively demeaning. The use of a commode may be a necessity in the short term, but in the medium term it is undignified, particularly when other viable options exist. Likewise, a flannel wash may have a certain biological functionality, but again it is demeaning. The courts and the ombudsman have sought to develop the concept of 'dignity' when seeking to explain the inadequacies of such service responses.

In *R (A, B, X and Y)* v. *East Sussex CC and the Disability Rights Commission (No 2)* [2003][15] it was held that:

The recognition and protection of human dignity is one of the core values – in truth the core value – of our society and, indeed, of all the societies which are part of the European family of nations and which have embraced the principles of the [European Convention on Human Rights].

Baroness Hale of Richmond[16] made much the same point, when she observed that:

human dignity is all the more important for people whose freedom of action and choice is curtailed, whether by law or by circumstances such as disability. The Convention is a living instrument... We need to be able to use it to promote respect for the inherent dignity of all human beings but especially those who are most vulnerable to having that dignity ignored. In reality, the niceties and technicalities with which we have to be involved in the courts should be less important than the core values which underpin the whole Convention.

The local ombudsman has taken the same line in relation to the basic requirements of disabled people's services. She has held, for instance, that it is maladministration for a local authority to suggest that bathing is not an 'essential activity – unless there was an identified medical need'[17] and that 'the ability to properly manage bathing/washing with dignity is the entitlement of everybody'.[18]

Although the most common outcome of an assessment is the provision of services by the local authority, this need not be the case. Parents of disabled children, and disabled people themselves if they are aged 16 years or over, have the right to have direct payments in lieu of services, i.e. the cash equivalent of the service. They must, however, use the money so provided to purchase services to meet the needs identified by the local authority. Direct payments are considered below.

Services for disabled children
Services under Section 17 of the Children Act 1989

As we note on p.77, once the needs of a disabled child have been identified, then Section 17 of the Children Act 1989 specifies that the social services department must ensure that a range of support services are available in order to safeguard and promote the child's welfare. The basic aim of such services is 'to promote the upbringing of such children by their families'.

The services that can be provided under the Children Act in respect of the needs of a disabled child are almost unlimited, including, by Section 17A,[19] direct payments (i.e. cash) in lieu of services.

Schedule 2, Part I of the 1989 Act deals further with the provision of services for children in need. It gives an illustration of the types of service that may be provided, but it is clear that this list is not exhaustive. The list comprises:

- advice, guidance and counselling
- occupational, social, cultural or recreational activities

- home help (which may include laundry facilities)
- facilities for, or assistance with, travelling to and from home for the purpose of taking advantage of any other service provided under this Act or of any similar service
- assistance to enable the child concerned and his or her family to have a holiday.

The guidance to the Children Act (Para. 2.11, Vol. 2, Family Support) summarises the breadth of powers available to social services authorities in such cases:

> This general duty is supported by other specific duties and powers such as the facilitation of 'the provision by others, including in particular voluntary organisations of services' (section 17(5) and Schedule 2). These provisions encourage SSDs to provide day and domiciliary services, guidance and counselling, respite care and a range of other services as a means of supporting children in need (including children with disabilities) within their families. The Act recognises that sometimes a child can only be helped by providing services for other members of his families (section 17(3)) 'if it [the service] is provided with a view to safeguarding or promoting the child's welfare'... The SSD may make such arrangements as they see fit for any person to provide services and support 'may include giving assistance in kind, or in exceptional circumstances in cash' (section 17(6)). However, where it is the SSD's view that a child's welfare is adequately provided for and no unmet need exists, they need not act.

The duties owed to disabled children are underwritten by a requirement (in Para. 6 of Part 1 of Schedule 2 to the Act) that authorities provide services designed to minimise the effect on disabled children within their area of their disabilities and to give such children the opportunity to lead lives that are as normal as possible.

Services under Section 2 of the Chronically Sick and Disabled Persons Act 1970

Disabled children are entitled to receive services under Section 2 of the Chronically Sick and Disabled Persons Act 1970 (see p.77) as well as under Section 17 of the 1989 Act. The interplay between these two provisions is of some complexity, but in practical terms if the child needs a service that could be provided under the 1989 or the 1970 Act, then as a matter of law it must be provided under the 1970 Act.[20] Although this question may appear solely of interest to students of jurisprudence, it is not an entirely academic question, since the duty under the 1970 Act is considered by the courts to be more enforceable than that under the 1989 Act.[21]

Once a local authority has carried out an assessment of the needs of a disabled child and decided that the provision of services under Section 2 is necessary in order to meet the child's needs, then the authority is under an absolute duty to provide these services. The services that can be provided under Section 2 are described below.

Practical assistance in the home

This includes services concerned primarily with the maintenance of the home (e.g. house cleaning, ironing, decorating, etc.) and those concerned with the personal care of the disabled person (e.g. help with getting out of and into bed, dressing, cooking, laundry, etc.).[22] Although a rigid policy of not providing the former services under Section 2 would be unlawful,[23] it is the case that personal care generally will be of higher priority in any system of eligibility criteria.

A sitting service, i.e. where a person 'sits' with the disabled child and thereby allows his or her usual carers to have a break, is a service under this heading. It is often referred to as 'respite care' and is considered further below.

Provision of radio, television, library, etc.

The service described consists of the social services authority providing, or helping with the acquisition of, equipment to satisfy a recreational need. Such equipment could include a personal computer, a hi-fi system, etc. However, in general, social services would not provide such equipment unless it was satisfied that it was necessary in order to meet a social care need.

Provision of recreational/educational facilities

This covers two separate services:

- Recreational facilities: included within this provision are traditional day centres as well as such recreational activities as outings and so on.

- Educational facilities: the educational service required in this case may be either home-based or otherwise and may include funding of the personal care requirements of students so as to enable them to pursue their studies, even if those studies are undertaken outside the local authority's area.[24]

Travel and other assistance

This will cover the provision of travel to and from a day centre or other recreational activity.

Home adaptations/disabled facilities

Social services departments are obliged to provide assistance to enable necessary adaptations to be carried out in the disabled child's home and to provide any 'additional facilities designed to secure his greater safety, comfort or convenience'. Grant assistance known as disabled facilities grants may also be available to cover the cost of significant home adaptations; this is considered on p.271.

Adaptations

Home adaptations may concern such matters as stair lifts, ground-floor extensions, doorway widening, ramps, wheelchair-accessible showers, and so on. Where such work is required, the local authority will arrange for a detailed assessment to be carried out, often by an occupational therapist. The test is whether the works are necessary in order to meet the needs of the disabled child by securing his or her greater safety, comfort or convenience. If the work is needed, then an application can be made for grant assistance by way of a disabled facilities grant.

Additional facilities

Social services departments are obliged to provide disabled children with those 'additional facilities' that are needed in order to secure the child's greater safety, comfort or convenience. This includes all manner of fittings and gadgets such as handrails, alarm systems, hoists, movable baths, adapted switches and handles, and so on. Guidance25 on the nature of this duty states:

> equipment which can be installed and removed with little or no structural modification to the dwelling should usually be considered the responsibility of the [social services] authority. However, items such as stair lifts and through-floor lifts, which are designed to facilitate access into or around the dwelling, would, in the view of the Secretaries of State, be eligible for disabled facilities grant. With items such as electric hoists, it is suggested that any structural modification of the property – such as strengthened joists or modified lintels – could be grant aidable under the disabled facilities grant, but that the hoisting equipment itself should be the responsibility of the [social services] authority. [Social services] authorities can, under s17 of the HASSASSA Act, charge for the provision of equipment. If the [social services] authority choose to make only a revenue charge (for example to cover maintenance), or not to charge at all, they would retain ownership of the equipment, and be able if they so wished to re-use it in another property if no longer required by the original recipient. [Social services] authorities are encouraged to make maximum use of their opportunities to recover and re-use equipment such as stair lifts, and to foster local arrangements for direct provision of such equipment where this can be done effectively and economically.

Holidays

The 1970 Act requires local authorities to assist disabled children to take holidays, if the authority considers this necessary. This duty is in addition to the power enjoyed by social services departments under the Children Act (noted above), although strictly speaking the duty under the 1970 Act extends only to the disabled child and any carer essential to enable the holiday to take place,[26] whereas under the Children Act the local authority power enables a holiday to be provided for the whole family.

Meals

The duty under the 1970 Act to provide disabled children with meals (when considered necessary by the social services department) covers the provision of meals within their own homes as well as at day centres, etc.

Telephone and ancilliary equipment

Although reference in the Act to the provision of a telephone and other ancilliary equipment may in general be of more relevance to the needs of disabled adults, the duty extends to other equipment such as amplifiers/inductive couples for personal hearing aids and visual transmission machines such as minicoms, faxes and modems for email transmission.

Laundry assistance under Schedule 8 of the NHS Act 1977

Schedule 8 of the 1977 Act enables social services authorities to provide a laundry service for households where such help is required owing to the presence of (among others) a person who is 'handicapped as a result of having suffered from illness or by congenital deformity'.

There is an overlap here with the power of the health services (in limited situations) to provide laundry assistance.

Direct payments

Section 17A of the Children Act 1989[27] enables social services departments to provide to the parents or others with parental responsibility of disabled children, or disabled children aged 16 years or over, direct payments instead of providing the social care services that the child has been assessed as needing. In simple terms, a direct payment is the cash equivalent of the service that the local authority would have provided.

In general, social services are compelled to make direct payments instead of providing services, the key provisions being as follows:

- *Direct payments must relate to the social services assessment*: a direct payment can be made only once an assessment has been completed, and the direct payment monies must be used to purchase services to meet the social care needs identified in the assessment as 'needing to be met'.

- *The ability of the direct payment recipient to 'manage'*: the recipient of the direct payment (i.e. the disabled person if aged 16 years or over or a person with parental responsibility for the disabled child) must be capable of managing the direct payment monies 'alone or with assistance'. This means that he or she must have sufficient mental capacity to handle the monies responsibly, even if relying heavily on the advice and support of another.

- *Prohibited services*: direct payments cannot be used to purchase services provided by the local authority or for lengthy periods of residential care home accommodation, although they can be used for regular periods of residential respite care. Direct payments cannot be used to pay for services provided by a family member if that family member lives in the same household as the disabled person, unless the local authority agrees to such an arrangement.

- *The amount of the payment*: a direct payment must be enough to purchase services to meet the disabled person's assessed needs. In general, it should be no more expensive than the amount the local authority would pay if it had to provide the service itself. If it is felt that the amount awarded is insufficient, then the procedure for challenging this is via the complaints procedures (see p.241).

- *The obligations upon the recipient of direct payments*: the recipient of a direct payment must keep sufficient records in order to satisfy the local authority that the money has been spent on purchasing services to meet his or her assessed needs.

Details on all these matters are provided in guidance issued both in England[28] and Wales.[29]

Respite/short-break care

Respite or short-break care is, as we have noted, a highly valued service by carers and, where the service provides appropriate stimulation and support, by disabled children (see p.63).

We have considered the obligations of the NHS to provide such a service (see p.126), but the duty will more commonly be that of the social services department.

In order to obtain the support of social services for such a service, there must first be an assessment that concludes that respite care should be provided as part of the care plan. If the assessment fails to determine that respite care is required, or if there is a dispute as to the amount or quality of that care, then the assessment should be challenged through the complaints process (see p.241).

As we have noted (p.257), once the local authority has assessed the service as being required, it must make it available and cannot use financial resource constraints as a reason for not providing the service. If it seeks to use this reason, then again the complaints process should be invoked.

Even if the local authority constraint concerns the lack of suitable facilities rather than financial resources, that alone is not a satisfactory reason for failing to provide the care. In such cases, the local authority must make urgent and determined efforts to find a suitable provider. This may involve searching outside its area, discussing with voluntary and private sector providers the possibility of creating a purpose-made service, the local authority itself (possibly in conjunction with the health authority or primary care trust) providing the service via a new in-house initiative, or the use of direct payments (see above). In short, the local authority must take the matter seriously and, by purposively pursuing a systematic search, demonstrate that the assessed need will be met as soon as is reasonably practicable.

A 2002 local government ombudsman's complaint[30] gives a clear indication of what the law requires in this respect. It concerned the care plan of a young adult with multiple and profound mental and physical disabilities. In 1994, her needs were assessed and provision was made for her to have one weekend per month respite care in a residential unit, paid for by the local authority but provided by a charitable organisation. In 2000, the family was notified that owing to funding problems, the unit was to close at weekends. Although the council had no record of its assessment, it argued that the need was for three days' respite care a week, not necessarily at weekends. The family made a formal complaint, arguing that weekend respite was essential, as it gave them a substantial break – as during the week, their daughter was at a residential special school.

The complaints panel noted that the 1994 assessment was 'not as sophisticated as current assessments' but concluded that since it did not specify an entitlement to weekend respite there was no obligation to provide this. The ombudsman found it 'astonishing that the Council acknowledges managing…regular periods of respite care for six years with neither a proper assessment nor a care plan'. However, having regard to the records of the service provider and the history of weekend service provision, the ombudsman was satisfied that weekend respite had been agreed. She then stated:

> The Council says that because it was not responsible for the closure of [the respite facility] it cannot be held responsible for the withdrawal of [the complainant's] provision. I do not accept this. It is the Council, not [the charitable provider], which has statutory responsibility for providing for [the complainant's] needs. If [the respite facility] could not, for whatever reason, meet those needs, the Council had a duty to find, in the locality, somewhere else where [the complainant] would feel equally settled and in which her parents would have confidence.

The ombudsman reached the same conclusion in a complaint concerning adult respite care arrangements that broke down because of problems with the centre providing the care (which included an allegation of abuse during a respite period). The ombudsman noted:[31]

> I understand why the Council found it difficult to identify alternative opportunities for respite care. And I appreciate the fact that the solution proposed [by the parents] requires resources that the department did not necessarily have. But there is case law to say that a want of resources in a particular budget does not excuse the council from carrying out its statutory duty.

Vouchers for respite care

Sections 3 and 7 of the Carers and Disabled Children Act 2000 provide for social services to run short-term break voucher schemes. In essence, the local authority, having assessed a need for periods of respite care, gives the disabled person or the carer, if the disabled person is a child or lacks sufficient mental capacity, a voucher or series of vouchers. These can then be used to pay for a specified period of respite, which the service provider then redeems for cash from the local authority. Voucher schemes are designed to offer flexibility in the timing of carers' breaks and choice in the way services are delivered to disabled people while their usual carer is taking a break.

Regulations[32] have been made (in England but not, as yet, in Wales) that describe in detail the way local authority voucher schemes should operate. Further details of the scope of the scheme can be found at www.acecarers.org.uk.

Social services' responsibilities towards carers

Since 1995, three major Acts have addressed the specific needs of carers. The Carers (Recognition and Services) Act 1995 contains the core statutory responsibilities and introduced the concept of a carer's assessment. The Carers and Disabled Children Act 2000 extended the rights of carers to include the right to support services and for these services to be made available by way of direct payments and vouchers (see above). The Carers (Equal Opportunities) Act 2004 extended the obligations in relation to assessments. It introduced a statutory obligation on social services to inform carers of their rights and requires carer's assessments to consider whether the carer works or wishes to work and/or is undertaking, or wishes to undertake, education, training or any leisure activity.

The Carers (Recognition and Services) Act 1995

The 1995 Act provides recognition for carers by requiring the social services department, if so requested, to carry out a separate assessment of the carer when it is assessing the disabled child's needs. The carer can be of any age (i.e. adult or child) and there may be more than one carer in any particular household.

In order to qualify for such an assessment, the carer must be providing or intending to provide a substantial amount of care on a regular basis.[33] The guidance accepts that the Act essentially entitles all parents of disabled children to a Carers Act assessment when their child is also being assessed,[34] since they all provide substantial and regular care. This will also be the case, in general, even if the disabled child is living away from home, provided the parents have regular contact, since that contact will be of substantial importance to the child and be 'regular'.[35] Separate guidance has in any event indicated that the word 'substantial' should be given a wide interpretation that fully takes into account individual circumstances.[36]

All such 'regular and substantial' carers, including sibling carers, are entitled to such an assessment, provided they make a formal request. The guidance, however, requires social workers to 'inform any carer who appears eligible under this Act of their right to request an assessment'.[37]

The Act entitles qualifying carers to an assessment of their ability to provide and continue to provide care. A typical example might be an assessment that disclosed that the child's parent still had to manually carry the disabled child when moving him or her around the home. Because the child had grown, this was now posing a risk of back strain on the parent, which would impair the 'ability to continue to provide care' (see pp.69 and 162). Likewise, if a non-disabled sibling was going through a difficult period, this might result in the parent being 'unable to provide care'.

If, as a consequence of such an assessment, it transpires that the carer is no longer able (or willing[38]) to provide the same level of care, then the authority will have to decide whether to change the service user's care plan by increasing the services provided by another agency or agencies in order to compensate.

The Carers and Disabled Children Act 2000

The 2000 Act added to the rights enjoyed by carers by (among other things) making available the possibility of direct payments for children's services and vouchers for respite care (both considered above). The other changes introduced by the 2000 Act are mostly directed at assisting carers of disabled people aged 16 years or over, by entitling them to:

- an assessment, even if the disabled person for whom they care refuses to have an assessment carried out on their own care needs
- receive directly from social services any service that helps them care for the disabled person.

Support of this nature has always been available to carers of children below the age of 16 years, since by virtue of Section 17(3) of the Children Act 1989 carers have always been entitled to support services if this assistance thereby promoted and safeguarded the well-being of the disabled child.

The Carers (Equal Opportunities) Act 2004

As noted above, the 2004 Act extended the rights of carers to include the right to have their employment, education, training and leisure wishes considered. Before the enactment of this Act, it was suggested incorrectly by a few local authorities that a separate carer's assessment for a parent carer was unnecessary, since a holistic assessment under the Children Act 1989 would address their needs fully.[39] With the enactment of the 2004 Act, this view is no longer tenable.

Parent carers, like all other qualifying carers, now have the right to have their employment, training, education and leisure aspirations addressed. This is of considerable value, since previously some authorities have been resistant to the idea of providing services that would enable a parent carer to return to work or maintain employment. In any carer's assessment, reliance can be placed on the government view that all 'carers who wish to work to have the right to work' (see Para. 4.43 above). The English practice guidance to the 2000 Act identified the importance of providing such assistance, stating at Para. 36:

> People with parental responsibility for disabled children will also benefit from joining or re-joining the workforce. Such carers often face difficulties re-entering the workforce because of lack of suitable child-care services. Many parents of disabled children would like to return to work and, if they were able to do so, would benefit socially and emotionally as well as financially.

The problems that parent carers experience in relation to maintaining employment are considerable and are not only due to the substantial demands often made by a disabled child over and above those made by a non-disabled child. The additional problem concerns the shortage of childcare facilities able to care for disabled children. For example, many working parents can benefit from the existence of after-school clubs to provide childcare, but these clubs may not be able or be prepared to care for disabled children with challenging or specialist needs.

Young carers

The Carers (Recognition and Services) Act 1995 applies to all carers, irrespective of their age. Carers who are under the age of 18 years generally are referred to as 'young carers'. They are eligible, in addition to the benefits detailed above, to services in their own right.

There is no legislation that refers specifically to young carers. Guidance concerning young carers has, however, been issued by the Social Services Inspectorate (CI(95)12). The guidance adopts a definition of a 'young carer' as 'a child or young person who is carrying out significant caring tasks and assuming a level of responsibility for another person, which would usually be taken by an adult'. Such duties as are owed to young carers by a social services authority are contained primarily in the Children Act 1989 and in the guidance issued by the Department of Health (Vol. 2, *Family Support*, and Vol. 6, *Children with Disabilities*).

As we have noted (see p.74), Section 17(1) of the Children Act 1989 places a general duty on social services authorities to safeguard and promote the welfare of children within their area who are in need and empowers authorities to provide almost unlimited services towards this goal.

In relation to young carers, one is not in general concerned with disabled children, and accordingly it is necessary to establish that the child comes within category (a) or (b). Because of the prevalent resource shortages within social services authorities, the criteria for obtaining services or funding under Section 17 have become increasingly severe. In a number of authorities, the position was reached that they were only considering a non-disabled child to be in need if his or her name was on the child protection register. Such a high threshold for accessing services effectively ruled young carers out; the fear of social services' child protection powers being a major reason why many young carers and their families avoid making contact with such authorities.[40]

In order to improve the help available to young carers, it was necessary for such restrictive definitions of 'in need' to be curtailed. The has been achieved by the Social Services Inspectorate issuing specific guidance on young carers as a Chief Inspector's 'guidance letter' on 28 April 1995. Annex A at Para. 1.1 refers to (among other things) research that it states:

> has demonstrated that many young people carry out a level of caring responsibilities which prevents them from enjoying normal social opportunities and from achieving full school attendance. Many young carers with significant caring responsibilities should therefore be seen as children in need.

The key issue, therefore, is whether the young carer's caring responsibilities are 'significant'. In this respect, the practice guidance LAC (96)7 points out at Para. 15.2 that young carers should not be expected to carry out 'inappropriate' (i.e. age-inappropriate) levels of caring.

If the young carer's caring responsibilities are significant, then he or she will be eligible for an assessment and, possibly, services under the Children Act 1989. The young carer will, in addition, almost certainly be entitled to a carer's assessment if the care provided is 'regular and substantial'. Obviously, in such cases, only one combined assessment will be carried out, although inevitably there will be policy and practice differences as to whether it is a children's team or an adult care social worker who actually does the assessment.

The Children Act 1989 assessment procedures and service provision arrangements for young carers are the same as for any other child and are detailed above. Section 17(1)(b) emphasises that a principal purpose for the provision of services to children in need is to promote the upbringing of such children by their families.

The power of social services departments to charge for services

Children's social services are empowered to charge for the services they provide under the Children Act 1989.

Charging for non-accommodation services under the Children Act

Section 29(1) deals with charging for non-accommodation services and empowers the authority to recover 'such charge as they consider appropriate'. This is subject to the following restrictions:

- No person can be charged while in receipt of income support or of any element of child tax credit (other than the family element) or working tax credit or of an income-based jobseeker's allowance (Section 29(3)).

- Where the authority is satisfied that a person's means are insufficient for it to be reasonably practicable for him or her to pay the charge, the authority cannot require him or her to pay more than he or she can reasonably be expected to pay (Section 29(2)).

Section 29(4) specifies who can be charged, namely the parents, unless the young person is aged 16 years or older, in which case the child can be charged.[42]

Authorities are empowered to recover outstanding charges 'summarily as a civil debt'.[43] Where a service is assessed as being required, the authority must provide it, even if the liable person refuses to pay the assessed charge.

Charging for accommodation services under the Children Act

Schedule 2, Part III Children Act 1989 empowers but does not oblige local authorities to charge for the cost of accommodating children. The rules are the same as for non-accommodation services, except in addition:

- the local authority cannot charge a sum greater than it would normally be prepared to pay if it had placed a similar child with local authority foster parents

- provision is made for the local authority to serve what is known as a 'contribution notice', which it is able to enforce through the Magistrates Court if necessary; the latter can also arbitrate on any dispute as to the reasonableness of such a notice.

Notes

1 [2003] UKHL 57, [2003] 3 WLR 1194. Lord Scott (also part of the majority) was of the opinion that at the very least it was 'implicit in this provision that the local authority will assess the actual needs of a child in need whenever it appears necessary to do so' (Para. 117).

2 The duty to undertake an assessment under s.47(1) NHS and Community Care Act 1990 arises when it appears that a person may be entitled to support under various statutory provisions, one being Para. 3 of Schedule 8 NHS Act 1977, which provides for support to disabled people, regardless of age (i.e. includes disabled children).

3 Para. 3 of Schedule 2.

4   The Children Act 1989: Guidance and Regulations, Vol. 6, *Children with Disabilities*. London: HMSO, Para. 6.4.

5   The Children Act 1989: Guidance and Regulations, Vol. 6, *Children with Disabilities*. London: HMSO, Para. 5.7.

6   Lord Laming (2003) *The Victoria Climbié Inquiry: Report of an Inquiry*. CM 5730. London: The Stationery Office.

7   Extracted, with necessary changes, somewhat incongruously from HSC 2002/001 and LAC (2002)1. Guidance on the Single Assessment Process for Older People. January 2002 Annex E pp.24–25. In Wales, broadly similar wording is adopted in the UFSAMC 2002 Policy Guidance, Para. 2.44.

8   The local ombudsman has held that care plans should specify the frequency of services – for instance, of respite care. Complaint 03/C/16371 against Stockton-on-Tees Borough Council 18 January 2005.

9   In England as (2000), London: The Stationery Office; accessible at www.doh.gov.uk/scg/cin.htm. In Wales as (2001), London: The Stationery Office.

10   1 CCLR 119, p.128.

11   Para. 3.1 *Care Management and Assessment: A Practitioners' Guide* (London: HMSO, 1991). Although this is guidance concerning the care plans for disabled adults, it must hold equally true for disabled children's services.

12   In *R v. Islington LBC ex p. Rixon* [1996] *The Times* 17 April; 1 CCLR 119 Sedley J put it thus: 'The practice guidance...counsels against trimming the assessment of need to fit the available provision.'

13   [1998] 1 CCLR 251.

14   *R v. Southwark LBC ex p. Khana and Karim* [2001] 4 CCLR 267 (CA).

15   [2003] EWHC 167 (Admin), [2003] 6 CCLR 194, at Para. 86.

16   Paul Sieghart Memorial Lecture 2004: What Can the Human Rights Act Do for my Mental Health? Accessible at www.bihr.org/transcript_hale.doc. In making these observations, Baroness Hale placed significant reliance on Watson, J. (2002) *Something for Everyone: The Impact of the Human Rights Act and the Need for a Human Rights Commission*. London: British Institute of Human Rights.

17   Complaint 02/A/11294 against Wycombe District Council 20 October 2004.

18   Complaint 02/C/8679, 8681 and 10389 against Bolsover District Council 30 September 2003.

19   Inserted by s.7 Carers and Disabled Children Act 2000.

20   *R v. Bexley LBC ex p. B* [1995] 3 CCLR 15.

21   R (G) v. Barnet LBC and others [2003] UKHL 57, [2003] 3 WLR 1194.

22   Disabled children are also entitled to such services under Para. 3 of Schedule 8 NHS Act 1977, which requires/enables social services departments to provide 'on such a scale as is adequate for the needs of their area...home help for households where such help is required owing to the presence of a person who is suffering from illness, lying-in,...handicapped as a result of having suffered from illness or by congenital deformity' and 'the provisions of laundry facilities'. If the need is health-related, then laundry services can also be provided by the NHS.

23   The ombudsman has held that it is maladministration for a council to have criteria that stipulate that no domestic assistance can be provided unless accompanied by a need for personal care. Complaint 01/C/17519 against Salford CC 11 December 2003.

24   Circular LAC(93)12.

25   Para. 19 circular LAC(90)7.

26   *R v. North Yorkshire County Council ex p. Hargreaves (No 2)* 1 CCLR 331.

27   Inserted by s.5 of the Carers and Disabled Children Act 2000.

28   Direct Payments Guidance: Community Care, Services for Carers and Children's Services (Direct Payments) Guidance England 2003; accessible at www.dh.gov.uk/assetRoot/04/06/92/62/04069262.pdf.

29   Direct Payments Guidance: Community Care, Services for Carers and Children's Services (Direct Payments) Guidance Wales 2004; accessible at www.wales.nhs.uk/documents/direct-payment-policy-e-merge.pdf.

30 Complaint 01/C/03521 against North Yorkshire 19 August 2002.

31 Complaints against Bedfordshire County Council 02/B/16654 16 October 2003.

32 The Carers and Disabled Children (Vouchers) (England) Regulations 2003 SI no. 1216.

33 People who provide the care as a result of a contract of employment or as a volunteer placed by a voluntary organisation are excluded.

34 See Para. 18.1, Carers (Recognition and Services) Act 1995 Practice Guidance.

35 'Regular' should be distinguished from 'frequent' – the former connotes an event that recurs or is repeated at fixed times or at uniform intervals.

36 LAC (93)10 Appendix 4, Para. 8.

37 LAC (96)7 Para. 20.

38 Para. 9.8 of the practice guidance accompanying the Act states that social workers should not 'assume a willingness by the carer to continue, or continue to provide the same level of support'.

39 Para. 10, A Practitioner's Guide to Carers Assessments under the Carers and Disabled Children Act 2000.

40 Para. 17, Practice Guidance to Carers Act LAC (96)7.

41 Unless the service is being provided for a member of the child's family, in which case it is that family member who is charged.

42 S.29(5) Children Act 1989.

Disabled Facilities
Grants Materials

Disabled facilities grants (DFGs) are grants paid towards the cost of building works that are necessary in order to meet the needs of a disabled occupant. The housing authority is responsible for the administration and payment of the grant, although the original application may be instigated and referred to it by a social services authority after a community care assessment. The maximum mandatory grant is currently £25,000 in England[1] and £30,000 in Wales,[2] although local authorities have the discretion to make higher awards.[3] The grant is payable to disabled occupants who are either owner-occupiers or tenants (including housing association, council tenants and certain licensees).

The relevant statutory provision for disabled facilities grants is Part I of the Housing Grants, Construction and Regeneration Act 1996, upon which detailed guidance has been issued by the Office of the Deputy Prime Minister (ODPM) in England: *Delivering Housing Adaptations for Disabled People* (2004).

The housing authority is responsible for the administration of the disabled facilities grant, through all stages from initial enquiry (or referral by the social services authority) to post-completion approval. As part of this obligation, the housing authority must decide whether it is 'reasonable and practicable' to carry out the proposed adaptation works. It must also consult the social services authority in order to obtain its view as to whether the proposed works are 'necessary and appropriate'.

Mandatory grants

These apply to work that is aimed at:

- making the dwelling safe
- facilitating access and provision to:
    - the principal family room
    - a room used for sleeping (or providing such a room)
    - a room in which there is a lavatory, a bath or shower and a washbasin (or providing such a room)

- providing a room usable for sleeping
- providing a bathroom
- facilitating preparation and cooking of food
- providing heating, lighting and power.

Eligibility

All owner-occupiers, tenants (council, housing association and private) and licensees[4] are potentially eligible to apply for DFGs, as are landlords on behalf of disabled tenants.

Eligibility for a DFG (for an adult) is dependent upon satisfying a means test. The financial circumstances of only the disabled occupant[5] and his or her partner are assessed, not those of other members of the household. There is no longer a means test for adaptations for a disabled child.

Timescales

Under Section 34 of the 1996 Act, the housing authority must approve or refuse a grant application as soon as is reasonably practicable and in any event not more than six months after the date of application. It is, therefore, essential that the completed application is lodged with the housing authority at the earliest opportunity, as time runs from that date. The guidance stresses that 'local authorities should not use pre-application tests as a way of delaying applications or avoiding their statutory duty to process applications within 6 months'.

The ombudsman has criticised on numerous occasions the failure of councils to prioritise referrals to ensure that those in greatest need have their grant processed with expedition and the failure of district and county councils to have agreed protocols to ensure that the processing of DFG applications are not delayed by, for instance, avoiding the need to queue twice – once for the social services input and then again for the housing authority determination.[6]

Section 36 of the Act provides local authorities with a discretion to notify the grant applicant that payment of their mandatory DFG will not be made until a date not more than 12 months following the date of the application. The guidance states that this:

> should enable authorities to manage their resources better between financial years by prioritising cases. However, this power should be used only in exceptional circumstances and not where the applicant would suffer undue hardship. There is no expectation that the contractor would complete the work in advance of the date the grant has been scheduled for payment. The 12 month period for completion of grant assisted works is not affected although the date from which this runs will be the date in the notification of the authority's decision.

Given that there is a legal duty on councils to provide such adaptations, the ombudsman has made it clear that she 'does not accept that lack of resources is an acceptable reason for excessive delays in helping people whose need have been clearly assessed and accepted' and that she 'would generally regard any delay beyond six months as unjustified'.[7]

The guidance note on DFGs issued by the ODPM in 2004[8] provides a table at Para. 9.5 that constitutes a 'possible approach' that local authorities could adopt for each stage from the initial enquiry about services, which may or may not result in a DFG, to completion of adaptations work. The table (reproduced here as Table 1) assumes an average grant cost of £5000. For smaller cases, the time will be less; for complex cases with major building work, several extra weeks' work would be involved.

Table 1

Indicative time targets (working days)	Priority ranking in assessment		
	High	Medium	Low
Referral to allocation/response (including screening, prioritisation and preliminary test of resources form issued) (NB where complex needs are identified some time may elapse before the need for adaptation is clarified and the process proceeds)	2	2	2
Assessment carried out within	3	15	40
Recommendation and report prepared and forwarded	2	5	5
Notice to disabled person of recommendation and application form issued	2	2	2
Home visits to assist in completion of form, measure up and consult on proposals	5	15	30
Preparation of schedule and drawings	10	20	30
Second home visit to confirm proposals	5	15	30
Issue specification to contractors, concurrently seek confirmation of title, etc.	3	5	5
Await return of tenders; concurrently seek completion of full test of resources	30	30	30
Evaluate tenders, calculate and check DFG, issue confirmation of DFG	3	5	5
Date to start not exceeding	10	30	60

Table 1 cont.

Indicative time targets (working days)	Priority ranking in assessment		
	High	*Medium*	*Low*
Time on site will depend upon the size and complexity of works but allow 5 days per £5000 value for general building work, less when value includes major items of equipment such as stair lifts: for average DFG of £5000	5	5	5
Inspection on completion	1	2	5
Secure guarantees and documentation, advise on repair and maintenance, consult disabled person on satisfaction, consider any remaining needs	2	5	10
Total	**83**	**151**	**259**

Notes

1   The Disabled Facilities Grants and Home Repair Assistance (Maximum Amounts) (Amendment no. 2) (England) Order 2001 SI 2001 no. 4036.

2   The Disabled Facilities Grants and Home Repair Assistance (Maximum Amounts) (Amendment) (Wales) Order 2002 WSI 2002 no. 837 (W.99).

3   The Disabled Facilities Grants and Home Repair Assistance (Maximum Amounts) Order 1996.

4   S.19(5) extends eligibility for a disabled facilities grant to a range of licensees, e.g. secure or introductory tenants who are licensees, agricultural workers, and service employees such as publicans.

5   The disabled occupant may or may not be the applicant.

6   See, for instance, complaint 02/C/04897 against Morpeth BC and Northumberland CC 27 November 2003.

7   Complaint 02/C/8679, 8681 and 10389 against Bolsover District Council 30 September 2003.

8   ODPM (November 2004) *Delivering Housing Adaptations for Disabled People*, accessible at www.odpm.gov.uk/index.asp?id=1152864

Precedent Letters

Letter 1: Requesting the initial involvement of social services

Ms Jane Smith
Flat 11, Any Street
Anytown AnyShire AE15 7LB
Tel: 01234 56789

Director of Children's Services
Disabled Children's Section
Anyshire Council
Council Offices Shire
Street Anytown AE1 0BU

1 February 2006

Dear Director of Children's Services

Request for assistance: register of children with disabilities
Richard Smith born 30 October 2004

I would be most grateful if a social worker could contact me at the earliest opportunity in relation to the care needs of my above named son.

Richard was born on 30 October last year and has been diagnosed as having cerebral palsy.

I have not as yet had any formal contact with a social worker from your authority and understand that you are able to provide assistance in relation to a number of matters and particularly concerning:

1.   the entry of Richard's name on your register of children with disabilities

2.   the assessment of Richard's needs for care services and of myself under the Carers Act 1995 and the Carers and Disabled Children Act 2000

3.   the provision of practical help in coping with Richard's needs

4.   advice on what help I can expect from the other relevant agencies, details of voluntary groups in my area who I can also contact and also on the availability of social security benefits.

I am not presently working and am generally available most mornings (until about midday) on the above telephone number.

I look forward to hearing from you at the earliest opportunity.

Yours sincerely

Jane Smith

Letter 2: Expressing concern about failure of hospital discharge planning

Ms Jane Smith
Flat 11, Any Street
Anytown
AnyShire AE15 7LB
Tel: 01234 56789

The Senior Social Worker
Hospital Social Work Team
Shiretown General Hospital
Shire Street Anytown AE1 0BU

1 February 2006

Dear Senior Hospital Social Worker

Richard Smith born 30 October 2004
Expression of concern about failure of hospital discharge planning

I write to express my dissatisfaction with the arrangements that were made for Richard's discharge from Shiretown General Hospital. While this is not a formal complaint I do require from you a satisfactory response and an assurance that the continuing problems will be resolved and that there will be no re-occurrence of these difficulties.

I appreciate that some of my dissatisfaction arises because of the hospital's actions and I am accordingly writing to the trust manager in similar terms. However, since I understand that your authority and the trust have an obligation to 'work together', I require a full response from you as well as from the trust. The relevant facts are as follows: [here set out the facts, e.g.]

1.   Richard was born on 30 October last year and has been diagnosed as having cerebral palsy.

2.   He was admitted to the Peter Pan ward on 1 September 2005 for a prearranged heart operation and I accompanied him. He was discharged initially on 10 September but readmitted as an emergency on the 12th. His final discharge occurred on 20 September.

My dissatisfaction concerns the following matters:

1. At no stage did I receive any clear statement as to when Richard was likely to be discharged; indeed the likely time and date varied depending upon who I spoke to.

2. In my view Richard was prematurely discharged on 10 September; he had lost weight and was having difficulty feeding.

3. No arrangements were made for me to travel home with Richard on the 10th (or indeed on the 20th) despite my having no access to a car. Eventually my mother, who lives some distance away, had to arrange for a friend to drive me home, for which I paid a contribution to the petrol of £15.00 on each occasion.

4. On return home, I found that no liaison had occurred with the community nurse or my GP. The nurse left a message on my answerphone sometime before I arrived home on 10th September saying she hoped to drop in after the weekend.

5. I was left without any means of support and no one had explained to me what I should expect in the way of back-up and health/social care services.

6. On night of 12 September when Richard had not fed for 24 hours I contacted the GP out of hours who immediately arranged for Richard to be admitted as an emergency.

7. As a result of, etc.

I understand that this state of affairs is contrary to good practice and that Richard and I have a right to expect adequate health and social care support services and for the arrangements that are being made, to be properly co-ordinated and clearly explained to me. There has been a serious failure in relation to both the discharge planning and service provision arrangements for Richard and I therefore look forward to hearing from you as a matter of urgency.

Yours sincerely

Jane Smith

cc. Director of Children's Services
Anyshire Council

A 'mirror' letter (i.e. one in almost identical terms) is then sent to the senior hospital manager but it is copied to the Primary Care Trust (or Local Health Board in Wales).

Letter 3: Complaint to children's social services

Ms Jane Smith
Flat 11, Any Street,
Anytown,
AnyShire AE15 7LB
Tel: 01234 56789

Director of Children's Services
Disabled Children's Section
Anyshire Council
Council Offices
Shire Street
Anytown AE1 0BU

1 February 2006

Dear Director of Children's Services

Formal Complaint:
Richard Smith born 30 October 2004

I ask that you treat this letter as a formal complaint concerning the discharge by your authority of its functions in respect of myself and my son Richard Smith. I require the complaint to be investigated under the formal complaints process under the Children Act 1989 (as amended). My complaint is:

[Here set out as precisely as possible:

(a)   what it is that is being complained about

(b)   the names of the key social workers who the complaints investigator will need to speak to;

(c)   the dates of the relevant acts/omissions;

If possible also enclose copies of any relevant papers.]

What I want to achieve by making this complaint is [here set out as precisely as possible what you want to be the result of your complaint: i.e. an apology, a changed service provision, an alteration to practice, compensation, etc.].

I understand that your complaints receiving officer will wish to contact me in order to investigate this complaint. I suggest that this be done by [here give a telephone contact number and the time/days you are normally available or some other convenient way you can be contacted].

Yours sincerely

Jane Smith

cc. Anyshire Council Chairperson
Children's Services Committee

Letter 4: Expressing concern about the failure of the NHS to provide adequate speech or language therapy assistance

Ms Jane Smith
Flat 11, Any Street,
Anytown,
AnyShire AE15 7LB
Tel: 01234 56789

The Manager
Shiretown Community NHS Trust
Shire Street
Anytown AE1 0B

1 February 2006

Dear NHS Community Trust Manager

Formal Complaint: Speech/Language Therapy
Richard Smith born 30 October 2002

I write concerning the failure by your trust to provide adequate speech and language therapy assistance to meet the needs of my son, Richard. As you know:

1. Richard has multiple and profound physical and mental impairments [describe briefly his impairments and in particular how his communication difficulties manifest themselves].

2. On 5 November 2004 the Shiretown social services department requested that your trust contribute towards the assessment of his need for care and health services.

3. The subsequent assessment of his needs concluded that it was essential that he receive speech and language therapy in order to enable him to engage in general social activity and in particular to express preferences concerning his health and social care needs

4. I believe that the importance of appropriate communication assistance for disabled children such as Richard has been stressed in much official guidance, as well as the need for health and social services to work together to ensure that they co-ordinate their responses to meet the assessed needs (i.e. the National Service Framework for Children's Services and the Department of Health's Social Care Group, para. 9.2 Disabled Children: Directions for Their Future Care 1998).

5. The importance of Richard being able properly to express his wishes and opinions is, I also understand, a 'convention right' (as articles 8 and 10) protected by the Human Rights Act 1998.

The reason why I am dissatisfied with your authority's response to his needs for language and speech therapy are: *[here explain in as much detail as possible what the trust has failed to do and what it needs to do in order to provide a satisfactory service to Richard].*

I am very concerned that there has been such delay in providing appropriate speech and language therapy and accordingly ask that you treat this letter as a formal complaint about this failure. I want rapid steps to be taken to ensure that he does receive the help he needs.

I am copying this letter to the health and social services authorities. Please acknowledge receipt.

Yours sincerely

Jane Smith

cc. Director of Patient Care
the Primary Care Trust (or Local Health Board in Wales)
and the Director of Children's Services.

Note: The most direct route to obtaining speech and language therapy is through a statement of special educational needs since the LEA has an 'absolute and non-delegable' obligation to arrange provision detailed in Part 3 of the statement (see p.125). If, therefore, the child has a statement requiring the provision of speech therapy a letter should be written to the LEA highlighting the failure to make this service available and stating that (1) it is required to make this service available, by virtue of Section 324(5)(a)(i) of the Education Act 1996; and (2) in the case of *R* v. *London Borough of Harrow ex parte M* (1997) this was held to be an 'absolute and non-delegable' obligation.

Letter 5: Requesting the initial involvement of LEA for child under 5 years old

Ms Jane Smith
Flat 11, Any Street,
Anytown,
AnyShire AE15 7LB
Tel: 01234 56789

Chief Education Officer
Children's Services Department
Anyshire Council
Council Offices
Shire Street Anytown
AE1 0BU

1 October 2005

Dear Chief Education Officer

**Special Educational Needs Assessment:
Richard Smith born 30 October 2004**

I formally request that your department carry out an assessment of my son's special educational needs in accordance with your duties under [section 331 (if aged under 2 years)] / [section 329 (if aged 2 to 5 years)] of the Education Act 1996.

Richard's special educational needs have not previously been assessed and I believe that it is necessary for such an assessment to be made.

Richard was born on 30 October last year and has been diagnosed as having cerebral palsy.

[Here explain briefly why it is believed that s/he will probably have significantly greater difficulty in learning than the majority of children of his/her age; and/or has a disability that prevents or hinders him/her from making use of educational facilities of a kind generally provided for children of his age.]

[Here give details, including names and addresses, etc. of any health or social services contacts, etc. with whom you have had contact and with whom it would be sensible for the LEA to liaise.]

I am not presently working and am generally available most mornings (until about midday) on the above telephone number.

I look forward to hearing from you at the earliest opportunity.

Yours sincerely

Jane Smith

Letter 6: Requesting access to files

Applicant's name
[Address]

Director of Children's Services/
Director of the Primary Carer Trust/Local Health Board
Director of the NHS Trust/
Director of Housing Department etc. [Address]

1 February 2006

Access to Personal Information – Data Protection Act 1998
Name and date of birth of disabled child

I formally request that you give me access to the personal information held by your authority relating to my *[personal circumstances][son's/ daughter's personal circumstances and I confirm that he/she lacks sufficient mental capacity to make the request in his/her own name]*.

The information I require to be disclosed is all personal information which your authority holds which relates to *[myself][my son/daughter]*. *[If possible describe as precisely as possible the information that is sought, including for instance where the information is likely to be located, the nature of the information and the dates between which it was collected.]*

I understand that I am entitled to receive this information within 40 days. I also understand that you may wish me to pay a fee for the processing and copying of this information and *[I confirm that I am willing to pay such reasonable sum as you may require (subject to the statutory maximum)]* or *[in order to expedite matters I enclose a cheque in the sum of £10, being the statutory maximum, and would be grateful if you could refund to me, if appropriate, any excess]*.

Please confirm receipt of this request.

[Signature]

References

Abberley, P. (1992) 'Counting Us Out: A Discussion of the OPCS Surveys.' *Disability, Handicap and Society 7*, 2, 139–155.

Abberley, P. (1996) 'Disabled by Numbers.' In R. Levitas and W. Guy (eds) *Interpreting Official Statistics.* London: Routledge.

Abbott, P. and Sapsford, R. (1992) 'Leaving it to Mum: "Community Care" for Mentally Handicapped Children.' In P. Abbott and R. Sapsford (eds) *Research into Practice: A Reader for Nurses and the Caring Professions.* Buckingham: Open University Press.

Abbott, D., Morris, J. and Ward, L. (2000) *Disabled Children and Residential Schools: A Survey of Local Authority Policy and Practice.* Bristol: Norah Fry Research Centre, University of Bristol.

Ahmad, W. (2000) *Ethnicity, Disability and Chronic Illness.* Buckingham: Open University Press.

Ahmad, W. and Atkin, K. (1996) 'Ethnicity and Caring for a Disabled Child: The Case of Sickle Cell or Thalassaemia.' *British Journal of Social Work 26*, 755–775.

Aldgate, J., Bradley, M. and Hawley, D. (1995) *Report to the Department of Health on the Use of Short-Term Accommodation in the Prevention of Long-Term Family Breakdown.* London: HMSO.

Anderson, H. (1995) *Disabled People and the Labour Market.* Birmingham: West Midlands Low Pay Unit.

Appleton, P. and Minchom, P. (1991) 'Models of Parent Partnership and Child Development Centres.' *Child: Care, Health and Development 17*, 27–38.

Appleton, P., Boll, V., Everett, J., Kelly, A., Meredith, K. and Payne, T. (1997) 'Beyond Child Development Centres: Care Coordination for Children with Disabilities.' *Child: Care, Health and Development 23*, 1, 29–40.

Argent, H. and Kerrane, A. (1997) *Taking Extra Care: Respite, Shared and Permanent Care for Children with Disabilities.* London: BAAF.

Aries, P. (1973) *Centuries of Childhood.* Harmondsworth: Penguin.

Association of Metropolitan Authorities (1994) *Special Child: Special Needs. Services for Children with Disabilities.* London: Association of Metropolitan Authorities.

Atkin, K. (1992) 'Similarities and Differences between Informal Carers.' In J. Twigg (ed) *Carers: Research and Practice.* London: HMSO.

Atkinson, N. and Crawforth, M. (1995) *All in the Family: Siblings and Disability.* London: NCH Action for Children.

Audit Commission (1992) *Getting in on the Act.* London: HMSO.

Audit Commission (1994) *Seen But Not Heard: Coordinating Community Child Health and Social Services for Children in Need.* London: HMSO.

Audit Commission (1995) *United they Stand.* London: HMSO.

Audit Commission (2003) *Services for Disabled Children. A Review of Services for Disabled Children and their Families.* Wetherby: Audit Commission Publications.

Baldwin, S. (1985) *The Costs of Caring. Families with Disabled Children.* London: Routledge and Kegan Paul.

Baldwin, S. and Carlisle, J. (1994) *Social Support for Disabled Children and their Families: A Review of Literature.* Edinburgh: HMSO.

Baldwin, S. and Glendinning, C. (1982) 'Children with Disabilities and their Families.' In A. Walker and P. Townsend (eds) *Disability in Britain: A Manifesto of Rights.* Oxford: Martin Robertson.

Baldwin, S. and Glendinning, C. (1983) 'Employment, Women and their Disabled Children.' In J. Finch and D. Groves (eds) *A Labour of Love: Women, Work and Caring.* London: Routledge and Kegan Paul.

Ball, M. (1998) *Disabled Children: Directions for Their Future Care.* London: Department of Health (in association with Social Services Inspectorate and the Council for Disabled Children).

Ballard, K., Bray, A., Shelton, E. and Clarkson, J. (1997) 'Children with Disabilities and the Education System: The Experience of Fifteen Fathers.' *International Journal of Disability, Development and Education 44,* 3, 229–241.

Barn, R. (1993) *Black Children in the Public Care System.* London: Batsford (in association with British Agencies for Adoption and Fostering).

Barnes, C. (1991) *Disabled People in Britain and Discrimination.* London: Hurst/University of Calgary Press (in association with the British Council of Organisations of Disabled People).

Barnes, C. and Mercer, G. (eds) (1996) *Exploring the Divide: Illness and Disability.* Leeds: Disability Press.

Barton, L. (1986) 'The Politics of Special Educational Needs.' *Disability, Handicap and Society 1,* 3, 273–290.

Baxter, C., Kamaljit, P., Ward, L. and Nadirshaw, Z. (1990) *Double Discrimination: Issues and Services for People with Learning Difficulties from Black and Ethnic Minority Communities.* London: King's Fund Centre.

Bebbington, A. and Miles, J. (1989) 'The Background of Children who Enter Local Authority Care.' *British Journal of Social Work 19,* 5, 349–368.

Beecham, J., Chadwick, O., Fidan, D. and Bernard, S. (2002) 'Children with Severe Learning Disabilities: Needs, Services and Costs.' *Children and Society 16,* 168–181.

Beecher, W. (1998) *Having a Say! Disabled Children and Effective Partnership, Section 2: Practice Initiatives and Selected Annotated References.* London: Council for Disabled Children.

Begum, N. (1992) *Something to be Proud of: The Lives of Asian Disabled People and Carers in Waltham Forest.* London: Waltham Forest Race Relations Unit and Disability Unit.

Beresford, B. (1994) *Positively Parents: Caring for a Severely Disabled Child.* York: Social Policy Research Unit/HMSO.

Beresford, B. (1995) *Expert Opinions: A National Survey of Parents Caring for a Severely Disabled Child.* Bristol: Policy Press.

Beresford, B. (1997) *Personal Accounts: Involving Disabled Children in Research.* London: HMSO.

Beresford, B. (2004) 'On the Road to Nowhere? Young Disabled People and Transition.' *Child: Care, Health and Development 306,* 581–587.

Beresford, B. and Oldman, C. (2002) *Housing Matters: National Evidence Relating to Disabled Children and their Housing.* Bristol: Policy Press.

Beresford, B., Sloper, P., Baldwin, S. and Newman, T. (1996) *What Works in Services for Families with a Disabled Child?* Barkingside: Barnardo's.

Beresford, B., Tozer, R., Rabiee, P. and Sloper, P. (2004) 'Developing an Approach to Involving Children with Autistic Spectrum Disorders within Health and Social Care Research.' *British Journal of Learning Disabilities 32,* 4, 180–185.

Berridge, D. (1996) *Fostercare: A Research Review.* London: HMSO.

Berridge, D. and Brodie, I. (1998) *Children's Homes Revisited.* London: Jessica Kingsley Publishers.

Bertoud, R., Lakey, J. and McKay, S. (1993) *The Economic Problems of Disabled People.* London: Policy Studies Institute.

Bethell, J. and Harrison, M. (2003) *Our Life, Our Say! A Good-Practice Guide to Young Disabled People's Peer Mentoring Support.* Brighton: Pavilion, for the Joseph Rowntree Foundation.

Biehal, N., Clayden, J., Stein, M. and Wade, J. (1995) *Moving On: Young People and Leaving Care Schemes.* London: HMSO.

Bignall, T., Butt, J. and Pagarani, D. (2002) *Something to Do: The Development of Peer Support Groups for Young Black and Minority Ethnic Disabled People.* Bristol: Policy Press.

Blackburn, C. (1991) *Poverty and Health: Working with Families.* Buckingham: Open University Press.

Blackburn, C. and Read, J. (2005) 'Using the Internet? The Experience of Parents of Disabled Children.' *Child: Care, Health and Development 31,* 5, 507–515.

Blackburn, C., Read, J. and Hughes, N. (2005) 'Carers and the Digital Divide: Independent Predictors of Internet Use among Carers in the UK.' *Health and Social Care in the Community 13,* 201–210.

Bone, M. and Meltzer, H. (1989) *The Prevalence of Disability among Children. OPCS Surveys of Disability in Great Britain, Report 3.* London: HMSO.

Booth, T. (1999) 'Inclusion and Exclusion Policy in England: Who Controls the Agenda?' In F. Armstrong, D. Armstrong and L. Barton (eds) *Inclusive Education: Policy, Contexts and Comparative Perspectives.* London: Fulton.

Booth, T. and Potts, P. (eds) (1983) *Integrating Special Education.* Oxford: Blackwell.

Booth, T. and Swann, W. (1987) *Including Pupils with Disabilities.* Milton Keynes: Open University Press.

Booth, T., Swann, W., Masterson, M. and Potts, P. (eds) (1992) *Curricula for Diversity in Education.* London: Routledge (in association with the Open University).

Broad, B. (1998) *Young People Leaving Care: Life after the Children Act 1989.* London: Jessica Kingsley Publishers.

Bullock, R., Little, M. and Milham, S. (1993) *Going Home: The Return of Children Separated from their Families.* Aldershot: Avebury.

Burkhart, L. (1993) *Total Communication in the Early Childhood Classroom.* Elderburg: Burkhart.

Butt, J. and Mirza, K. (1996) *Social Care and Black Communities.* London: HMSO.

Cameron, C. and Statham, J. (1997) 'Sponsored Places: The Use of Independent Day-Care Services to Support Children in Need.' *British Journal of Social Work 27,* 85–100.

Cameron, R. (1997) 'Early Interventions for Young Children with Developmental Delay: The Portage Approach.' *Child: Care, Health and Development 23,* 1, 11–27.

Carers UK (2003) *Missed Opportunities: The Impact of New Rights for Carers.* London: Carers UK.

Cass, H., Price, K., Reilly, S., Wisbeach, A. and McConachie, H. (1999) 'A Model for the Assessment and Management of Children with Multiple Disabilities.' *Child: Care, Health and Development 25,* 191–211.

Cavet, J. (1998) 'Leisure and Friendship.' In C. Robinson and K. Stalker (eds) *Growing Up With Disability.* London: Jessica Kingsley Publishers.

Cavet, J. and Sloper, P. (2004) 'Participation of Disabled Children in Individual Decisions about Their Lives and in Public Decisions about Service Development.' *Children and Society 18,* 278–290.

Chailey Young People's Group with Sue Virgo (1998) 'Group Advocacy in a Residential Setting.' In C. Robinson and K. Stalker (eds) *Growing Up With Disability.* London: Jessica Kingsley Publishers.

Chamba, R., Ahmad, W., Hirst, M., Lawton, D. and Beresford, B. (1999) *On the Edge: Minority Ethnic Families Caring for a Severely Disabled Child.* Bristol: Policy Press.

Clements, L. and Read, J. (2003) *Disabled People and European Human Rights.* Bristol: Policy Press.

Clements, L. and Smith, P. (1999) *A 'Snapshot' Survey of Social Services' Responses to the Continuing Care Needs of Older People in Wales.* Cardiff: Cardiff Law School.

Connors, C. and Stalker, K. (2003) *The Views and Experiences of Disabled Children and Their Siblings.* London: Jessica Kingsley Publishers.

Contact a Family (2003) *We're Listening.* London: Contact a Family; accessible at www.cafamily.org.uk/ wmids/WeAreListeningFull.pdf.

Contact a Family (2004) *Working with Families Affected by a Disability or Health Condition from Pregnancy to Pre-School.* London: Contact a Family; accessible at www.cafamily.org.uk/wales/Families_With_ Disability_E.pdf.

Coote, A. (2005) 'Comment.' *Community Care* 17 February, p.18.

Corbett, J. and Barton, L. (1992) *A Struggle for Choice: Students with Special Needs in Transition to Adulthood.* London: Routledge.

Council for Disabled Children (2004) *Come On In. A Practical Guide for Children's Services. The Disability Discrimination Act 1995, Part 3: Access to Goods and Services.* London: Council for Disabled Children.

Coventry Who Cares (1984) *Barbara's Case Conference.* Coventry: CRIS.

Cross, M. (1992) 'Abusive Practices and Disempowerment of Children with Physical Impairments.' *Child Abuse Review 1,* 3, 194–197.

Crow, L. (1996) 'Including All of our Lives.' In J. Morris (ed) *Encounters with Strangers: Feminism and Disability.* London: Women's Press.

Cuckle, P. and Wilson, J. (2002) 'Social Relationships and Friendships among Young People with Down's Syndrome in Secondary Schools.' *British Journal of Special Education 29,* 66–71.

Cunningham, C. (1983) 'Early Support and Intervention: The HARC Infant Project.' In P. Mittler and H. McConachie (eds) *Parents, Professionals and Mentally Handicapped People: Approaches to Partnership.* London: Croom Helm.

Cunningham, C. (1994) 'Telling Parents their Child has a Disability.' In P. Mittler and H. Mittler (eds) *Innovations in Family Support for People with Learning Disabilities.* Chorley: Lisieux Hall.

Cunningham, C., Morgan, P. and McGucken, R. (1984) 'Down's Syndrome: Is Dissatisfaction with Disclosure of Diagnosis Inevitable?' *Developmental Medicine and Child Neurology 26,* 33–39.

Dalrymple, J. and Burke, B. (1995) *Anti-Oppressive Practice: Social Care and the Law.* Buckingham: Open University Press.

Dearden, C. and Becker, S. (2004) *Young Carers in the UK: The 2004 Report.* London: Carers UK.

Department of Education and Science (DES) (1978) *Special Educational Needs (The Warnock Report).* London: HMSO.

Department for Education and Employment (DfEE) (1998) *Excellence for All Children, Meeting Special Educational Needs.* London: The Stationery Office.

Department for Education and Employment (DfEE) (2000) *Connexions: The Best Start in Life for Every Young Person.* London: The Stationery Office.

Department for Education and Skills (DfES) (2001) *Special Educational Needs: Code of Practice.* Nottingham: DfES Publications.

Department for Education and Skills (DfES) (2003a) *Every Child Matters.* London: The Stationery Office.

Department for Education and Skills (DfES) (2003b) *Disabled Children in Residential Placements*; accessible at www.teachernet.gov.uk/docbank/index.cfm?id=6462.

Department for Education and Skills (DfES) (2003c) *Together from the Start: Practical Guidance for Professionals Working with Disabled Children (Birth to Third Birthday) and their Families.* Nottingham: DfES Publications.

Department for Education and Skills (DfES) (2005) *Every Child Matters* website www.everychildmatters. gov.uk/aims/strategicoverview/integratedprocesses.

Department for Education and Skills (DfES) and Department of Health (DH) (2004) *National Service Framework for Children, Young People and Maternity Services.* London: The Stationery Office.

Department of Health (DH) (1976) *Fit for the Future: The Report of the Committee on Child Health Services (Court Report).* Cmnd 6684. London: HMSO.

Department of Health (DH) (1991) *Patterns and Outcomes in Child Placement: Messages from Current Research and their Implications.* London: HMSO.

Department of Health (DH) (1997) *Providing Therapists' Expertise in the New NHS: Developing a Strategic Framework for Good Patient Care.* London: HMSO.

Department of Health (DH) (1998a) *Disabled Children: Directions for their Future Care.* London: HMSO.

Department of Health (DH) (1998b) *Quality Protects.* London: The Stationery Office.

Department of Health (DH) (1999) *Working Together to Safeguard Children: A Guide to Inter-Agency Working to Safeguard and Promote the Welfare of Children.* London: The Stationery Office.

Department of Health (DH) (2000a) *Assessing Children in Need and their Families: Practice Guidance.* London: The Stationery Office.

Department of Health (DH) (2000b) *Quality Protects: Disabled Children, Numbers, Categories and Families.* London: Department of Health.

Department of Health (DH) (2001a) *Carers and Disabled Children Act: Practice Guidance.* London: The Stationery Office.

Department of Health (DH) (2001b) *Valuing People: A New Strategy for Learning Disability for the 21st Century.* London: The Stationery Office.

Department of Health (DH) (2003) *Discharge from Hospital: Pathway, Process and Practice.* London: The Stationery Office.

Department of Health (DH) (2004) *Improving Services for Wheelchair Users and Carers: Good Practice Guide.* London: The Stationery Office.

Department of Health (DH), Department for Education and Employment (DfEE) and Home Office (2000) *Framework for Assessing Children in Need and their Families.* London: The Stationery Office.

Disability Alliance (2005) *The Disability Rights Handbook.* London: Disability Alliance Educational and Research Association.

Dobson, B. and Middleton, S. (1998) *Paying to Care: The Cost of Childhood Disability.* York: Joseph Rowntree Foundation/York Publishing Services.

Dobson, B. and Middleton, S. (2001) *The Impact of Childhood Disability on Family Life.* York: Joseph Rowntree Foundation/York Publishing Services.

Dyson, S. (1987) *Mental Handicap: Dilemmas of Parent–Professional Relations.* London: Croom Helm.

Dyson, S. (1992) 'Blood Relations: Educational Implications of Sickle-Cell Anaemia and Thalassaemia.' In T. Booth, W. Swann, M. Masterson and P. Potts (eds) *Curricula for Diversity in Education.* London: Routledge (in association with the Open University).

Dyson, S. (1998) '"Race", Ethnicity and Haemoglobin Disorders.' *Social Science and Medicine 47, 1, 121–131.*

Family Focus (1984) *Swimming Against the Tide: Working for Integration in Education.* Coventry: CRIS.

Ferguson, T. and Kerr, A. (1960) *Handicapped Youth.* Oxford: Oxford University Press.

Flynn, M. and Hirst, M. (1992) *This Year, Next Year, Sometime…? Learning Disability and Adulthood.* London and York: National Development Team and Social Policy Research Unit.

Flynn, M., Cotterill, L., Hayes, L. and Sloper, T. (1998) 'Innovation in Supporting Adults with Learning Disabilities.' In C. Robinson and K. Stalker (eds) *Growing Up With Disability.* London: Jessica Kingsley Publishers.

Flynn, R. (2002) *Short Breaks: Providing Better Access and More Choice for Black Disabled Children and their Parents.* Bristol: Policy Press.

Frank, J. (2002) *Making it Work: Good Practice with Young Carers and their Families.* London: The Children's Society and the Princess Royal Trust for Carers.

French, S. (1996) 'Out of Sight, Out of Mind: The Experience and Effects of "Special" Residential School.' In J. Morris (ed) *Encounters with Strangers: Feminism and Disability.* London: Women's Press.

Gandhi, M.K. (1982) *An Autobiography.* London: Penguin.

Glendinning, C. (1983) *Unshared Care: Parents and their Disabled Children.* London: Routledge and Kegan Paul.

Glendinning, C. (1986) *A Single Door: Social Work with the Families of Disabled Children.* London: Routledge and Kegan Paul.

Glendinning, C., Kirk, S., Guiffrida, A. and Lawton, D. (2001) 'Technology-Dependent Children in the Community: Definitions, Numbers and Costs.' *Child: Care, Health and Development 27,* 321–334.

Goodey, C. (1991) *Living in the Real World: Families Speak about Down's Syndrome.* London: Twenty-One Press.

Gooding, C. (1994) *Disabling Laws, Enabling Acts: Disability Rights in Britain and America.* London: Pluto Press.

Gordon, D., Adelman, L., Ashworth, K., Bradshaw, J., Levitas, R., Middleton, S., *et al.* (2000a) *Poverty and Social Exclusion in Britain.* York: York Publishing Services for JRF.

Gordon, D., Parker, R. and Loughran, F. with Heslop, P. (2000b) *Disabled Children in Britain. A Re-analysis of the OPCS Disability Surveys.* London: The Stationery Office.

Gough, D., Li, L. and Wroblewska, A. (1993) *Services for Children with a Motor Impairment and their Families in Scotland.* Glasgow: Public Health Research Unit, University of Glasgow.

Graham, H. (1985) 'Providers, Negotiators and Mediators: Women as the Hidden Carers.' In E. Lewin and V. Olesen (eds) *Women, Health and Healing Towards a New Perspective.* New York: Tavistock.

Graham, H. (1993) *Hardship and Health in Women's Lives.* Brighton: Harvester Wheatsheaf.

Greco, V. and Sloper, P. (2004) 'Care Co-Ordination and Key Worker Schemes for Disabled Children: Results of a UK-Wide Survey.' *Child: Care, Health and Development 30,* 13–20.

Green, J.M. and Murton, F. E. (1996) 'Diagnosis of Duchenne Muscular Dystrophy: Parents' Experiences and Satisfaction.' *Child: Care, Health and Development 22,* 113–128.

Gregory, S. (1991) 'Challenging motherhood: mothers and their deaf children.' In A. Phoenix, A. Woollett and E. Lloyd (eds) *Motherhood, Meanings and Practices.* London: Sage.

Hale, B. (2004) 'Paul Siegart Memorial Lecture 2004: What Can the Human Rights Act Do for my Mental Health?' www.bihr.org/transcript_hale.doc.

Hall, D. (1997) 'Child Development Teams: Are they Fulfilling their Purpose?' *Child: Care, Health and Development 23,* 1, 87–99.

Harker, M. and King, N. (1999) *An Ordinary Home: Housing and Support for People with Learning Disabilities.* London: IDEA.

Harrison, J. and Woolley, M. (2004) *Debt and Disability: The Impact of Debt on Families with Disabled Children.* York: Contact a Family and the Family Fund.

Hasler, F., Campbell, J. and Zarb, G. (1999) *Direct Routes to Independence: A Guide to Local Authority Implementation of Direct Payments.* London: PSI/NCIL.

Hatton, C., Akram, Y., Shah, R., Robertson, J. and Emerson, E. (2004) *Supporting South Asian Families with a Child with Severe Disabilities.* London: Jessica Kingsley Publishers.

Haylock, C., Johnson, A. and Harpin, V. (1993) 'Parents' Views of Community Care for Children with Motor Disabilities.' *Child: Care, Health and Development 19,* 209–220.

Henderson, R. and Pochin, M. (2001) *A Right Result? Advocacy, Justice and Empowerment.* Bristol: Policy Press.

Hevey, D. (1992) *The Creatures Time Forgot.* London: Routledge.

Hirst, M. (1987) 'Careers of Young People with Disabilities Between Ages 15 and 21.' *Disability, Handicap and Society 2,* 61–74.

Hirst, M. and Baldwin, S. (1994) *Unequal Opportunities.* London: HMSO.

Humphries, S. and Gordon, P. (1992) *Out of Sight: The Experience of Disability 1900–1950.* Plymouth: Northcote House Publishers.

Hussain, Y., Atkin, K. and Ahmad, W. (2002) *South Asian Disabled Young People and Their Families.* Bristol: Policy Press.

Jackson, S. and Thomas, N. (1999) *On the Move Again.* Barkingside: Barnardo's.

Jigsaw Partnerships (1994) *Strategies for Change. Youthwork with Young Disabled People.* Lancashire: Jigsaw Partnerships and Lancashire County Council Youth and Community Service.

Jones, L., Atkin, K. and Ahmad, W. (2001) 'Supporting Asian Deaf Young People and Their Families: The Role of Professionals and Services.' *Disability and Society 16,* 1, 51–70.

Kagan, C., Lewis, S. and Heaton, P. (1998) *Caring to Work: Accounts of Working Parents of Disabled Children.* London: Family Policy Studies Centre.

Kagan, C., Lewis, S., Heaton, P. and Cranshaw, M. (1999) 'Enabled or Disabled? Working Parents of Disabled Children and the Provision of Child-Care.' *Journal of Community Applied Social Psychology 9,* 369– 381.

Kelly, D. and Warr, B. (1992) *Quality Counts: Achieving Quality in Social Care Services.* London: Whiting and Birch.

Kennedy, M. (1992) 'Not the Only Way to Communicate: A Challenge to the Voice in Child Protection Work.' *Child Abuse Review 1,* 169–177.

Kennedy, M. (1996) 'The Sexual Abuse of Disabled Children.' In J. Morris (ed) *Encounters with Strangers: Feminism and Disability.* London: The Women's Press.

Kerr, S and McIntosh, J. (2000) 'Coping when a Child has a Disability: Exploring the Impact of Parent-to-Parent Support.' *Child: Care, Health and Development 26,* 4, 309–322.

Kirk, S. and Glendinning, C. (2004) 'Developing Services to Support Parents Caring for a Technology-Dependent Child at Home.' *Child: Care, Health and Development 30,* 209–218.

Knight, A. (1998) *Valued or Forgotten? Independent Visitors and Disabled Young People.* London: National Children's Bureau.

Laming, Lord (2003) *The Victoria Climbié Inquiry: Report of an Inquiry.* London: The Stationery Office.

Lawton, D. (1989) 'Very Young Children and the Family Fund.' *Children and Society 3,* 3, 212–225.

Lawton, D. (1998) *Complex Numbers: Families with more than One Disabled Child.* York: Social Policy Research Unit, University of York.

Lawton, D. and Quine, L. (1990) 'Patterns of Take-Up of the Family Fund, the Characteristics of Eligible Non-Claimants and the Reasons for not Claiming.' *Child: Care, Health and Development 16,* 33–53.

Leighton Project, with Simon Grant and Daisy Cole (1998) 'Young People's Aspirations.' In C. Robinson and K. Stalker (eds) *Growing Up With Disability.* London: Jessica Kingsley Publishers.

Lewis, A. (1995) *Children's Understanding of Disability.* London: Routledge.

Lonsdale, S. (1990) *Women and Disability.* Basingstoke: Macmillan.

Loughran, F., Parker, R. and Gordon, D. (1992) *Children with Disabilities in Communal Establishments: A Further Analysis and Interpretation of the Office of Population Censuses and Surveys Investigation.* Bristol: University of Bristol.

MacDonald, H. and Callery, P. (2004) 'Different Meanings of Respite: A Study of Parents, Nurses and Social Workers Caring for Children with Complex Needs.' *Child: Care, Health and Development 30,* 3, 279–288.

MacHeath, C. (1992) 'Maresa.' In J. Morris (ed) *Alone Together: Voices of Single Mothers.* London: Women's Press.

Marchant, R. and Cross, M. (1993) 'Places of Safety: Institutions, Disabled Children and Abuse.' In *ABCD Reader.* London: NSPCC.

Marchant, R. and Martyn, M. (1999) *Make it Happen: Communication Handbook.* Brighton: Triangle.

Marchant, R. and Page, M. (1992) 'Bridging the Gap: Investigating the Abuse of Children with Multiple Disabilities.' *Child Abuse Review 1,* 179–183.

Marchant, R., Jones, M. and Julyan, A. (1999) *Listening on all Channels: Consulting with Disabled Children.* Brighton: Triangle.

Marsh, P. and Treseliotis, J. (eds) (1993) *Prevention and Reunification in Child Care.* London: Batsford.

Masson, J., Harrison, C. and Pavlovic, A. (1999) *Lost Parents.* Aldershot: Avebury.

McCarthy, M. (1999) *Sexuality and Women with Learning Disabilities.* London: Jessica Kingsley Publishers.

McConachie, H. (1997) 'The Organisation of Child Disability Services.' *Child: Care, Health and Development 23,* 1, 3–9.

McConkey, R. and Adams, L. (2000) 'Matching Short-Term Break Services for Children with Learning Disabilities to Family Needs and Preferences.' *Child: Care, Health and Development 26,* 429–444.

McConkey, R. and Smyth, M. (2003) 'Parental Perceptions of Risks with Older Teenagers who have Severe Learning Difficulties Contrasted with the Young People's Views and Experiences.' *Children and Society 17,* 18–31.

McConkey, R., Nixon, T., Donaghy, E. and Mulhern, D. (2004) 'The Characteristics of Children with a Disability Looked After Away from Home and their Future Service Needs.' *British Journal of Social Work 34,* 561–576.

Meltzer, H., Smyth, M. and Robus, N. (1989) *Disabled Children: Services, Transport and Education. OPCS Surveys of Disability in Great Britain, Report 6.* London: HMSO.

Middleton, L. (1999) *Disabled Children: Challenging Social Exclusion.* Oxford: Blackwell.

Milham, S., Bullock, R., Hosie, K. and Haak, M. (1986) *Children Lost in Care: The Family Contacts of Children in Care.* Aldershot: Gower.

Minkes, J., Robinson, C. and Weston, C. (1994) 'Consulting the Child: Interviews with Children using Residential Respite Services.' *Disability and Society 9,* 1, 561–571.

Mitchell, W. and Sloper, P. (2000) *User-Friendly Information for Families with Disabled Children: A Guide to Good Practice.* York: York Publishing Services for the Joseph Rowntree Foundation.

Mitchell, W. and Sloper, P. (2001) 'Quality in Services for Disabled Children and their Families: What can Theory, Policy and Research on Children's and Parents' Views Tell Us?' *Children and Society 15,* 237–252.

Mitchell, W. and Sloper, P. (2003) 'Quality Indicators: Disabled Children's and Parents' Prioritisations and Experiences of Quality Criteria when Using Different Types of Support Services.' *British Journal of Social Work 33,* 8, 1063–1080.

Mittler, P. and McConachie, H. (eds) (1983) *Parents, Professionals and Mentally Handicapped People.* London: Croom Helm.

Morris, J. (1991) *Pride Against Prejudice.* London: Women's Press.

Morris, J. (1993) *Independent Lives: Community Care and Disabled People.* Basingstoke: Macmillan.

Morris, J. (1995) *Gone Missing? A Research and Policy Review of Disabled Children Living Away from their Families.* London: Who Cares? Trust.

Morris, J. (1998a) *Still Missing? Vol. 1: The Experiences of Disabled Children Living Away from their Families.* London: Who Cares? Trust.

Morris, J. (1998b) *Still Missing? Vol. 2: Disabled Children and the Children Act.* London: Who Cares? Trust.

Morris, J. (1998c) *Accessing Human Rights: Disabled Children and The Children Act.* Barkingside: Barnardo's.

Morris, J. (1998d) *Don't Leave Us Out: Involving Children and Young People with Communication Impairments.* York: York Publishing Services.

Morris, J. (1999a) *Move On Up: Supporting Disabled Children in their Transition to Adulthood.* Barkingside: Barnardo's.

Morris, J. (1999b) *Hurtling into the Void. Transition to Adulthood for Young Disabled People with 'Complex Health and Support Needs'.* Brighton: Pavilion Publishing.

Morris, J. (2003) *The Right Place? A Parents' Guide to Choosing a Residential Special School.* York: York Publishing Services.

Mukherjee, S., Beresford, B. and Sloper, P. (1999) *Unlocking Keyworking: An Analysis and Evaluation of Keyworker Services for Families with Disabled Children.* Bristol: Policy Press/Community Care.

Murray, P. (2000) 'Disabled Children, Parents and Professionals: Partnership on Whose Terms?' *Disability and Society 15,* 4, 683–698.

Murray, P. and Penman, J. (1996) *Let Our Children Be.* Sheffield: Parents with Attitude.

National Association of Citizens Advice Bureaux (NACAB) (1994) *Unequal Opportunities: CAB Evidence on Discrimination in Employment.* London: National Association of Citizens Advice Bureaux.

National Society for the Prevention of Cruelty to Children (NSPCC) (2001) *Two Way Street: Training Video and Handbook about Communicating with Disabled Children and Young People.* Leicester: NSPCC National Training Centre.

Neil, E. and Howe, D. (2004) *Contact in Adoption and Permanent Foster Care: Research, Theory and Practice.* London: BAAF.

Newton, D. (1995) *Inclusion in the Early Years: A Report on the Work of a Partnership between Save the Children and Birmingham Social Services.* Birmingham: Birmingham City Council Social Services Department/Save the Children.

Noyes, J. (1999) *'Voices and Choices': Young People who Use Assisted Ventilation – Their Health and Social Care and Education.* London: The Stationery Office.

Office for National Statistics (ONS) (2002) *Living in Britain.* London: National Statistics Online.

Office for National Statistics (ONS) (2004) *The Health of Children and Young People.* London: National Statistics Online.

Oldman, C. and Beresford, B. (1998) *Homes Unfit for Children: Housing Disabled Children and their Families.* Bristol: Policy Press.

Oliver, M. (1996) *Understanding Disability.* London: Macmillan.

Page, R. and Clark, G. (eds) (1977) *Who Cares? Young People in Care Speak Out.* London: National Children's Bureau.

Parker, R. (1998) 'Counting with Care: A Re-Analysis of OPCS data.' In M. Ball (ed) *Disabled Children: Directions for their Future Care.* London: Department of Health (in association with the Social Services Inspectorate and the Council for Disabled Children).

Parker, R., Ward, H., Jackson, S., Aldgate, J. and Wedge, P. (eds) (1991) *Looking After Children: Assessing Outcomes in Child Care.* London: HMSO.

Phillips, R. (1998) 'Disabled Children in Permanent Substitute Families.' In C. Robinson and K. Stalker (eds) *Growing Up With Disability.* London: Jessica Kingsley Publishers.

Preston, G. (2005) *Helter Skelter: Families, Disabled Children and the Benefit System.* CASE Paper 92. London: Centre for the Analysis of Social Exclusion, London School of Economics.

Prewett, B. (1999) *Short-Term Break, Long-Term Benefit: Using Family-Based Short Breaks for Disabled Children and Adults.* York: JUSSR and Community Care.

Prewett, B. (2000) *The Views of Short Break Carers for Children who are 'Hard to Place'.* York: York Publishing Services.

Priestley, M. (1998) 'Childhood Disability and Disabled Childhoods: Agendas for Research.' *Childhood 5,* 2, 207–223.

Priestley, M. and Rabiee, P. (2002) 'Hopes and Fears: Stakeholder Views on the Transfer of Special School Resources Towards Inclusion.' *Inclusive Education 6*, 4, 371–390.

Prime Minister's Strategy Unit (PMSU) (2005) *Improving the Life Chances of Disabled People.* London: The Stationery Office.

Pugh, G. (ed) (1992) *Contemporary Issues in the Early Years.* London: Paul Chapman.

Pumpian, I. (1996) 'Foreword.' In D. Sands and M. Wehmeyer (eds) *Self-Determination across the Lifespan: Independence and Choice for People with Disabilities.* Baltimore, MD: Paul Brookes.

Quine, L. (1993) 'Working with Parents: The Management of Sleep Disturbance in Children with Learning Disabilities.' In C. Kiernan (ed) *Research into Practice? Implications of Research on the Challenging Behaviour of People with Learning Disability.* Clevedon: BILD.

Quine, L. and Pahl, J. (1986) 'First Diagnosis of Severe Mental Handicap: Characteristics of Unsatisfactory Encounters Between Doctors and Parents.' *Social Science and Medicine 22*, 53–62.

Quinton, D., Rushton, A., Dance, C. and Mayes, D. (1997) 'Contact between Children Placed Away from Home and their Birth Parents: Research, Issues and Evidence.' *Clinical Child Psychology and Psychiatry 2*, 3, 393–413.

Rabiee, P., Sloper, P. and Beresford, B. (2005) 'Desired Outcomes for Children and Young People with Complex Health Care Needs and Children who do not Use Speech for Communication.' *Health and Social Care in the Community 135*, 478–487.

Read, J. (1991) 'There was Never Really any Choice: The Experience of Mothers of Disabled Children in the United Kingdom.' *Women's Studies International Forum 14*, 6, 561–571.

Read, J. (1996) *A Different Outlook: Service Users' Perspectives on Conductive Education.* Birmingham: Foundation for Conductive Education.

Read, J. (1998) 'Conductive Education and the Politics of Disablement.' *Disability and Society 13*, 2, 279–293.

Read, J. (2000) *Disability, Society and the Family: Listening to Mothers.* Buckingham: Open University Press.

Read, J. and Clements, L. (1999) 'Research, the Law and Good Practice in Relation to Disabled Children: An Approach to Staff Development in a Local Authority.' *Local Governance 25*, 2, 87–95.

Read, J. and Clements, L. (2001) *Disabled Children and the Law: Research and Good Practice.* London: Jessica Kingsley Publishers.

Reisser, R. (1992) 'Internalised Oppression: How it Seems to Me.' In T. Booth, W. Swann, M. Masterson and P. Potts (eds) *Policies for Diversity in Education.* London: Routledge (in association with the Open University).

Reisser, R. and Mason, M. (1992) *Disability Equality in the Classroom.* London: Disability Equality in Education.

Residential Forum (1996) *Creating a Home from Home: A Guide to Standards.* London: Residential Forum/National Institute for Social Work.

Riddell, S. (1998) 'The Dynamic of Transition to Adulthood.' In C. Robinson and K. Stalker (eds) *Growing Up With Disability.* London: Jessica Kingsley Publishers.

Roberts, K. and Lawton, D. (1999) 'Financial Assistance for Families with Severely Disabled Children and Transport Costs.' *Children and Society 13*, 333–345.

Roberts, K. and Lawton, D. (2001) 'Acknowledging the Extra Care Parents Give their Disabled Children.' *Child: Care, Health and Development 27*, 307–319.

Robinson, C. (1996) 'Breaks for Disabled Children.' In K. Stalker (ed) *Developments in Short-Term Care: Breaks and Opportunities.* London: Jessica Kingsley Publishers.

Robinson, C. and Jackson, P. (1999) *Children's Hospices: A Lifeline for Families?* London: National Children's Bureau.

Robinson, C. and Stalker, K. (1993) *Out of Touch: Non-Users of Respite Care Services.* Bristol: Norah Fry Research Centre.

Rowe, J. and Lambert, L. (1973) *Children Who Wait: A Study of Children Needing Substitute Families.* London: Association of British Adoption Agencies.

Russell, P. (1988) 'Community Approaches to Serving Children and their Families.' In D. Towell (ed) *An Ordinary Life in Practice.* London: King Edward's Hospital Fund for London.

Russell, P. (1991) 'Working with Children with Physical Disabilities and their Families – The Social Work Role.' In M. Oliver (ed) *Social Work: Disabled People and Disabling Environments*. London: Jessica Kingsley Publishers.

Russell, P. (1995) *Positive Choices: Services for Disabled Children Living Away from Home*. London: Council for Disabled Children.

Russell, P. (1996) 'Short-Term Care: Parental Perspectives.' In K. Stalker (ed) *Developments in Short-Term Care*. London: Jessica Kingsley Publishers.

Russell, P. (1998) *Having a Say: Disabled Children and Effective Partnership in Decision Making, Section 1: The Report*. London: Council for Disabled Children.

Russell, P. (2003) '"Access and Achievement or Social Exclusion?" Are the Government's Policies Working for Disabled Children and their Families?' *Children and Society 17*, 215–225.

Ryan, S. (2005) '"Busy Behaviour" in the "Land of the Golden M": Going Out with Learning Disabled Children in Public Places.' *Journal of Applied Research in Intellectual Disabilities 18*, 65–74.

Scope (2003) *Right from the Start*. London: Scope.

Sebba, J. and Sachdev, D. (1997) *What Works in Inclusive Education?* Barkingside: Barnardo's.

Sellick, C. and Thoburn, J. (1996) *What Works in Family Placement?* Barkingside: Barnardo's.

Shah, R. (1992) *The Silent Minority: Children with Disabilities in Asian Families*. London: National Children's Bureau.

Shah, R. (1997) 'Services for Asian Families and Children with Disabilities.' *Child: Care, Health and Development 23*, 1, 41–46.

Shaw, L. (1998) 'Children's Experiences of School.' In C. Robinson and K. Stalker (eds) *Growing Up With Disability*. London: Jessica Kingsley Publishers.

Shaw, M., Dorling, D., Gordon, D. and Davey Smith, G. (1999) *The Widening Gap: Health Inequalities and Policy in Britain*. Bristol: Policy Press.

Sheik, S. (1986) 'An Asian Mothers' Self-Help Group.' In S. Ahmed, J. Cheetham and J. Small (eds) *Social Work with Black Children and their Families*. London: Batsford.

Simons, K. (1998) *Home, Work and Exclusion: The Social Policy Implications of Supported Living and Employment for People with Learning Disabilities*. York: York Publishing Services.

Sloper, P. (1999) 'Models of Service Support for Parents of Disabled Children: What Do We Know? What Do We Need to Know? *Child, Carer, Health and Development 25*, 85–99.

Sloper, P. and Turner, S. (1992) 'Service Needs of Families of Children with Severe Physical Disability.' *Child: Care, Health and Development 18*, 259–282.

Sloper, P. and Turner, S. (1993a) 'Risk and Resistance Factors in the Adaptation of Parents of Children with Severe Physical Disability.' *Child: Care, Health and Development 18*, 259–282.

Sloper, P. and Turner, S. (1993b) 'Determinants of Parental Satisfaction with Disclosure of Disability.' *Developmental Medicine and Child Neurology 35*, 816–825.

Sloper, P., Knussen, C., Turner, S. and Cunningham, C. (1991) 'Factors Related to Stress and Satisfaction with Life in Families of Children with Down's Syndrome.' *Journal of Child Psychology and Psychiatry 32*, 655–676.

Sloper, P., Mukherjee, S., Beresford, B., Lightfoot, J. and Norris, P. (1999) *Real Change not Rhetoric: Putting Research into Practice in Multi-Agency Services*. Bristol: Policy Press.

Sloper, P., Turner, S., Knussen, C. and Cunningham, C. (1990) 'Social Life of School Children with Down's Syndrome.' *Child: Care, Health and Development 16*, 235–251.

Smith, A. (1994) 'A Damaging Experience: Black Disabled Children and Educational and Social Services Provision.' In N. Begum, M. Hill and A. Stevens (eds) *Reflections: Views of Black Disabled People on their Lives and Community Care*. London: CCETSW.

Smyth, M. and Robus, N. (1989) *The Financial Circumstances of Families with Disabled Children Living in Private Households. OPCS Surveys of Disability in Great Britain, Report 5*. London: HMSO.

Social Services Inspectorate (1994) *Services to Disabled Children and their Families: Report of the National Inspection of Services to Disabled Children and their Families*. London: Department of Health.

Social Services Inspectorate (1995a) *Growing Up and Moving On: Report of an SSI Project on Transition Services for Disabled Young People.* London: Department of Health.

Social Services Inspectorate (1995b) *Opportunities or Knocks: National Inspection of Recreation and Leisure in Day Services for People with Learning Disabilities.* London: Department of Health.

Social Services Inspectorate (1997) *Moving on Towards Independence: Second Report on Transition Services for Disabled Young People.* London: Department of Health.

Social Services Inspectorate (1998) *Removing Barriers for Disabled Children: Inspection of Services to Disabled Children and Their Families.* London: Department of Health.

Soutter, J., Hamilton, N., Russell, P., Russell, C., Bushby, K., Sloper, P. and Bartlett, K. (2004) 'The Golden Freeway: A Preliminary Evaluation of a Pilot Study Advancing Information Technology as a Social Intervention for Boys with Duchenne Muscular Dystrophy and their Families.' *Health and Social Care in the Community 12*, 25–33.

Spastics Society (1992) *A Hard Act to Follow.* London: Spastics Society.

Stalker, K. (1991) *Share the Care: An Evaluation of Family Based Respite Care Services.* London: Jessica Kingsley Publishers.

Stalker, K. (1996) 'Principles, Policy and Practice in Short-Term Care.' In K. Stalker (ed) *Developments in Short-Term Care: Breaks and Opportunities.* London: Jessica Kingsley Publishers.

Stalker, K., Carpenter, J., Phillips, R., Connors, C., MacDonald, C., Eyre, J. and Noyes, J. (2003) *Care and Treatment? Supporting Children with Complex Needs in Healthcare Settings.* Brighton: Pavilion Publishing.

Stallard, B. and Lenton, S. (1992) 'How Satisfied are Parents of Pre-School Children who have Special Needs with the Services they have Received?' *Child: Care, Health and Development 18*, 197–205.

Standing Conference of Voluntary Organisations for People with a Learning Disability in Wales (SCOVO) (1989a) *Parents Deserve Better.* Cardiff: SCOVO.

Standing Conference of Voluntary Organisations for People with a Learning Disability in Wales (SCOVO) (1989b) *Practical Steps to Better Practice: Better Early Counselling in Wales.* Cardiff: SCOVO.

Statham, J. (1996) *Young Children in Wales: An Evaluation of the Implementation of The Children Act 1989 on Day Care Services.* London: Thomas Coram Research Institute.

Statham, J. and Read, J. (1998) 'The Pre-School Years.' In C. Robinson and K. Stalker (eds) *Growing Up with Disability.* London: Jessica Kingsley Publishers.

Stein, M. (1997) *What Works in Leaving Care?* Barkingside: Barnardo's.

Strong, P. (1979) *The Ceremonial Order of the Clinic, Doctors and Medical Bureaucracies.* London: Routledge and Kegan Paul.

Stuart, M. and Baines, C. (2004) *Progress on Safeguards for Children Living Away from Home: A Review of Action Since the People Like Us Report.* York: York Publishing Services.

Swann, W. (1987) 'Statements of Intent: An Assessment of Reality.' In T. Booth and W. Swann (1987) *Including Pupils with Disabilities.* Milton Keynes: Open University Press.

Thoburn, J. (1990) *Success and Failure in Permanent Family Placement.* Aldershot: Gower Avebury.

Thoburn, J. (1994) *Child Placement: Principles and Practice.* Aldershot: Arena.

Thomas, C. (1999) *Female Forms: Experiencing and Understanding Disability.* Buckingham: Open University Press.

Thompson, G., Ward, K. and Wishard, J. (1995) 'The Transition to Adulthood for Children with Down's Syndrome.' *Disability and Society 10*, 325–340.

Thompson, N. (1993) *Anti-Discriminatory Practice.* London: Macmillan.

Thornton, P., Sainsbury, R. and Barnes, H. (1997) *Helping Disabled People to Work: A Cross-National Study of Social Security and Employment Provisions. A Report for the Social Security Advisory Committee.* London: The Stationery Office.

Townsley, R. and Robinson, C. (2000) *Food for Thought.* Bristol: Norah Fry Research Centre, University of Bristol.

Townsley, R., Abbott, D. and Watson, D. (2003) *Making a Difference? Exploring the Impact of Multi-Agency Working on Disabled Children with Complex Healthcare Needs, their Families, and the Professionals who Support Them.* Bristol: Policy Press.

Tozer, R. (1999) *At the Double: Supporting Families with Two or More Disabled Children.* London: National Children's Bureau.

Traustadottir, R. (1991) 'Mothers Who Care: Gender, Disability and Family Life.' *Journal of Family Issues 12*, 2, 211–228.

Twigg, J. and Atkin, K. (1994) *Carers Perceived Policy and Practice in Informal Care.* Buckingham: Open University Press.

Utting, W. (1991) *Children in the Public Care.* London: HMSO.

Utting, W. (1997) *People Like Us: The Report of the Review of the Safeguards for Children Living Away from Home.* London: The Stationery Office.

Voice for the Child in Care (1998) *Shout to be Heard: Stories from Young People in Care about Getting Heard and Using Advocates.* London: Voice for the Child in Care.

Walker, A. (1982) *Unqualified and Underemployed: Handicapped Young People in the Labour Market.* London: Macmillan.

Ward, L. (1997) *Seen and Heard: Involving Disabled Children and Young People in Research and Development Projects.* York: Joseph Rowntree Foundation.

Ward, L., Mallet, R., Heslop, P. and Simons, K. (2003) 'Transition Planning: How Well does it Work for Young People with Learning Disabilities and their Families?' *British Journal of Special Education 30*, 132–137.

Warner, N. (1992) *Choosing with Care.* London: HMSO.

Watson, D., Lewis, M., Townsley, R., Abbott, D. and Cowen, A. (2004) *All Together Better: A Guide for Families of a Disabled Child with Complex Health Care Needs.* York: The Family Fund and Norah Fry Research Centre.

Webb, A. and Wistow, G. (1986) *Planning, Need and Scarcity: Essays on the Personal Social Services.* London: Allen and Unwin.

Westcott, H. (1991) *Institutional Abuse of Children: From Research to Policy – A Review.* London: NSPCC.

Westcott, H. (1993) *Abuse of Children and Adults with Disabilities.* London: NSPCC.

Westcott, H. (1998) 'Disabled Children and Child Protection.' In C. Robinson and K. Stalker (eds) *Growing Up With Disability.* London: Jessica Kingsley Publishers.

Who Cares? Trust (1993) *Not Just A Name.* London: National Consumer Council.

Williams, F. (1993) 'Women and Community.' In J. Bornat, C. Pereira, D. Pilgrim and F. Williams (eds) *Community Care: A Reader.* Basingstoke: Macmillan.

Williams, G. (1996) 'Representing Disabilities: Some Questions of Phenomenology and Politics.' In C. Barnes and G. Mercer (eds) *Exploring the Divide: Illness and Disability.* Leeds: Disability Press.

Wright, J. and Ruebain, D. (2002) *Taking Action! Your Child's Right to Special Education* (3rd edn). Birmingham: Questions Publishing Company.

Wynne Oakley, M. and Masson, J. (2000) *Official Friends and Friendly Officials.* London: NSPCC.

Yerbury, M. (1997) 'Issues in Multidisciplinary Teamwork for Children with Disabilities.' *Child: Care, Health and Development 23* 1, 77–86.

Younghusband, E., Birchall, D., Davie, R. and Kellmer Pringle, M. (1970) *Living with Handicap.* London: National Children's Bureau.

Subject Index

Index of Legislation and Guidance

Note: This index includes legal cases, statutes, regulations, policy guidance, codes of practice and practice guidance. Figure 4.1 (p. 72) illustrates the relative importance of each.

Author Index